D0458904

Revolution and Intervention:

The Diplomacy of Taft and Wilson with Mexico, 1910–1917

The MIT Press   Cambridge, Massachusetts, and London, England

Revolution and Intervention:

The Diplomacy of Taft and Wilson with Mexico, 1910–1917

P. Edward Haley

To my mother and my wife

Contents

How to respond to revolution abroad has become a central issue of American foreign policy. The employment of force by the United States to intervene in a revolutionary civil war in Vietnam has opened deep divisions in America and has become a rallying point for those who deny the relevance to the twentieth century of the traditional moral and philosophical bases of American society.

The purpose of this essay is to provide a study of America's past response to revolution abroad which will aid in understanding and formulating the nation's present and future response. America's diplomatic response to the Mexican Revolution from 1910 to 1917 is examined in detail. The Mexican Revolution was chosen because the fierce regulation of private property and foreign investment in Mexico, the emphasis on social welfare and the deemphasis of political freedom seemed to link it closely to the other major revolutions of the twentieth century. Moreover, communism played a negligible role in the Mexican Revolution. One can thus examine America's response to a major revolution free of the incubus of anticommunism. I hope this will prove useful to those interested in determining the influence of anticommunism on America's response to later revolutions.

Response to revolution in another country can be classified in two ways. First, response to revolutionary violence when one or several movements or factions compete for power, with or without an *ancien régime:* major differences with foreign governments result from the destruction incident to revolutionary warfare and from the desire of foreign governments to control the outcome of the revolution for strategic, ideological, or commercial reasons. Second, response to revolutionary government when the internal struggle for power has been decided: differences with foreign governments arise over the internal and external policies of the newly established revolutionary government. A foreign government could, of course, object to the internal and external policies of a revolutionary movement before that movement won control of the entire country. The coming to power, nonetheless, transforms the revolutionaries into agents of the entire country and offers a convenient distinction.

This essay deals with the first sort of response: the response of the United States government to revolutionary struggle in

Mexico. It takes account of what we are not and what we cannot do and suggests what we are and what we can do.

The access to primary material enjoyed by scholars in the United States is without parallel in the history of the world. The bulk and variety of available primary material alone threatens to overwhelm the individual scholar. The librarians, archivists, and clerks at the Library of Congress and the National Archives I found to be helpful and courteous, often solicitous of the projects of the many scholars they serve, intent on opening to inquiry as well as preserving their vast stores of material. Americans, more than any other people, have an opportunity to learn from their past. After prolonged study of the response of the United States to the Mexican Revolution, I believe that the Mexican revolutionary experience, particularly Mexico's revolutionary diplomacy, could and should exert greater influence in Latin America than any other, including the Cuban and American revolutionary experiences.

Acknowledgments

One completes a major undertaking with pride in personal achievement and with gratitude for the kindness of others without whose concern and assistance one's own accomplishment would have been immeasurably diminished. I am indebted to Robert E. Osgood, Director of the Washington Center of Foreign Policy Research, who assisted me at every stage in the writing of this essay. I am grateful to Herbert S. Dinerstein of the School of Advanced International Studies, Johns Hopkins University, for his helpful comments and deep understanding, which sharpened my own efforts and gave the essay much of its contemporary relevance. Throughout long months and years of intellectual and professional preparation I have been sustained and inspired by my wife, Elaine Seagrave Haley.

While a research assistant at the Washington Center of Foreign Policy Research, I benefited from the constructive criticisms of my fellow researchers, Charles R. Planck, now of the State University of New York at Buffalo, and Naomi Schweisow, who read the earliest drafts of the manuscript. André Kaspi of the University of Paris and Leon Boothe of the University of Mississippi, fellows with me for a time in the perpetual community of Wilson scholars at the Library of Congress, unselfishly shared their understanding of Woodrow Wilson. Richard S. Wheeler of Clarement Men's College and the Claremont Graduate School read sections of the manuscript and suggested a number of helpful revisions. Grateful acknowledgment is made to Houghton Mifflin Company for permission to quote from *A History of Mexico,* third edition, revised and enlarged, by Henry Bamford Parkes, copyright 1960 by Houghton Mifflin Company.

Claremont Men's College provided a grant that helped to defray the expense of preparing the manuscript for publication. Mrs. Mae Gordon typed the earliest drafts from handwritten copy. Special thanks go to Mrs. Norma Campbell for her enthusiasm and her interest in the work and for her skillful typing and editorial help, and to Georgia Barron and Carolyn Emigh for assistance in reading proof.

P. Edward Haley
Claremont, California
August 1969

Revolution and Intervention:

The Diplomacy of Taft and Wilson with Mexico, 1910–1917

P. Edward Haley

Presidents Woodrow Wilson (*left*) and William Howard Taft, Inauguration Day, March 4, 1913 (Prints and Photographs Division, Library of Congress)

Introduction

A government's diplomatic response to foreign revolution is shaped by its overall approach to foreign policy. Response to revolution, whether interventionist or indifferent, hostile or sympathetic, can be understood as part of a larger effort at conceptualization of and adaptation to international politics.

During the eighteenth and nineteenth centuries America's weakness and isolation from the major centers of conflict, her tradition of noninvolvement, and the dominance among American statesmen of a limited conception of the nation's interests helped prevent the nation from becoming embroiled in conflicts arising from revolutions in Europe and Latin America. By the beginning of the twentieth century, however, the United States had become a great power with colonial responsibilities in the Far East. The traditional American approach to foreign affairs—that of a weak, isolated neutral—could no longer determine and justify the nation's foreign policy.

The need for a new approach to foreign policy was met in two different ways, both eminently American and both destined to survive World War II in uneasy synthesis. Theodore Roosevelt responded with a sort of loudmouthed, undeveloped realism. Roosevelt saw international affairs in terms of conflicting national interests. He understood power politics viscerally and instinctively if not intellectually and accepted the use of force as necessary and right. Taft's foreign policy was a variant of Rooseveltian realism. What distinguished the Taft administration from its predecessor was the outspoken zeal with which it sought to expand America's overseas markets and investments.

DOLLAR DIPLOMACY

"Dollar diplomacy" proceeded from a belief widely accepted around the turn of the century that industrialized nations either secured outlets overseas for their surplus goods and capital or succumbed to stagnation and revolution at home and defeat and humiliation abroad. Though Taft and his secretary of state, Philander C. Knox, emphasized dollar diplomacy, they did so to protect what they understood to be American interests and with a thorough understanding of the exigencies of power politics.

To these men economic expansion abroad—the acquisition of

foreign markets and investments—was a vital national interest.[1] But this by no means exhausted their motives for action or their understanding of foreign affairs. Taft, Knox, and other members of the administration were sensitive to and held definite views about the importance of power, military security, and the use of force in international affairs. In Central America and the Caribbean, security was the first concern of the Taft administration. Commercial expansion played an instrumental role, designed to guarantee and make workable the protection of American security interests. Knox, in particular, hoped by the injection of American capital and advisers to prevent the financial misconduct and endemic political instability that invited intervention by the great European powers. He was delighted that this would aid American commercial expansion, which he also considered a vital national interest, and one feels he never quite understood the furor raised by his frank association of security with economic expansion abroad:

It is the fashion to style this "Dollar Diplomacy," the phrase being originally intended in a disparaging sense. It seems, on the contrary, to be a creditable and happy phrase. If the American dollar can aid suffering humanity and lift the burden of financial difficulty from States with which we live on terms of intimate intercourse and earnest friendship, and replace insecurity and devastation by stability and peaceful self-development, all I can say is that it would be hard to find better employment.[2]

A different situation existed in China from the American standpoint. The China policy of the Taft administration makes sense only when understood primarily as an attempt to hold open the vast Chinese market for American goods and investment. "National" and "commercial" interests are often set off against one another by scholars anxious to refute or substantiate the case for economic factors as determinants of American foreign policy. In Taft's case the correct view seems to be that commer-

---

[1] See Philander C. Knox Papers, Library of Congress, Accession 3686, Bound Pamphlets (hereinafter cited as Knox papers); and Wilbur J. Carr Papers, Library of Congress, Correspondence and Accessions 12,014 and 12,015, Box 17 (hereinafter cited as Carr Papers).
[2] Address, December 11, 1911, Knox Papers, Accession 3686, Bound Pamphlets. See also "The Monroe Doctrine and Some Incidental Obligations in the Caribbean Zone," January 19, 1912, *ibid.*, and Willard Straight, "The Politics of Chinese Finance," address before the East Asiatic Society of Boston, May 2, 1913, *ibid.*

cial expansion in China, or at least the maintenance of an opportunity for future commercial expansion there, was regarded as a vital national interest. No useful opposition of "national" and "economic" interests can be made because the two were regarded as coincident. The United States would soon need a share of China's market if it did not already, and if the European nations and Japan carved out exclusive spheres that need could not be met. In China, the Taft administration again attempted preventive action, directed to preserving future markets rather than, as in the Caribbean, to protecting the physical security of North America.

Taft and his advisers were aware of the larger interests in China of Japan and the great European powers. They recognized the resulting limits on the means available to the United States to maintain access to the Chinese market. Japan and Russia would fight, had fought one another in fact, to defend their interests in China. Taft and Knox did not need Theodore Roosevelt to remind them, though he did of course, that the American people would never support a war with Japan or Russia in the Far East. Thus it was out of the question for the United States unilaterally to support China unless it could at the same time defend China against the Japanese, who were certain to regard such an American initiative as a hostile act. If, on the other hand, the United States became a member of the "club" of nations presiding over China's fate, it seemed to Taft and Knox that a number of advantages would follow. First, the United States would gain concrete vested interests in China, as in fact almost happened with the railway and currency loans, and would thus acquire more than a moral right to a voice in questions affecting China. Second, as a member of the group of nations with interests in China the United States would work from within to preserve Chinese sovereignty and an open Chinese market. Taft and Knox knew that the action of the group would always represent the course least objectionable to all members. This would favor the limited and somewhat altruistic American objectives and counter the more aggressive Japanese and Russian designs. Taft and Knox wished to join the group and then to use it.

Though he was Roosevelt's nominee, Taft and his supporters represented the Republican party's "Old Guard." Taft's desire to protect American interests through dollar diplomacy complemented his administration's domestic harmony with big business.

Taft, understandably, responded to the Mexican Revolution by seeking to protect American lives and investments in Mexico. He nonetheless transcended the pattern set by the political origins of his administration and his approach to foreign policy in two ways. Taft believed in a strict interpretation of the constitutional prerogatives of the president and accepted, far more than did Roosevelt or Wilson, the restraints on presidential action imposed by a traditional view of America's role in the world. These beliefs led him to refrain from using force against Mexico without the consent of Congress. Though he seldom if ever spoke of it publicly, Taft seems to have reacted strongly against Roosevelt's expansion of the powers of the president. Taft's beliefs also led him to emphasize neutrality toward Mexico and abstention from involvement in Mexico's internal affairs. Ultimately, Taft was ready to use force in Mexico to protect American lives and property. But he reacted with patience and foresight to the revolutionary violence in Mexico and was acutely aware that American intervention might so provoke the Mexican people as to bring about the very destruction of American interests he desired to forestall.

WILSON'S NEW DIPLOMACY

Woodrow Wilson offered a different approach. In his conduct of American foreign policy, Wilson emphasized the force of morality in international affairs and the efficacy of nontraditional, nonviolent means in achieving idealistic foreign-policy objectives. As a person may condemn and desire to transcend sin or personal weakness, Wilson desired to lead other nations to transcend their traditional patterns of action in international affairs, characterized in the early twentieth century by the balancing of power and by worldwide economic rivalry and colonial exploitation. If Wilson's foreign policy was marked by his insistence on the force of morality, it also reflected in the Far East and in Europe an awareness of the advantages of international pluralism and of the need to balance power, as well as the eventual return to and skillful use of military force and commercial power. Wilson's opposition to Japanese expansion in China, for example, evolved from a repudiation of dollar diplomacy to the conscious thwarting of Japanese aims by financial diplomacy and American military participation in the occupation of Siberia. In Europe, Wilson hoped to achieve a peace without victory that would eliminate German militarism but preserve Germany as a member of the European system.

Though he had not studied statecraft before becoming president, Wilson had studied the lives of famous European statesmen. Wilson believed that great statesmen led their nations by discovering high principles and imposing them on all who resisted their will.[3] To this belief in total commitment to principle as the hallmark of great leaders Wilson added an awareness of the growing importance of foreign affairs in American life. If he had devoted little attention to foreign affairs before becoming president, Wilson had realized that the United States had grown rich and great and strong and had become, as never before, a significant actor on the international stage. He ranked the Battle of Manila with the Battle of Trenton in historic importance for the United States and regarded the victory over Spain as a crucial turning point in American history.[4]

Early in his career Wilson believed that democracy represented the "wave of the future" and would spread around the world.[5] Twenty years later he realized that he had been overoptimistic. The failure of democracy to spread led him to observe: "It is no longer possible to mistake the reaction against democracy. The nineteenth century was above all others a century of democracy; and yet the world is no more convinced of the benefits of democracy as a form of government at its end than it was at its beginning."[6] Wilson saw in this proof that other peoples had learned through trial and error that democratic institutions could not be imposed on societies unready for them. He agreed with Tocqueville that democratic government succeeded in the United States,

not because of its intrinsic excellence, but because of its suitability to the particular social, economic, and political conditions of the

---

[3] See Ray Stannard Baker and William E. Dodds, eds., *The Public Papers of Woodrow Wilson,* 6 vols. (New York: Harper Brothers, 1925–1927) (hereinafter cited as *Public Papers*). *College and State, 1875–1913,* 1: 15–16, 54, 59. See also "Abraham Lincoln: A Man of the People," address, February 12, 1909, *ibid.,* 2: 94. For a pioneer study of the relation between Wilson's beliefs and his foreign policy see Harley Notter, *The Origins of the Foreign Policy of Woodrow Wilson* (Baltimore: Johns Hopkins Press, 1937).
[4] *Public Papers: College and State,* 1: 426. See also *ibid.,* 2: 330–331, 360–361.
[5] *Ibid.,* 1: 76.
[6] *Ibid.,* p. 396.

people of the country for whose use and administration it had been framed. . . . No other people could expect to succeed by the same means, unless these means equally suited their character and stage of development. Democracy, like every other form of government, depended for its success upon qualities and conditions which it did not itself create, but only obeyed.[7]

Wilson's views on political development and on the tutelary responsibilities of developed peoples offset these pessimistic insights about the future of democracy. To Wilson, political development occurred organically, by evolution over centuries. A backward nation, unaccustomed to self-government, could not be expected to make democratic institutions work. Discipline had to precede liberty: "Discipline—discipline generations deep."[8]

Wilson applied this view of political development to the Philippines and concluded that the United States must retain the islands long enough to prepare them for democratic self-government.[9] Wilson did not stop there. In the past, he observed, Americans had acted "under an odd mixture of selfish and altruistic motives."[10] Now, as a world power and guardian of subject peoples, the United States could lay aside the old, selfish motives and concentrate on its new mission as teacher and example to mankind. A crucial part of this mission involved the political development of the Orient. "The East is to be transformed, whether we will or no," Wilson wrote:

The standards of the West are to be imposed upon it; nations and peoples which have stood still the centuries through are to be quickened and made part of the universal world of commerce and ideas which has so steadily been a-making by the advance of European power from age to age. It is our peculiar duty, as it is also England's, to moderate the process in the interests of liberty: to impart to the peoples thus driven out upon the road of change, so far as we have the opportunity or can make it, our own principles of self-help; teach them order and self-control in the midst of change; impart to them, if it be possible by contact and sympathy and example, the drill and habit of law and obedience which we long ago got out of the strenuous processes of English history; secure for them, when we may, the free intercourse and the natural development which shall make them at least equal

---

[7] *Ibid.*, pp. 396–397.
[8] *Ibid.*, p. 433.
[9] *Ibid.*, p. 434.
[10] *Ibid.*, p. 404.

members of the family of nations. In China, of course, our part
will be indirect, but in the Philippines it will be direct.[11]

With the exception of the Philippines, where the United States
had just suppressed an "insurrection," there is no provision in
this view for the use of military force to compel the peoples
of the Orient to accept American instruction on political development. In fact, Wilson specifically limited the American role
to "contact and sympathy and example." The potential open-
endedness of Wilson's concept of the duty of the United States
suggests itself, nonetheless, particularly in light of Wilson's ac-
tivistic moralism and the difficulties of teaching democracy to
what Wilson called "undeveloped peoples."

Wilson entered office opposed to "material interests" and committed to a program of social and economic reform. Roosevelt's
progressivism envisioned a benevolent partnership of big business
and big government acting together in the public interest. Wilson
held out the somewhat illusory prospect of a restoration of com-
petition that would preserve individual entrepreneurship. He desired to make room for the little man and to protect the welfare
and liberty of the American people against the greed and power
of giant financial and industrial concerns. In the end, Wilson's
achievements matched Roosevelt's objectives more closely than
his own, but Wilson's opposition to economic exploitation at
home made him sympathetic to rebellion against injustice and
oppression in Mexico.

When he became president, Wilson acted as though the tutelary
responsibilities of the United States included Mexico and the
Caribbean countries as well as Asia. At each crucial juncture
in the Mexican Revolution, Wilson appeared with a plan for
mediation, conciliation, and compromise. His efforts at conciliation were consistently unsuccessful for two reasons. First, the
Mexican factions were engaged in a struggle to the death that
could have been stopped only if the United States had conquered
and subdued Mexico, a course abhorrent to Wilson. From the
beginning of his administration, Wilson's Mexican policy was
caught between his sympathy for the revolutionaries and their
cause and his desire to control Mexico's destiny, a desire that
grew out of his concept of political development and his belief
in the tutelary role of the United States in the world. Second,
the outbreak of war in Europe and the eventual belligerency

[11] *Ibid.,* pp. 412–413.

of the United States preempted the thought and resources of the American government and limited its involvement in the Mexican Revolution.

The analysis that follows documents the responses of the Taft and Wilson administrations to the Mexican Revolution. It also provides a basis for a number of generalizations about the policies of Taft and Wilson and about the general problem of responding to foreign revolution.

I. Protecting American Lives and Property:
The Response of the Taft Administration, 1910–1913

1 Revolutionary Mexico: The Setting of Conflict

For centuries Mexicans had hoped and dreamed of putting an end to the stagnant, oppressive regime that had evolved from Spanish colonial antecedents. In studying Mexico's history, one is constantly impressed by the durability and consistency of the ideals of Mexican revolutionaries. José María Morelos, active a century before Carranza and Obregón, believed in racial equality, the breaking up of *haciendas* into small holdings for the peasants, the confiscation of the rich, universal suffrage, and parliamentary government, concepts that formed the credo of most twentieth-century Mexican revolutionaries.

Though Mexico won its independence from Spain early in the nineteenth century and acquired a veneer of modernization, these changes had little meaning for most Mexicans. Under Porfirio Díaz, in spite of the construction of railroads and factories, Mexico seemed to be a society neither feudal nor capitalist suffering from the worst abuses of both. The hacienda system expanded. In Lower California thirty million acres were allotted to one individual; seventeen million acres went to another individual in Chihuahua. "By 1910 nearly half of Mexico belonged to less than three thousand families, while of the ten millions of Mexicans engaged in agriculture more than nine and a half millions were virtually without land."[1] The wages of a peon had remained twenty-five to forty centavos a day for a century, while the cost of corn alone had increased four times. The initial attempts of factory workers to organize were brutally suppressed. The government consisted of the friends of the dictator or local politicians too powerful for him to control who were willing to recognize the federal government in exchange for a share in the spoils. The legislature and judiciary were handpicked by the dictator. Foreigners complained of corrupt officials and lazy workers, but the tranquillity of the country and the size of the profits made them supporters of the status quo.

Americans were the largest single investors in Mexico. Their interests were worth more than the sum of all foreign investments.[2] Foreigners had an enormous stake in Mexico:

---

[1] Henry Bamford Parkes, *A History of Mexico,* 3d ed., rev. and enl.; (Boston: Houghton Mifflin Company, 1960), p. 306.
[2] Interested persons and the contemporary American press assigned a value of $1 billion to American interests in Mexico. Most historians

Mexico, it was said, had become the mother of aliens and the stepmother of her own children. American interests—the Hearsts, the Guggenheims, United States Steel, the Anaconda Corporation, Standard Oil, McCormich, Doheny—owned three quarters of the mines and more than half the oil fields; they owned sugar plantations, and—along the American border—enormous cattle ranches. The American investment in Mexico, which by 1910 had grown to more than a billion dollars, exceeded the total capital owned by the Mexicans themselves. The English were interested in oil, in precious metals, in public utilities, and in sugar and coffee The textile mills belonged mainly to the French. Spaniards—still hated as *gachupines*—almost monopolized retail trade, acquired large *haciendas,* and owned the notorious tobacco fields, graveyard of thousands of convict laborers, in the Valle Nacional. Few of the foreign immigrants acquired Mexican citizenship. The foreign colonies lived in isolation, reserving all the more responsible and highly paid positions in their industries for men of their own race, accumulating wealth which they proposed one day to take home, and openly voicing their contempt for the nation which they were exploiting.[3]

Mexico passed through three crises during the Taft administration: the overthrow of the aged dictator, Porfirio Díaz in 1911; the difficulties experienced by the successful revolutionary leader, Francisco Madero, in establishing his government throughout 1912; and the overthrow of the Madero regime by Victoriano Huerta in February 1913. In responding to each crisis Taft acted to maximize the protection afforded American lives and property.

The Taft administration expired before organized government in Mexico broke down and before the Mexican revolutionaries who rose against Huerta had formulated a coherent, radical program. Thus it is unclear how Taft would have handled the problems that confronted President Wilson. Taft's caution, his limited construction of presidential powers, and his limited objectives stand out, as does his appreciation of the difficulties of acting effectively in Mexico without precipitating the very attacks on American lives and property he sought to prevent.

---

have accepted this figure. At the time the State Department in its own confidential estimate gave the much lower figure of $331 million, which may have represented the value of the physical plants alone, excluding all loans and securities. See *Memo on "The Mexican Situation,"* prepared by J. R. Clark Jr., Solicitor for the Department of State, Knox Papers, Correspondence, 19: 3106–3107.

[3] Parkes, *History of Mexico,* pp. 308–309.

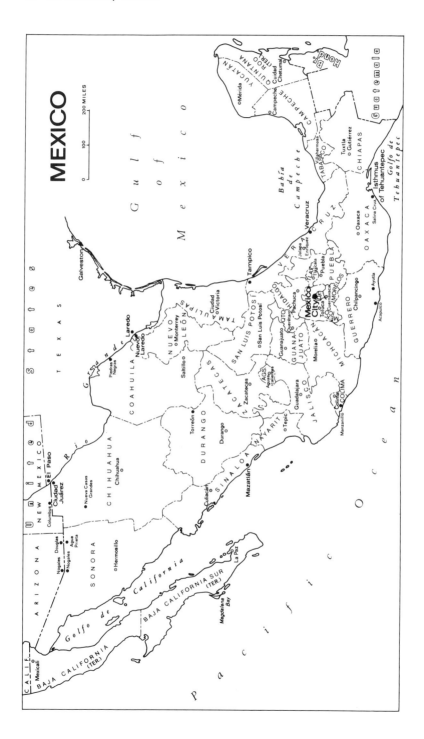

Taft and Knox regarded security interests as vitally important in Central America, and they frequently said so in trying to defend dollar diplomacy. But security interests go virtually unmentioned in connection with the revolution in Mexico. The Taft administration acted to preserve and protect American interests in Mexico out of their belief in the crucial importance of foreign markets for national survival. Taft revealed his concerns in a letter to his wife written during a political tour of the United States on the occasion of a meeting with Díaz on the Mexican–United States border.

There is a great fear, and I am afraid a well-founded fear, that should [Díaz] die, there will be a revolution growing out of the selection of his successor. As Americans have about $2,000,000 [sic] of capital invested in the country, it is inevitable that in case of a revolution or internecine strife we should interfere, and I sincerely hope that the old man's official life will extend beyond mine, for that trouble would present a problem of the utmost difficulty. I am not quite sure at whose instance the meeting was had, but I do know I had received a communication, perhaps directly from the old man, of an informal character, saying how glad he would be to have such a meeting brought about. He thinks, and I believe rightly, that the knowledge throughout his country of the friendship of the United States for him and his Government will strengthen him with his own people, and tend to discourage revolutionists' efforts to establish a different government.[4]

"The old man's official life" ended because of the failure and collapse of the old order rather than the irresistible success of the new.[5] Just six months after Francisco Madero had declared against Díaz, the dictator resigned the presidency and sought exile in Spain. He did so with the gratitude and admiration of the American government. President Taft wrote to Díaz:

. . . to express my warm feeling of friendship and admiration for you as a man, a statesman, and as a patriot. After your long and faithful service to Mexico and the Mexican people, it arouses in me the profoundest feeling of sympathy and sorrow to see what you have done temporarily forgotten. Even now, however, your disinterested love of your country shows itself in your willingness

---

[4] W. H. Taft to Helen H. Taft, October 17, 1909, The Papers of William H. Taft, Library of Congress, Ser. 8, 7: 460–461 (hereinafter cited as Taft Papers).

[5] See E. J. Hobsbawn, *The Age of Revolution, Europe 1789–1848* (London: Weidenfeld and Nicholson, 1962), for a view of this as a common revolutionary sequence.

to lay down your high office and to become an exile if only you can thus compose the unhappy differences between your countrymen and bring peace again, and the prosperity which is dependent on peace.

Into your highly honorable retirement, I would send this message of high appreciation and good will with the fervent prayer that your well earned leisure, your freedom from responsibility after many years of heavy burdens, and the retrospect of a grand work of development of your people done by you may give you the happiness and peace of mind you so richly deserve. . . .

With you, I sincerely hope that peace will come to Mexico and that upon the foundations which you reared, may be erected a permanent state in which order will prevail, due process of law be maintained and prosperity be consequently restored.[6]

Taft expressed his respect for Díaz in full knowledge of the corruption, poverty, and tyranny that existed in Mexico. To Taft and to most of his administration, Díaz had accomplished a great deal considering what he had to work with. Moreover, foreign investment had been welcomed by Díaz and had prospered under his regime. Taft, Knox, and especially the American ambassador to Mexico, Henry Lane Wilson, believed that, because of the poverty and ignorance of most Mexicans, Mexico could not for the foreseeable future achieve any workable sort of democratic governmental system. Only after a long period of education and economic development would Mexico be "ready" for democracy.[7] During the interim the United States, according to this view, should work to preserve the status quo, which could and would be changed only by gradual evolution.

THE IMPORTANCE OF AMBASSADOR HENRY LANE WILSON

Taft trusted the judgment of his ambassador to Mexico, Henry Lane Wilson, to an extent that should make any diplomat envious. Wilson exerted a decisive influence on the response of

---

[6] W. H. Taft to Porfirio Díaz, June 7, 1911, Taft Papers, Ser. 8, 24: 258–259.
[7] In this connection it is interesting to compare the reasons advanced by Taftian conservatives to justify a dictatorship of the right in Mexico with the similar reasons given by some social scientists and some critics of current American foreign policy to justify dictatorships of the left in the underdeveloped countries of today. For an example of the latter, see Robert L. Heilbroner, "Counter-Revolutionary America," *Commentary* 43, no. 4 (April 1967): 31–38. Mexico offers a qualified refutation of both views.

the Taft administration to the Mexican Revolution. At every crucial point one finds the ambassador's views and recommendations shaping policy.

Wilson gained his position in the American diplomatic corps as a reward for his connections with and services to the Republican party.[8] He possessed little training relevant to his new career and was an activist by temperament, altogether in conflict with Talleyrand's warning *"Surtout, messieurs, pas trop de zèle."* In Mexico, Wilson took seriously his position as the diplomatic representative of the United States. He worked hard at his daily tasks which, until Madero declared against Díaz, largely consisted of running interference for American firms wrongly brought to court or otherwise entangled in the web of the Díaz regime's corruption. Wilson's political dispatches reflected his own biases. With a conservative's insight into politics and human nature, Wilson perceived and predicted the twists and turns of the Mexican Revolution as it progressed from Madero's mild reformist coup to the wild brutality of Pancho Villa and the bloody and apparently unconquerable rebellion led by Emiliano Zapata. If Wilson saw beyond the revolutionary turmoil, he thought only in terms of what would have been destroyed, and above all in terms of loss of American lives and harm to his country's economic primacy in Mexico. Ambassador Wilson's overwhelming desire for stability and law and order in Mexico, in the face of the terrible odds he understood and reported accurately, led him to yearn for a strong man to emerge who would force the lid back on Mexico's cauldron of troubles and preserve America's position in the country. The only changes he could foresee as a result of the revolution promised to diminish the American position in Mexico, and Wilson bemoaned their arrival while he worked to defeat them. He distrusted the future and the capacity of Mexicans to make something better than that which they destroyed. His reasoning went along these lines: The Mexican people are too poor, too ignorant, and too unaccustomed to self-government to accomplish anything permanent at the end of the period of anarchy that seems likely to ensue after Madero gains power. After all the slaughter and destruction, a strong leader like Díaz will have to take power to restore peace and order to Mexico. Nothing will have changed except

---

[8] See Henry Lane Wilson, *Diplomatic Episodes in Mexico, Belguim, and Chile* (Garden City, N.Y.: Doubleday, 1927). Wilson's brother was the boss of the Republican party in the state of Washington.

that thousands will have died and American interests will have
been ruined. Since, according to this view, the revolution could
not be justified in any sort of cost-benefit evaluation, it ought
to be shortened. If a capable dictator took control soon enough,
the inevitable end of coercive government would have been
reached without the damaging period of extremism and civil
war. The rather lengthy quotes that follow provide insight into
the ambassador's views, a peculiar mixture of understanding
and shortsightedness, that exercised great influence on policy.
   On October 31, 1910, Wilson filed a summary of the political
situation in Mexico that amounted to a scathing critique of
the Díaz regime:
Theoretically, Mexico is a federal Republic similar in form to ours,
certain specified rights being reserved to the States and certain
others exercised by the Central Government. Like ours, the Central
Government is divided into three branches, viz.: the Legislative,
Executive and Judicial, but this is a nominal division only, as practically, the legislative and judicial branches are subordinate to and
in a very large measure the creatures of the executive. The members
of both branches of the Legislature must be in political accord
with the executive and it is not in the least wise controverted
that in order to be elected either a deputy or a senator, executive
approval is an absolute essential; the law making power is thus
virtually in the hands of the executive. The control of the Executive
over the judiciary is even more absolute and more clearly defined
than that exercised over the legislative branch. Though a form
of election is gone through, the President actually names and re-
moves at pleasure all of the fifteen judges of the Supreme Court
and all the judges of the minor Federal Courts. Having thus control
of the initiation and enactment of the laws of the Republic, through
representatives of his own choosing, and of the interpretation of
the laws and of the administration of justice, through an attached
and subservient judiciary, it is not difficult to see that the President
of the Republic is really an autocrat ruling and governing through
republican forms and maintaining his rule by the use of those
instrumentalities which inherently belong to the Executive, namely:
the army and the police.[9]

---

[9] U.S., National Archives, General Records of the Department of State,
Record Group 59; Internal Affairs of Mexico, 1910–1929, H. L. Wilson
to Knox, October 31, 1910, 812.00/355. Hereinafter only the decimal
number and date are cited. How much of this dispatch was composed
by Wilson and how much by other members of the embassy, like Fred
Morris Dearing, is an open question. Though Dearing performed admirably
in the Latin American Division in Washington, his departure from the
embassy deprived Wilson of the counsel of an experienced, perceptive,
and judicious subordinate.

Of the general conditions that contributed to unrest and opposition Wilson wrote:

Concentration of wealth and lands.
It is probably capable of demonstration that the great mass of the wealth of the country is in the hands of 10% of its population. . . . It is not at all an uncommon thing to find millions of acres in a single holding and some large land holders, like Molina and Terrazas, have passed the 10,000,000 mark. Probably ten millions of the population of Mexico do not own a foot of land nor have other means than that derived from toil.

The growing middle class.
This class, while not an evil, is a danger. Its existence springs from the better things which the Government has done and from the example and influence of the so-called American invasion. All over the Republic a class of sturdy tradesmen, usually of Indian blood, has developed. This class is industrious, intelligent, takes an acute interest in public affairs, is impatient of existing conditions, and constantly exerting a stronger and wider influence. Usually this class is opposed to the present Government and utterly hostile to the group of men [*Cientificos*] supposed to be its moving force. It may easily be supported that in the event of a crisis the vast majority will rise to the support of ambitious men offering remedies for present evils.[10]

The ambassador saved his strongest condemnation for the judiciary, calling it "weak and debauched," and adding that it was only by the "utmost vigilance and by pressure upon the President, upon the Foreign Office, by unofficial communications to Governors, and by almost daily visits by [an American] representative to the judges here in Mexico, that I have been able to prevent the grossest injustice and the rankest outrages to persons and property of American citizens."[11]

Wilson had ample reason to dislike both the system Díaz had created and its operation. Instead, he warned: "Under the circumstances it will be easily understood that the permanence of specific conditions, the prevalence of order, the security of invested capital, both domestic and foreign, and the maintenance of cordial relations with contiguous nations depends in a large measure, if not entirely, upon the character of the Executive. . . ."[12] President Díaz, aged and increasingly infirm, was apparently at the mercy of his ministers, who exploited their rank and attacked American interests for their own gain. Wilson

[10] *Ibid.*
[11] *Ibid.*
[12] *Ibid.*

ended his dispatch with a warning that seemed to imply the necessity of American intervention in Mexico at some future time:

The evils and dangers which surround the administration of President Diaz are real, in spite of the vast amount of good which it has conferred upon the country. In the natural order of things he must soon pass away, and the state of affairs which may follow his decease, while it cannot be predicted with certainty, ought nevertheless to be the subject of serious consideration by our Government, a vast number of whose citizens, some with their wealth and some with their persons, have staked their faith on the stability of this Republic.[13]

This dispatch still reflected the belief, shared by President Taft, that Díaz would remain in office until forced to retire by sickness or old age. Late in November 1910, Ambassador Wilson reported that the revolutionary movement launched by Madero in October 1910 was being suppressed.[14] In a dispatch dated November 26, he discussed Madero's movement against Díaz as though it had been entirely defeated. But he pointed out (1) that despite poor organization and leadership the movement had "ramified throughout the Republic and was remarkable for its intensity and bitterness showing deep-seated antipathy and antagonism to the Government"; (2) that the upper and lower classes remained aloof, though openly sympathetic with the movement against Díaz; and (3) that the Mexican government was deeply apprehensive and had difficulty in dealing with "an unorganized and leaderless movement."[15] Speaking in the past tense he concluded that "during the recent disturbances in the North, the danger did not result from the strength and respectability of the movement but from the circumstances that a few successes by the revolutionists would have brought about a serious and active movement in all the great centers against the present Government."[16] On December 12, Ambassador Wilson reported the defeat of all organized resistance against the government.[17] On December 16 he stated that his earlier telegram had been based on "verbal official information" given in anticipation of victory, which had not yet been consummated.[18] And on December 29 the ambassador reported that,

---

[13] *Ibid.*
[14] H. L. Wilson to Secretary of State, November 25, 1910, 812.00/474.
[15] H. L. Wilson to Secretary of State, November 26, 1910, 812.00/517.
[16] *Ibid.*
[17] H. L. Wilson to Secretary of State, December 12, 1910, 812.00/563.
[18] H. L. Wilson to Secretary of State, December 16, 1910, 812.00/567.

although he had great difficulty securing reliable information, "it is certain, however, that the Government's reverses have been in some cases severe, and the fact that the local press is severely censored demonstrated considerable [governmental] apprehension and timidity."[19] The characteristics that marked Wilson's later political reporting were already in evidence: the situation is defined so that any change, short of the installation of another iron-fisted dictator, is considered dangerous; the telegrams swing wildly from reports of total governmental success to reports of "serious reverses," and the domestic Mexican political climate is depicted in an ominous light.

---

[19] H. L. Wilson to Secretary of State, December 29, 1910, 812.00/622.

As the new year began, the movement against Díaz steadily
gained strength, and on February 16, 1911, Ambassador Wilson
reported: "The revolutionary situation in a general way is becoming worse."[1] Throughout this period the Mexican government made a great effort to enlist the aid of the United States
in suppressing Madero's movement. Mexico's appeals for the
United States to stop the movement of men and supplies across
the border, to prevent the dissemination of anti-Díaz propaganda, to halt the flow of arms to the revolutionaries, and to
arrest Madero and the other revolutionary leaders presented another aspect of the Mexican Revolution to which the American
government had to respond.

ARMS AND NEUTRALITY

During a conversation with Ambassador Wilson, President Díaz
characterized the activities of Madero's followers in the United
States, particularly their purchase and shipment of arms to Mexico, as a breach of neutrality. He asked for energetic action
by the American government to stop these practices.[2] Knox's
reply outlined the position taken by the Taft administration until
March 1912, when an arms embargo resolution was voted by
Congress. According to international law, Knox wrote, "Mere
trade in arms, ammunition and other articles of contraband
is considered legal and subject to no penalty save the loss of
the goods if captured in the trade."[3] Knox then cited the statu-
tory authority under which persons could be prosecuted in the
United States for hostile acts committed on American territory
against a nation with which the United States was at peace.
In brief, these "neutrality acts" forbid accepting a commission
to serve against another state, enlisting in service against another
state, fitting out vessels for use against another state, and preparing a military expedition against another state. Knox concluded
that: "from the circumstance stated in your conversation with

---

[1] H. L. Wilson to Secretary of State, February 16, 1911, 812.00/798.
But even at his strongest Madero could count on less than 17,500 fighting
men. See Howard F. Cline, *The United States and Mexico,* rev. ed.,
enl. (Cambridge, Mass.: Harvard University Press, 1965), p. 122.
[2] H. L. Wilson to Secretary of State, November 16, 1910, 812.00/447.
[3] Knox to American Embassy, Mexico, December 14, 1910, 812.00/447.

the President of Mexico, it does not appear that the incident mentioned by him falls within any of the rules of international law on neutrality, or within the American laws on the same subject. In future conversations with the President you will have the above rules and statutes in mind."[4]

When the Mexican government asked for the arrest of Maderistas in Presidio, Texas, alleging, among other charges, that they had slandered the Mexican government, Knox replied that arrests could be made only if the parties named carried out any of the acts prohibited by the neutrality statutes. He added, "It should be recalled that since under the American Constitution liberty of speech and of the press is guaranteed, mere propaganda in and of itself would probably not fall within these statutes and would not be punishable thereunder."[5]

Together, the Mexican embassy in Washington and the Mexican government made almost daily requests for aid in suppressing the revolutionaries. Their pleas lacked the evidence needed to convict Maderistas in an American court of law, and the conduct of the Mexican government showed little proof of an intention or ability to police the Mexican side of the border. To a complaint from the Mexican ambassador that the revolutionaries enjoyed what amounted to asylum in the United States, Knox replied: "I venture to remind your excellency that the mere fact that a man is engaged in revolutionary undertakings in another country does not render his presence in the United States illegal."[6] To a request that Madero and his colleagues be arrested in San Antonio for violation of the neutrality laws, Knox answered:

This Government has spared and will spare no effort in its endeavors to see that its international obligations are fully met, but, as you are aware, notwithstanding the numerous charges which have been heretofore made against various persons regarding their unneutral conduct on American territory, it has, so far, been impossible for this Government to secure evidence of such unneutral conduct sufficient to justify putting the accused parties upon trial, to say nothing of securing a conviction.[7]

To an overzealous American consul along the border, Wilbur J. Carr, director of the consular service, wrote: "this Govern-

---

[4] *Ibid.*
[5] Knox to de la Barra, November 28, 1910, 812.00/499.
[6] Knox to de la Barra, January 24, 1911, 812.00/654.
[7] Knox to de la Barra, January 24, 1911, 812.00/655.

ment can not be regarded and is not to be regarded as an insurer
of the peace in Mexico, nor as a policeman charged with the
maintenance of order along its northern border."[8]

After pointing out that the activities of the Mexican government seemed to be confined to reporting rumored incursions,
Carr stated: "The policing of the Mexican border is a matter
for the Mexican Government, and not for this Government,
and while this Government will continue to use every legitimate
endeavor to prevent illegal and hostile expeditions, it can not
be charged with the responsibility of preventing the legal importation of arms and ammunition into Mexico, nor the exclusion
from Mexico of bands of unorganized Mexican citizens who are
returning to their native land. . . ."[9]

Carr instructed the consul as follows:
You will, therefore, while continuing to be most vigilant in preventing violations of the neutrality of the United States, which this
Government has the strongest desire to observe, be certain to keep
strictly within the law, and have especial care that you take no
action which will, under the circumstances given above, appear
to shift the responsibility of maintaining peace on the Mexican
side of the border from the Mexican Government, where it belongs,
to this Government, where it does not belong.[10]

The traditional legalism of this position is apparent. The United
States government had often in cases involving revolution in
Latin America attempted to make this sort of basic division
of responsibility and obligation. The long and inhospitable land
border with Mexico made control extremely difficult, and many
Americans living along the border sympathized with the anti-
Díaz forces. But the American government did more than its
share to police the border. The Díaz regime fell because of its
own corruption and its inability to defend itself or to enforce
its laws, not as a result of American support for the regime's
opponents. The following excerpts from reports of the commanding generals of the departments of Texas and Colorado describe
the situation along the border. Brigadier General J. W. Duncan
wrote of the Texas department:
From information gleaned all along the line I am convinced that
the populace along the border on both sides of the river, not only
Mexican but to some extent American, are in sympathy with the

---

[8] Carr to Ellsworth, January 25, 1911, 812.00/672a. This was sent to
all border consuls.
[9] *Ibid.*
[10] *Ibid.*

revolutionary movement in Mexico, and that they will aid and comfort where they can when running no special risk.

Our troops produce a moral and restraining effect and will be able from time to time to apprehend or capture material and parties attempting to cross into Mexico, but on the other hand small parties and small quantities of material can probably be gotten through from time to time without discovery.

I found no patrolling on the part of the Mexican authorities on the Mexican side of the border, only one instance of a patrol having been seen was reported to me.[11]

Brigadier General W. S. Schengler wrote of the Colorado department:

Since my arrival, I have made every effort to inform myself upon the situation, and must admit a difficulty in arriving at satisfactory conclusions. I am satisfied that our guard and patrol of the border is as effective as it is possible to make it. I am satisfied that the number of arms and recruits for the revolutionary ranks which get across the border is very small. I am satisfied that most of the rumors as to the recruits procured on American soil and of arms and ammunition smuggled across the border are enormously exaggerated. . . .

West of Juarez and El Paso there are no Mexican federal troops worthy of being classed as soldiers, and the inferiority of the enlisted men is only equalled by the incapacity of the officers in command of them. The so-called revolutionists are divided into bands without a common leader and without apparent coordination. South of El Paso the uniform seems to consist of a certain straw hat. Farther west it is a broad brimmed black hat with a band of red, white, and green. . . . It is easy for these people to procure arms and ammunition, for they simply have to find out where such exist in ranches or small villages in Mexico, and then proceed to go and take them. . . .[12]

The American government's policy of diplomatic and commercial neutrality had been fashioned in the State Department, and its punctiliousness reflected the legal background and training of virtually the entire upper level of the department. It did not go unchallenged. The letter sent by Carr to the border consuls evoked a letter of protest to Knox from the attorney general, G. W. Wickersham. The chief of the Justice Department's Bureau of Investigation, Stanley W. Finch, had been sent to the border to direct the efforts of the Justice Department, in cooperation with those of the War and Treasury departments,

---

[11] Duncan to Adjutant General, dated February 25, 1911, 812.00/968.
[12] Schengler to Adjutant General, March 5, 1911, 812.00/974.

to prevent violations of the neutrality laws. Finch apparently complained to his chief of the restrictive orders given the consuls by the State Department. Wickersham's letter to Knox, missing from the State Department's files, was evidently based on Finch's reports and the personal misgivings of the attorney general. Huntington Wilson, in a memo to Knox on February 18, called Wickersham's letter "extremely outrageous" and asked if Knox had been present at a cabinet meeting when President Taft had, according to the attorney general, directed that the border should be policed as effectively as possible and that the flow into Mexico of arms, ammunition, and men should be halted. Knox indicated that he had been present, but that the idea had been to do only that which was legal. In rebuttal, Knox took the attorney general's letter to the president together with his unsigned reply.[13] Knox was determined to avoid an "exercise of neutrality so aggressive as to become un-neutral," and his position carried with the president.

"MANEUVERS" ALONG THE BORDER
On balance, the formal neutrality of the United States benefited the Maderistas and undermined Díaz. Although Madero had won no major battles by the winter of 1911, he had revealed the Díaz regime to be hollow and impotent. Ambassador Wilson found the situation deeply alarming. He took advantage of a visit to the United States to confer with President Taft. As a result of their meeting, Taft mobilized 20,000 troops and sent them to the border. He acted apparently without consulting the State Department. Knox was vacationing in Florida, and Taft explained what he had done and why in a long letter to the secretary:
On Monday [March 6, 1911] after you left I had a call from Ambassador Wilson. He was anxious to see me, and I gave him a full opportunity for a talk. His view of the situation in Mexico was very pessimistic. He said that all of Mexico was boiling; that disturbances in the north and south were merely symptomatic of a condition in the body politic which made him afraid of an outburst at any moment; that all that was necessary was a successful leader and the explosion would come. He said that Americans were very solicitous as to what would happen when the explosion did come; that the spirit of anti-Americanism, which had mani-

---

[13] 812.00/780. This includes all related correspondence except the missing letter from the attorney general.

fested itself in the riots, was still existent, and that they were looking to the United States with the utmost concern for protection should the explosion come which they thought was possible at any time. I had two or three letters from different parts of Mexico from private persons that confirmed this view, and have also had personal interviews.[14]

Taft wrote that he had then discussed the situation with the secretary of the navy, George von L. Meyer, the secretary of war, J. M. Dickinson, and the army chief of staff and the chief of naval operations. The navy had been planning maneuvers in the Gulf of Mexico for several months, and the army was more than willing to act: "[General] Wood and Dickinson said that they would send down enough to make 16,000 troops without great effort, and that they could make the movement useful for the Army, and as this was just the season for maneuvers in Texas they thought it would be an excellent thing for the Army and the Navy to have a mobilization at Galveston, San Antonio and Los Angeles."[15]

Taft then told Knox his motives for ordering the mobilization: I concluded that the doing of this would strengthen the forces for law and order in Mexico and would put both parties on notice in that Republic that we were ready to defend our rights if occasion arose. I concluded that it would have a very healthful effect with reference to the care which might be exercised by the combatants in respect of American citizens and American property, and that the presence of troops near at hand might have a very healthful effect all along the border in stopping the crossing and re-crossing of filibustering expeditions which make their field of action in both countries and supply the insurrectors with ammunition.[16]

In his letter of instructions to General Wood, later treated by Taft as a document for limited public circulation, Taft gave this version of his motives:
It seems my duty as Commander-in-Chief to place troops in sufficient number where if Congress shall direct that they enter Mexico to save American lives and property, an effective movement may be promptly made. Meantime, the movement of the troops to Texas and elsewhere near the boundary, accompanied with sincere assurances of the utmost goodwill toward the present Mexican Government and with larger and more frequent patrols along the border to prevent insurrectionary expeditions from American soil, will

---

[14] Taft to Knox, March 11, 1911, Taft Papers, Ser. 8, 24: 351–352.
[15] *Ibid.*, p. 352.
[16] *Ibid.*, p. 353.

hold up the hands of the existing government and will have a
healthy moral effect to prevent attacks upon Americans and their
property in any subsequent general internecine strife.[17]

Taft denied that he contemplated intervention and even ques-
tioned whether he had the right to use force in this way without
the permission of Congress.

The assumption by the Press that I contemplate intervention on
Mexican soil to protect American lives or property is of course
gratuitous, because I seriously doubt whether I have such authority
under any circumstances, and if I had, I would not exercise it
without express congressional approval. . . . My determined purpose, however, is to be in a position so that when danger to American lives and property in Mexico threatens, and the existing government is rendered helpless by the insurrection, I can promptly
execute congressional orders to protect them with effect.[18]

Taft intended to capitalize on the deterrent effects on the revolutionaries and on the domestic critics of his Mexican policy,
but he went through the appropriate motions to disguise his
precise motives. The day after the interview with Ambassador
Wilson, the president instructed the State Department to reassure
the Mexican government that the maneuvers should not be a
cause for alarm. Throughout, the administration maintained that
the mobilization was ordered as a part of normal field training,
and on March 9 a cover story was published giving a scenario
for an attack on Galveston by the navy.[19] The same day the
cover story was released, the secretary of the navy notified the
State Department that enroute from Panama to San Diego the
U.S.S. *Princeton* would call at the west coast ports of Salina
Cruz, Acapulco, and Manzanillo and that the *Yorktown* would
also be sent to ports on the Pacific Coast.[20] News of this caused
a furor in Mexico and prompted the Mexican ambassador to
ask for an explanation. President Taft reassured the ambassador,
ordered the ships away, and wrote a note to the secretary of
navy expressing surprise that the ships had been sent, since this
had not been mentioned at the March 6 meeting. He instructed
the secretary to keep naval maneuvers north of the border and

---

[17] *Ibid.*, pp. 142–143.
[18] *Ibid.*, p. 143.
[19] U.S., Department of State, Division of Information, Confidential Series
A, no. 72, Mexico, no. 6, "Disorders in Mexico," March 25, 1911, p.
47, hereinafter cited as Confidential Series A.
[20] Acting Secretary of Navy to Secretary of State, March 9, 1911,
812.00/912.

to "see that these small fry do not appear any more in Mexican ports."[21]

A number of personal letters written by Taft to friends and to friendly members of the press reveal the same general picture of the president's reasons for ordering the "maneuvers." Taft and Theodore Roosevelt still remained on good terms at the time of the mobilization, and on March 14, eight days after the decision to mobilize, Roosevelt wrote to Taft:

I don't suppose that there is anything in this war talk, and I most earnestly hope that we will not have to intervene even to do temporary police duty in Mexico. But just because there is, I suppose, one chance in a thousand of serious trouble such as would occur if Japan or some other big power were to back Mexico, I write. Of course I would not wish to take any part in a mere war with Mexico—it would not be my business to do peculiarly irksome and disagreeable and profitless police duty of the kind that any occupation of Mexico would entail. But if by any remote chance—and I know how remote it is—there should be a serious war, a war in which Mexico was backed by Japan or some other big power, then I would wish immediately to apply for permission to raise a division of cavalry, such as the regiment I commanded in Cuba. . . . I ask, Sir, that instead of treating this as a boast, you will remember that in the war with Spain our regiment was raised, armed, equipped, mounted, dismounted, drilled, kept two weeks on transports, and put through two victorious aggressive fights in which it lost nearly a quarter of the men engaged, and over one-third of the officers, a loss greater than that suffered by any but two of the twenty-four regular regiments in the same army corps; and all this within less than sixty days.[22]

In his reply, which began "My dear Theodore," Taft went out of his way to explain his actions to Roosevelt. He promised to grant Roosevelt's wish for a division if the occasion arose, but he doubted that Japan would get involved: "As I write, however, I have not the slightest idea that there will be any war in which Japan will take a part, and I sincerely hope that there will be no trouble at all and no need to do other than exercise our troops in guarding the border and in maneuvers in Texas."[23]

Further on, Taft returned to the question of Japanese involve-

[21] Taft to Meyer, March 14, 1911, Taft Papers, Ser. 8, 24: 279.
[22] Theodore Roosevelt to W. H. Taft, March 14, 1911, Taft Papers, Ser. 7, casefile 26.
[23] Taft to Roosevelt, March 22, 1911, Taft Papers, Ser. 8, 24: 205.

ment: "The suggestion that Japan has any interest in the matter seems to me to be wholly gratuitous. The truth is, our new [immigration] treaty with Japan has put us on the best basis possible with that country and there is nothing she would like less than a controversy with us at present."[24]

Taft told Roosevelt of the alarming interview with Ambassador Wilson and of the subsequent meeting with the navy and army officials. He also repeated what he had written to General Wood about having an adequate force in readiness "where it could be used should the explosion that Wilson feared take place and chaos ensue, in which case I should ask Congress to authorize me to send a force into Mexican territory to preserve American lives and property which would certainly be exposed to a great deal of danger." With regard to the ships in Mexican waters, he wrote:

I found, to my surprise, however, that the Navy, in addition to having mobilized a force at Galveston and San Diego, had also sent a few small boats north from Panama and Central America with a view to patrolling the Mexican coast. This attracted the attention of the Mexican Government, and they invited my attention to it, and I immediately reversed the orders as to those vessels. The Navy is anxious for a contest, and has to be held in leash. However, they now understand my exact position.[25]

Taft denied that he had "yielded to Wall Street influence" or acted on behalf of any specific American interests: "As a matter of fact, I have no communication of any sort with anybody representing any property in Mexico, except possibly Cecil Lyon, who was fearful of his plantation."[26] To his brother, Horace Taft, he wrote: "I observe that the Insurgents are preparing to attack me [for the mobilization]. The chief basis of the attack is that possibly this movement might, if carried through, save a billion dollars to wicked Americans who have invested their money in Mexico. To use United States troops for the defense of American capitalists and American property is horrible."[27]

It had been necessary, Taft wrote to Roosevelt, to conceal the actual reasons for the mobilization in order to protect the ambassador and to avoid excessive damage to Mexican-American rela-

---

[24] *Ibid.*, p. 209.
[25] *Ibid.*, p. 207.
[26] *Ibid.*, p. 208.
[27] W. H. Taft to Horace Taft, March 16, 1911, Taft Papers, Ser. 8, 24: 294.

tions. Taft, asking that the source of the information be kept secret, sent the substance of the reply to Roosevelt and a copy of his letter to General Wood to a number of newspapers, including the Richmond *Times Dispatch,* the Boston *Advertiser,* the Philadelphia *Public Ledger,* and the Los Angeles *Times.*[28] He sent another less complete version of events to a number of other papers, including the New York *Tribune* and the New York *Sun.*[29]

Secretary Knox remained in Florida, but he wrote the president a warm letter in support of his actions.[30] In a memorandum handwritten on the stationery of his hotel, the Royal Poinciana, Knox explored some of the problems raised by the uncertain situation in Mexico. He grappled with the difficulty of protecting the thousands of Americans scattered over Mexico and, in the process, revealed that he agreed with Taft's limited construction of executive powers:

This government does not undertake to furnish police protection for the lives and property of its citizens who reside in foreign countries.

Our inability to discharge such an obligation in respect to ["so vast"—deleted] such a country as Mexico over whose vast area are scattered tens of thousands of American citizens engaged in divers and disconnected occupations is obvious.

Our obligation to our citizens is to insist upon Mexico extending to them the full protection of her laws under which our citizens have elected to live and which protection is secured to them by treaty guarantees.

If Mexico refuses to comply with her treaty obligations it may be cause for declaring war. That Congress must decide.

The President cannot undertake to supersede and discharge the functions of the Mexican Government by invading her territory to furnish police protection to Americans without by so doing declaring the inadequacy of the Mexican government or its intentional refusal to protect Americans. This would be cause for war.[31]

An entry in Wilbur J. Carr's diary describing a discussion of Mexican affairs with the secretary provides additional insight into Knox's assessment of how to respond to the problems caused by the Mexican Revolution.

---

[28] See Taft Papers, Ser. 8, 24: 390–395, 404–405, 407–410.
[29] *Ibid.,* pp. 416–427.
[30] Knox to Taft, March 15, 1911, Knox Papers, Correspondence, 13: 2229–2230.
[31] Knox Papers, Correspondence, n.d., 14: 2280.

Easter Monday. Bright and sunny. . . . Called into conference
in Secretary's office in regard to Mexican situation. . . . Treasury
[had] closed customs house at Douglas, Ariz. opposite Agua Prieta
where Federals and insurrectors were fighting today. . . . Decided
we should deal with those in *de facto* control [of the customs].
Question as to how to protect Douglas from fire on Mexican side.
Agreed that would be justified in crossing line with troops, but
not desirable in interest of preventing injury to Americans in interior. Interesting discussion as to landing troops. John Hay said
to have held that troops could be landed anywhere to protect American interests. Knox said he did not believe Hay had so held without
having qualifications in his mind. . . . [Knox was] very much
against sending troops into Mexico because "if you do you will
never come out."
Interesting to note Knox's methods. No books merely questions
put to others, then application of answers to concrete cases. . . .
Mind works always along practical lines. Never theoretical.[32]

Knox had come to grips with two problems crucial to armed
intervention in another country. They were, first, controlling
the intervention and, second, being prepared and willing to accept all the consequences that might conceivably flow from the
intervention. With regard to controlling the intervention, Knox
believed that armed intervention in Mexico would have become
an unending task. Even if American forces could have "pacified"
the country, they could not have been withdrawn in the foreseeable future. Moreover, as soon as the occupation ended, the
old tensions and inequities in Mexican society would surface
and the struggle to resolve them would resume. Knox believed
that intervention and the hatred of America that would result
from it would precipitate the slaughter of Americans and the
destruction of their property. In Knox's view, armed intervention, given the situation that existed in Mexico, was an inappropriate means to the end of protecting American lives and
property in Mexico. He feared that the use of force would cause
destruction of the very lives and interests he sought to protect.
Last, Knox believed that one likely consequence of intervention
might be war between Mexico and the United States. A
declaration of war by Mexico would threaten and probably
defeat his policy, even if Americans and their interests weathered
the initial outpouring of anti-American sentiment. Knox refused
to duck either the potential openendedness of the smallest
expedition into Mexico territory or the possibility that the use

[32] Carr Papers, Diary, entry for April 17, 1911.

of force would defeat the ends he sought to achieve. Concern over these objections to armed intervention permeated the Taft administration, with the crucial exception of Ambassador Wilson, and exerted significant influence on American policy.

Madero's brief term as president of Mexico was distinguished by two traits: moderation and surprising longevity. Politically, Madero desired to give Mexico liberal democratic government. His ideas on social reform were vague, but he favored gradual change through legislation and compensation. Even so mild a platform lost him the support of the rich and of the foreign colony, but this did little damage numerically or militarily. At the same time, Madero's moderate reformism left him unable dramatically to improve the lot of the poor, most of whom desired land of their own. Possessing neither an effective political organization to implement even limited reforms nor a dependable and assuredly loyal army to detect and defeat all enemies of the regime, Madero floated on the troubled surface of Mexican politics. Unable to secure his government from repeated attempts at its overthrow, he nevertheless survived in office for fifteen months, drawing strength from the conflicting antagonisms of his opponents and, though it was a wasting asset, from the enthusiasm and idealism stirred by his movement's success against Díaz. The ease with which Victoriano Huerta and Félix Díaz toppled Madero's government testified to the shallowness of the regime's roots.

The record of American policy during the Madero regime is marked by a discrepancy: a discrepancy between the extreme and at times abusive pessimism of Ambassador Wilson's political reports about conditions in Mexico and the limited response of the American government to those reports. Essentially, the American response was limited to the prohibition in March 1912 of arms shipments to Mexico, almost immediately interpreted to allow shipments to the Madero government, and the dispatch, in September 1912, of a threatening protest. American business and commercial interests in Mexico remained undiminished after Madero took office, and the events surrounding the troop mobilization in March 1911 have shown that Taft relied heavily on his ambassador's advice. Given Ambassador Wilson's extreme pessimism, his access to the president and secretary of state, and the undeniably large American stake in Mexico, the question becomes why was the response so limited? The answers to this question can best be discovered by examining the most important events in Mexican-American relations during the Madero period. These were the disorders in early 1912 in northern Mexico and along the border resulting from the Orozco movement against Madero; the prohibition in March 1912 of arms shipments from the United States to Mexico; the sharp protest sent to the Mexican government by the United States in September 1912; the abortive uprising led by Félix Díaz in October 1912, and last, the successful overthrow of Madero in February 1913 by Huerta and Díaz.

MADERO'S EARLY DIFFICULTIES

Ambassador Wilson greeted the success of Madero against Díaz in May 1911 with predictions of the failure of all that Madero represented:

By far the gravest change about to be effected is the adoption of universal suffrage. When it is understood that, of the fifteen million Mexicans, over ten million are illiterate and wholly without the necessary training to fit them for the responsibilities of intelligent citizenship, some idea may be formed of the situation which will result from the adoption of universal suffrage. That it will result in orderly, peaceful and progressive government I very much doubt, but I expect, rather, to see ushered in a long period of corrupt practices in election, of violence at the polls and of armed settlement of the claims of various chieftains, ending eventually in the supremacy of the ablest and most forceful leader; the pendulum swinging back after years of trial, to conditions similar to those under which we are now living. . . .

I think you should become reconciled to the view that Mexico is entering upon a long period of turbulence and political unrest, and that she will continue to be a subject and a problem for the consideration and concern of our government.[33]

Changes more profound than the introduction of universal suffrage were taking place everywhere in Mexico. Slowly, tentatively, like an enormous serpent, the Mexican people were shedding the skin of a former life, not just their life under the Díaz dictatorship but the life forced on Mexico by the Spanish conquerors centuries before. This frightened the American ambassador and men like him, who detected anarchy in the slightest deviation from the old ways. Still, if one ignores the editorializing, the ambassador's reports offer a fascinating glimpse of a

[33] H. L. Wilson to Secretary of State, May 23, 1911, 812.00/1981.

revolution in process. When the functionaries of the Díaz government fled the sinking ship, Wilson reported: "the spectacle is now being witnessed of a new and untried army of patriots flocking to this capital and to the State capitals to take over the administration of government in the name of the revolutionary party. . . ."[34]

About conditions in general, he wrote: "Even more dangerous than the open acts of violence to which I have referred, is the spirit of disregard for law and authority, of contempt for the ordinary conventions and restraints of society, of insolence in the public highways, of industrial strikes based upon impossible demands, *which are all indications of a changed spirit among the people,* the tendencies and fruits of which cannot be clearly estimated."[35] (Italics added.)

On July 11, 1911, the ambassador reported the confirmation of his fears that "the success of the revolutionary movement of Mr. Madero might lead to a permanent disrespect for constituted authority and to a disturbance of established administrative methods."[36] And in September he returned to the widespread dissatisfaction that so much troubled him:

While order has been restored throughout the Republic [except in Sinaloa, Chiapas, Morelos, and Oaxaca] a spirit of unrest, of nervous tension, of dissatisfaction with any and all political programs, of lack of respect for law and the constituted authorities prevails everywhere. This spirit of discontent with all men and all measures is so dangerous in character that if it were cohesive and united it might easily be likened to a gunpowder or dynamite mine ready to burst into eruption at any moment.[37]

In the same report Wilson showed that he had already begun to repeat the stories belittling Madero personally. These stories plagued Madero in a way reminiscent of the personal propaganda beating suffered by Juan Bosch, the unsuccessful Dominican revolutionary of the 1960s:

There exists a very powerful and numerous opposition to Madero throughout the country among people who believe his policies to be impracticable, his intelligence dubious and his character lacking in firmness, vigor and consistency, but a large proportion of these elements believe that the sooner Madero has had his fling and is placed in power the sooner he will demonstrate his incompetence

---

[34] *Ibid.*
[35] H. L. Wilson to Secretary of State, June 23, 1911, 812.00/2181.
[36] H. L. Wilson to Secretary of State, July 11, 1911, 812.00/2219.
[37] H. L. Wilson to Secretary of State, September 22, 1911, 812.00/2384.

and lack of the qualities so essential at this moment, and that
his loss of popular favor and prestige will eventually result in loss
of power, leadership and, perhaps, the loss of the Presidency in
the new revolution which it is thought the anticipated misgovern-
ment will bring about.[38]

Ambassador Wilson's reports tended to hold center stage in
Washington and to color all consideration of Mexican policy.
Although President Taft requested detailed consular reporting
after mobilizing the troops in 1911, most of the consuls continued
to send infrequent and sketchy political dispatches. On two occasions, at least, thanks to F. M. Dearing acting as chargé
d'affaires, the State Department received detailed information
directly from the consuls. While these reports did not contradict
Ambassador Wilson's interpretations, they differed considerably
in emphasis and supplied a measure of the perspective and hard
local facts the Department missed in the ambassador's reports.
Dearing submitted one of these major supplementary reports
on September 5, 1911, coincident with the pessimistic reports
from the ambassador cited earlier. Dearing's report consisted
of the consuls' answers to a number of political and economic
questions asked by the embassy, including, "How do people at
large regard present conditions in the country as compared with
those of the last days of the Díaz regime?" "Have they confidence in the outcome of the revolution?" "Have they benefited
in any way from the revolutionary changes?" "Has the disarma-
ment of revolutionist soldiers been carried out?"

The answers of the consuls reflected personal and local bias,
but they revealed that certain conditions were common in all
states, save those cut off geographically from the course of events.
There was general unrest and uncertainty among all parts of
the population. This revealed itself in a number of ways, including open criticism of the current situation, in the prevalence
of a sort of anticipatory passivity, and in strikes. The old regime
had fallen, but a new one had not yet been securely established.
Business had declined by 25–30 percent, though it was not seriously disrupted in most places. Strikes had occurred against large
firms. The strikes remained essentially economic, though the unsettled situation probably encouraged the laborers to try for better wages and working conditions. Madero had steadily lost support since the resignation of Díaz. The longer the provisional
government remained in office, the more Madero lost. Substan-

---

[38] *Ibid.*

tial numbers of the revolutionary forces had not given up their arms. In short, an atmosphere of uncertainty prevailed, while the leading figure among the revolutionaries steadily lost support. Considerable numbers of armed men remained in the field. The industrial workers were making unprecedented demands for better pay and working conditions, while the upper classes and intellectuals remained aloof, discontented, and convinced of Madero's incompetence.

Though both sets of reports showed clearly the difficulties Madero faced, the consular survey indicated that events tended to move more slowly in the countryside than Ambassador Wilson implied. The tide of events had not swept out of control. As the consular reports showed, the general inclination was far more that of wait-and-see than the licentious breakdown of restraint reported by the ambassador. On the other hand, both sets of reports agreed that further disorders could easily occur should a reasonably competent leader emerge. This observation proved accurate, for Madero had to put down one after another uprising, led chiefly by ambitious generals who easily gathered money and recruits for their campaigns from dissatisfied Mexicans of all classes. The spasmodic agrarian revolt led by Emiliano Zapata was not of this sort. It fed on the land hunger of the peasants of Morelos and was kept alive by Zapata's virtuosity as a guerrilla leader.[39] Zapata's partisans never constituted a serious threat to Madero, but they and their chief eluded capture and continued to disrupt the consolidation of the Madero regime in the districts southwest of Mexico City. On February 2, 1912, for example, Ambassador Wilson reported that south of Mexico City "Government seems to be powerless to do more than hold urban centers."[40] Also in February, a former Maderista general, Pascual Orozco, began his attempt to unseat Madero. Ironically, Orozco was defeated by Victoriano Huerta, who later destroyed the regime he had saved. The violence in the south, the Orozco uprising, and several warnings from Ambassador Wilson prompted the Taft administration to strengthen the American forces along the border.[41]

The State Department received a second consular survey on

---

[39] See John Womack, *Zapata and the Mexican Revolution* (New York: Knopf, 1968).

[40] H. L. Wilson to Secretary of State, February 2, 1912, 812.00/2727.

[41] Knox to Taft, February 3, 1912, 812.00/2727; Memo from Office of Army Chief of Staff to State Department, February 6, 1912, 812.00/2754.

February 7. This time the conflict with Ambassador Wilson's
reports was unmistakable. The consuls reported significant political and economic improvement in all districts except those in
the southwest, where Zapata's revolt waxed and waned, and
in the extreme northeast soon to be the scene of the Orozco
uprising. The consul in Acapulco described the "entire state
of Guerrero" as being "in a state bordering on anarchy, and
there are not substantial guarantees of protection to either life
or property."[42] The consul in Ciudad Juárez mentioned laxity
in law enforcement and added prophetically, "There are many
who are waiting for the time when they can join a leader who
will allow them to compensate themselves with such spoils as
they can gather."[43] Strikingly different were the reports from
Aguascalientes ("political conditions appear very tranquil and
quite satisfactory"), Ciudad Porfirio Díaz ("political conditions . . . are excellent . . . Americans, in fact all foreigners,
apparently are perfectly satisfied with their treatment by Mexicans in authority"), Durango ("the political situation in this
State has cleared very much within the last month [January]"),
Torreón ("this district is very quiet with the exception of a
few robberies in the ranches by bandits who do not claim to
be revolutionists . . . business in all lines is increasing; a general
feeling of security exists"), Ensenada ("the opinion prevails here
that revolutionary troubles are over"), Hermosillo ("there are
no political troubles in the State at the present time; the few
outlaws in the State are being diligently pursued and most likely
will soon be wiped out"), Matamoros ("everything is perfectly
quiet here and everyone believes that there will be peace now"),
Oaxaca ("conditions both political and economical, in the entire
State of Oaxaca are practically normal"), and Monterrey ("a
large number of well-to-do Americans appear to be looking for
investments in this district").[44] Several of the reports deserve
to be quoted at length. From Nuevo Laredo the consul reported:
   Since the [defeat] of General Reyes all feeling of political unrest
has disappeared from this consular district. At no time have 10%
of the people here been in favor of a revolution and the consensus
of opinion is that President Madero was fairly elected and that
he should be given a chance to work out his policies. The citizens
here also believe that he will make a good president and that

---

[42] H. L. Wilson to Secretary of State, February 7, 1912, 812.00/2776.
[43] *Ibid.*
[44] *Ibid.*

Mexico will enjoy an era of unprecedented prosperity under his administration.[45]

The consul at Tampico, the heart of Mexico's oil industry, approached the lyric in his report: "Political conditions appear to be quiet and peaceful throughout this consular district. Great progress is being made in agricultural and industrial development; the laboring classes are employed at good wages; foreign capital is steadily coming in; new settlers are constantly arriving; in fact, Tampico is prosperous and has excellent prospects for still greater prosperity."[46]

Whatever allowances one makes for human error, bias, and incompetence, the reports show almost unanimous agreement that with one or two exceptions Mexico was returning to normal, that lawlessness had declined, and that the new government was widely accepted and even more widely tolerated. Huntington Wilson found the report "reassuring" and noted: "The report seems to show that the disturbances are in the nature of serious and widespread outlawry and have hardly sufficient cohesion to merit characterization as a 'revolution.' "[47]

Ambassador Wilson's political report for February painted an entirely different picture, one so different that it is hard to believe the consuls and the ambassador were discussing the same country. The ambassador wrote:

Events in Mexico have moved with startling rapidity over a wide extent of territory, indicating in the most forceful way the great measure of discontent, the general unrest, and the fulfillment in no inconsiderable degree of the predictions which I have made in former confidential dispatches relative to the unfitness of these people for self-government, the inability of the present administration to carry out the political program under which it assumed the Government, the loss of respect for law and for property and for life, the breaking down of the machinery of public administration, generally and locally, the licentiousness of the press, and the manifest tendency to elevate and place the ignorant, inefficient, and disorderly elements over the head of the intelligence, wealth, and traditionally leading families of the Republic.[48]

---

[45] *Ibid.*
[46] *Ibid.*
[47] Huntington Wilson to American Embassy, Mexico, February 21, 1912, 812.00/2776.
[48] H. L. Wilson to Secretary of State, February 20, 1912, 812.00/2889. F. M. Dearing in the Latin American Division in Washington had already begun to warn his superiors that Ambassador Wilson exaggerated the

According to the ambassador, Madero had been forced to work
with and rely on bureaucrats and legislators identified with the
Díaz regime. Reform thus went slowly, and this had lost Madero
the support of many of his own followers. The southern part
of the country was in a state of petty uprisings and brigandage.
The north had passed into "active rebellion." The center was
comparatively quiet, with "considerable political agitation." The
army was weak and had revolted twice. In short, the ambassador
described a country teetering on the brink of anarchy, its revolutionary president deserted by those who had raised him to power,
its roads unsafe, its citizens at the mercy of savage bandits and
rebellious generals. He closed his report with another demeaning
portrait of Madero: "In the meantime the President remains
serene and optimistic—an honest man of high ideals and patriotic purposes, dealing with a situation which he comprehends
very slightly and which he aggravates [by vacillation and
weakness]."[49]
The alarming if contradictory reports from Mexico, and the
risk that battles against Orozco in border towns would spill
across the border, led the State Department to propose two
courses of action to the president: (1) to send American troops
across the border when necessary to defend American soil, and
(2) to advise Americans to withdraw from Mexico.[50] These
were the first proposals made during a three-week search for
means by which the Taft administration could impress the Mexican government, secure protection for Americans and their property in Mexico and along the American side of the border, and
avoid war, the stimulation of anti-Americanism in Mexico, or
the appearance in the eyes of congressmen of exercising undue
executive prerogative. The measures considered by Taft and
the state department included firing across the border to suppress
incoming fire, crossing the border, advising the withdrawal of
American nationals, and obtaining from Congress, by way of
a joint resolution, advance approval for the use of force against
Mexico.[51]
Taft very quickly made clear his determination to avoid forceful

---

seriousness of conditions in Mexico. See Huntington Wilson to Taft,
February 17, 1912, 812.00/2881B.
[49] *Ibid.*
[50] Huntington Wilson to Taft, February 24, 1912, 812.00/2884A.
[51] Huntington Wilson sent Taft a draft of a congressional resolution on
March 1, 1912, 812.00/3005A.

intervention at all costs. On February 26, two days after the original proposals had been made, news reached Washington of an impending attack on Juárez by Orozco's forces, which almost certainly would result in firing into U.S. territory. Fred Dearing and J. R. Clark, solicitor for the state department, took the news to the president late the same evening, together with draft telegrams for strong warnings to the Mexican government and the consul at Juárez to prevent firing across the border. Taft approved the telegrams and then remarked, "You know I am not going to cross that line. That is something for which Congress will have to take the responsibility. But I suppose it will do no harm to threaten them a little."[52]

At Dearing's request the president agreed to read a memorandum giving the "department's views" on policy. The memorandum had been prepared by Clark and left at the White House earlier that evening. Clark's memo emphasized the difficulties and dangers likely to result from any hostile acts against Mexico. Posing the problem of firing on El Paso during an attack on Juárez, Clark identified three possible solutions. The United States (1) could advise Americans to withdraw from the danger zone and require compensation from the Mexican government for whatever damages were done; (2) could announce that the United States would not permit any Mexican force to put its back against the border and thus endanger American territory; and (3) could, if fire fell on American soil, suppress it by return fire or by the dispatch of troops across the border. For a number of reasons, Clark favored advising Americans to withdraw from danger. He argued that it would set a good precedent, one that would prove useful if the United States became involved in civil war or in war against an invading army. It would emphasize the impartiality of the United States in Mexican politics. Moreover, the Mexican people could not resent such a course, making it "the safest for the thousands of American citizens who are now in Mexico."[53] Returning the fire could be regarded by Mexico as an act of war, while the problem with crossing the border was that: "Once in Mexico, it is impossible to tell when we should be able to return. If the Mexican contestants refused to observe our warning not to fire into American territory

---

[52] Memo by F. M. Dearing, February 26, 1912, 812.00/2912.
[53] Memo by James Ruben Clark, February 26, 1912, Taft Papers, Ser. 6, casefile 95b—Mexico.

and desist from their intention only when actually driven from
their position by an armed force, it is probable we would have
to maintain such armed force in Mexico until a central Mexican
Government had again gained control."[54]

Clark compared the slight damage that could occur in El Paso
as a result of the fighting in Juárez to the probable "great loss
to American life in Mexico," and the certain "enormous property loss" that would follow if American troops returned the
fire or crossed the border. In large sections of Mexico the central
government was powerless, and anti-American sentiment was
widespread. "It is probable," Clark wrote, "that either the firing
into Mexico or the crossing of the border . . . by American
troops will put every American life in Mexico in jeopardy. . . ."[55]
Under such circumstances, the Mexican government
might do all it could to protect Americans, or it might find
such protection neither desirable nor possible. If returning the
fire or crossing the border sparked anti-American violence,
Americans in Mexico could be guaranteed full protection only
if the United States government itself attempted to provide it:

This obviously would mean the over-running of Mexico by a
large force, how large it is impossible to determine, but certainly
a force numbering far more than our regular army and perhaps
even the regular army plus the existing state militia. In other words,
this Government would have on its hands what in reality would
be a war of conquest of a people animated by the most intense
hatred for the conquering race. History has a sufficient number
of instances of this kind of conflict to demonstrate that such work
is not child's play . . . it would seem most unwise, if not indeed
much worse, to open fire upon Juarez or to invade Mexico unless
this Government is adequately prepared for war.[56]

Clark then considered and rejected the alternative of advising
Americans in Mexico to withdraw altogether from the country
and with the assistance of their government to seek compensation
for their losses. Once again the Americans in Mexico would
suffer. Mexico could not pay so enormous an indemnity, Congress would not indemnify them adequately, and territory seized
in war would not be adequate compensation. In addition, it
would be extremely difficult to evacuate the scattered thousands
of Americans in a reasonable time, and many, with their life's

---

[54] *Ibid.*
[55] *Ibid.*
[56] *Ibid.*

work at stake, probably would not leave at all. For these reasons, Clark opposed any action at El Paso until Americans in Mexico were able to protect themselves, either by acquiring arms or by leaving the country.

While Ambassador Wilson shared the belief that retaliation at Juárez would probably provoke attacks against Americans in Mexico, he believed it wise to advise their withdrawal from the country and for some time had been advising transient Americans to leave.[57] He also suggested the dispatch of warships to all the main Mexican ports on the Atlantic and Pacific coasts: "A naval demonstration will be useful not only in impressing the Mexican mind but may also be useful in taking off American refugees."[58] Though his recommendations were sought at every stage, the ambassador neither advocated nor opposed intervention, though he did point out that crossing the border might lead to much more.[59]

The steps finally taken by the American government reflected the president's firm rejection of intervention and the state department's deep concern for the vulnerability of Americans in Mexico and for the potential open-endedness of any sort of military action. On March 2 the president issued a proclamation admonishing Americans not to meddle in Mexican affairs and warning that the neutrality laws would be strictly enforced. In an explanatory press release the State Department described the proclamation as "fresh evidence of the determination of the administration to let the Mexicans settle their own differences."[60] On the same day, Ambassador Wilson received instructions authorizing him at his discretion to advise Americans to withdraw not from Mexico proper but from those localities within Mexico where conditions or prospects of lawlessness threatened personal safety.[61] Wilson promptly advised the withdrawal of Americans in the states of Chihuahua, Durango, Morelos, and Guerrero and in parts of the states of Coahuila, Zacatecas, Sinaloa, Vera-

---

[57] H. L. Wilson to Secretary of State, February 24, 1912, Confidential Series A, No. 82, Mexico, no. 11, p. 21.
[58] *Ibid.*, p. 23.
[59] *Ibid.*
[60] *Papers Relating to the Foreign Relations of the United States, 1912* (Washington, D.C.: Government Printing Office, 1919), p. 733 (hereinafter cited as *Foreign Relations (date)*).
[61] Huntington Wilson to American Embassy, Mexico, March 2, 1912, 812.00/3005D.

cruz, and Puebla. The administration also obtained from Congress authority to prohibit the export of arms "whenever the President shall find in any American country conditions of domestic violence which are promoted by the use of arms or munitions of war procured from the United States."[62] On March 14 Taft issued the necessary proclamation.[63] Two weeks later, after several requests, the president allowed arms shipments to go to the Madero government. This exception was consistent with Taft's desire to protect American lives and property in Mexico and considerably strengthened Madero in his efforts to consolidate his rule.

The easy initial successes of the Orozco movement deepened Ambassador Wilson's pessimism.[64] On April 14 he suggested that the president consider whether to send troops into Chihuahua and Guerrero to protect Americans against Orozco. He admitted in the same report the paucity of information available to him, but went on to counsel military intervention in Chihuahua and Guerrero, relying on "official private sources" whose greatest concern judging from their advice to the ambassador, was the overthrow of Madero.[65] Wilson's suggestion was rejected,[66] but a stern protest was sent to the Mexican government and to Orozco.[67] The protest was made largely for the record, however,[68] and Huerta's victories against Orozco in May signaled the end of this source of concern for both governments. Even this could not shake Ambassador Wilson, and in mid-May he reported that the defeat of the rebels in the North would not bring order to Mexico: "Believing as I do that the disease in the Mexican body politic is inherent I can see no cure for the situation until the Mexican people as a whole become aroused to the fact that the nation is fast drifting into anarchy and until its ablest and best citizens join in active and patriotic support of the present administration. Of this I see no signs at present."[69]

---

[62] *Foreign Relations, 1912,* pp. 745–746.
[63] *Ibid.*
[64] H. L. Wilson to Secretary of State, March 20, 1912, 812.00/3365, and March 29, 1912, 812.00/3430.
[65] H. L. Wilson to Secretary of State, April 13, 1912, 812.00/3590.
[66] Knox to American Embassy, Mexico, April 18, 1912, *ibid.*
[67] Confidential Series A, no. 83, Mexico, no. 12, May 7, 1912, p. 81.
[68] *Ibid.,* p. 78.
[69] H. L. Wilson to Secretary of State, May 15, 1912, 812.00/3963.

The State Department took a more optimistic view of the situation, as indicated in a memo prepared by the Latin American division to be used by a senator friendly to the administration in rebutting Senator Albert Fall's scathing denunciations of the Taft administration's Mexican policy. The memo advanced the view that though Americans and their property had suffered during the revolutions in Mexico, few lives had been lost. In the opinion of the Latin American division, Madero would serve out his term, "although he will do so with much difficulty and turbulence."[70]

A Severe Protest

This calm overview within the State Department makes it difficult to understand what followed. In early September the Taft administration made a most severe verbal and written protest to the Mexican government, a protest that bordered on an ultimatum. Though the wording of the protest was sharp and even threatening, the administration exercised great care to avoid setting a time limit and was reluctant to press the Madero government to meet its demands. This suggests that there had been no major shift in policy, no decision to use force, and that the protest was not prompted by a dramatic worsening of the situation in Mexico but by the requirements of Taft's campaign for reelection and by a desire to get all grievances "on the record" to serve as a basis for damage claims against the Mexican government.

Ambassador Wilson's reports alone were sufficient cause for deep concern in Washington, although the Latin American division's memo indicated that the ambassador's reports were not taken at face value. The administration desired to cover all angles, however, and on August 24 Huntington Wilson informed Ambassador Wilson that in accordance with the ambassador's suggestion the State Department had arranged for American naval vessels to make periodic visits to Mexican ports on the east and west coasts. The *Vicksburg* had already sailed for the west coast, and during the first week in September the *Des Moines* would begin similar visits to the east coast. Huntington

---

[70] Memo by Department of State, Latin American division, *Resumé of the Revolutionary Disturbances in Mexico since September, 1910,* July 29, 1912, 812.00/4540.

Wilson added, "It is the Department's intention to have naval
vessels call at Mexican ports every now and then during the
next eight or ten months for moral effect."[71]

In late August, Ambassador Wilson surpassed all his previous
descriptions of anarchy and incompetence in Mexico. His report
reached Huntington Wilson on September 3, the day before
a severe verbal protest was made to the Mexican ambassador.
Wilson reported that the states of Puebla, Oaxaca, Morelos,
Guerrero, and México were the scene of the most barbaric
destruction.

Entire villages have been burned, their inhabitants—men, women,
and children—slaughtered and mutilated indiscriminately; plantations have been ravaged and burned, trains have been blown up
and derailed, and passengers slaughtered like cattle; women have
been ravished and men mutilated with accompaniments of horror
and barbarity which find no place in the chronicles of Christian
warfare. It is impossible to accurately estimate the number of these
savages which are under arms, nominally under the command of
Zapata. . . . With this situation, as far as my observation goes,
the Government is either wholly incompetent or wholly impotent
to deal.[72]

Without in any way minimizing the cruelties of an agrarian
uprising, one reacts to such statements by questioning the reliability of the sources of information on which they are based
and by seeking a number of reports from different sources. The
State Department's attempts to do this were hampered by the
poor political reporting of the consuls. On September 7, in reply
to a letter from the department censuring the consuls for poor
political reporting, Ambassador Wilson pointed out that on "the
scene of the worst disturbances"—Puebla, Morelos, Michoacán,
and Guerrero, an area as large as Texas—there was only one
consular representative, in Puebla. He observed: "It is therefore
manifestly difficult if not impossible to secure information from
this vast region. . . ."[73] What were his sources, then, for the
ghastly details he had reported two weeks before? Not for another four months did the department discover proof that Ambassador Wilson based his repeated descriptions of anarchy and

---

[71] Confidential Series A, no. 87, Mexico, no. 13, September 17, 1912,
p. 63.
[72] H. L. Wilson to Secretary of State, August 28, 1912, 812.00/4899.
[73] H. L. Wilson to Secretary of State, September 7, 1912, 812.00/4902.

governmental failure on information taken uncritically from articles published in several irresponsible, pro-American newspapers in Mexico City, from anti-Maderists, and from disloyal members of Madero's own government.

The ambassador's report in late August also denied that the final defeat of Orozco's forces in the north would improve the situation. The rebel army had split into guerrilla bands that constituted an even greater threat to law and order and to American interests. The victory over Orozco reflected some prestige on the federal army but had accomplished little else. Summing up, the Ambassador stated:

In the midst of this appalling situation in the north and in the south the Federal Government sits apathetic, ineffective, and either cynically indifferent or stupidly optimistic. Its councils are divided and moved in contrary directions from one day to another by the preponderance of antagonistic elements. Whatever public action, therefore, is taken as a result of its deliberations may be expected to be incoherent, spasmodic, and advancing and receding conformably with the preponderance of the conservative or radical elements, or in response to the changeable gusts of public opinion.[74]

Having described the balancing act Madero was forced to perform, the ambassador then indicated he completely misunderstood it by attributing most of the government's hesitancy and advances and retreats to Madero's "character." He then repeated rumors about Madero's "mental weaknesses": "Peculiar stories are told of his irrelevancy, of his lack of memory, of his inaccurate information, and of his unreasonable and petulant reception of such matters as are ordinarily presented to a chief executive. I have had frequent occasion to notice these peculiarities myself."[75] Specifically, Wilson had in mind Madero's cold response to his complaints on behalf of American interests, and the ambassador compared Madero unfavorably with Díaz in this respect. Madero was pictured as conducting an anti-American campaign to benefit his family, which controlled him and exploited his high position for financial gain. Wilson alluded frequently to the need for stern measures that would force the Mexican government to protect American interests. In perhaps his strongest appeal to date, he said, "I feel that usual diplomatic methods have failed in impressing this Government with its responsibility, and I fear that, unless some well-defined and posi-

---

[74] H. L. Wilson to Secretary of State, August 28, 1912, 812.00/4899.
[75] *Ibid.*

tive course is adopted the injustice, abuses, and murders of American citizens will increase in number."[76]

On September 4, President Taft and Huntington Wilson, then acting secretary of state, met with the Mexican ambassador just prior to the latter's return to Mexico. Taft spoke of the friendliness of the American government toward the Madero government, mentioning the handling of the arms embargo as an example, and said the United States had a right to expect "more hearty consideration" of U.S. interests in Mexico. Taft then warned the ambassador that if the situation grew worse he would be forced to convene Congress and ask them for guidance. When the Mexican ambassador referred to the bad feeling created by Senator Fall's speeches and by the Magdalena Bay resolution, Huntington Wilson interposed that the crucial facts were three: (1) murderers went unpunished; (2) much evidence existed of hostility to American interests; and (3) the remedial actions of the Madero administration were not sufficiently energetic and zealous.

The interview was backed up by a severely written protest composed with the advice of Ambassador Wilson and finally delivered in Mexico City on September 17. In his instructions to deliver the note, Huntington Wilson revealed what were probably the administration's true reasons for choosing this moment to protest so fiercely and loudly: "The Department regards it as of the greatest importance that this note should be presented at the earliest possible moment and be a matter of record prior to the occurrence of any possible *coup d'état* of which several rumors have recently reached the Department. Date note September 15 and officially present it to the Minister for Foreign Affairs. . . ."[77] The note listed sixteen murders that had occurred since September 1910 about which little or nothing had been done. Punishment was demanded for those guilty of the thirteen oldest crimes, and also an investigation of the three most recent murders. The note cited the imprisonment of Ameri-

---

[76] *Ibid.*

[77] Acting Secretary of State H. Wilson to American Embassy, Mexico, September 16, 1912, Confidential Series A, no. 87, Mexico, no. 13., September 12, 1912, p. 124. Huntington Wilson was referring in part to a report from Consul Marion Letcher that General Huerta was planning to overthrow Madero. See *Foreign Relations, 1912,* pp. 847–848, and Letcher's report dated September 15, 1912, Confidential Series A, no. 89. Mexico, no. 15, November 21, 1912, p. 6.

cans "on frivolous and inadequate charges,"[78] and complained that Mexicans preyed upon American interests without hindrance from the Mexican government.

In addition to a catalogue of complaints, the note carried threats of a change in American policy if no improvements were made. At one point the Mexican government was told either to establish law and order or to confess that it could not do so. In the latter case, the U.S. government would "consider what measures it should adopt to meet the requirements of the situation."[79] The Taft administration stayed well away from an ultimatum, however, asking instead to be told as "promptly as possible" what the Mexican government intended to do to punish the murderers, to end "discrimination" against American interests, and to improve general conditions throughout Mexico.[80]

On the surface it appeared that the Taft administration might reverse its policy of neutrality and nonintervention, and Ambassador Wilson must have been gratified to see that the change followed so hard on his frightening reports of late August. But there is much to indicate that Wilson exaggerated the significance of the protest and wrongly viewed it as a crucial turning point in Mexican-American relations. The day he delivered the protest, for example, he reported to Washington that in the event of an unsatisfactory reply, "I think the Department should be advised that . . . vigorous and firm action of some sort will be necessary to maintain our relations and secure action relative to our just complaints."[81] Wilson had obliquely raised the question of intervention, and the department equivocated, rejecting military means for the present, but throwing the ball back to the ambassador: "As the Embassy has doubtless observed, the Department exercised the greatest care to keep the strong note absolutely distinct from and short of an ultimatum. . . . In the event the attitude of the Mexican Government is [unsatisfactory] the Department will await from you specific suggestions as to what action should next be taken."[82]

---

[78] *Foreign Relations, 1912*, p. 843.
[79] *Ibid.*, p. 845.
[80] *Ibid.*, p. 846.
[81] H. L. Wilson to Secretary of State, September 26, 1912, Confidential Series A, no. 88, Mexico, no. 14, p. 4.
[82] Secretary of State to American Embassy, Mexico, September 20, 1912, *ibid.*, p. 15.

The Mexican government made a dignified and devastating reply on November 22, challenging the U.S. government's allegations on every point. With regard to the sixteen alleged murders, for example, the Mexican reply pointed out that four had occurred prior to the revolution of 1910, that three convictions had been obtained, that two cases had been closed for want of evidence, and that in two cases the official investigation had produced no results.[83] There were no data in the Foreign Office on three of the cases, and the remaining men had been executed by the government as filibusters in Lower California. The reply was hardly "satisfactory," in Ambassador Wilson's terms, and throughout the few months left to the Madero regime he pushed in Washington and Mexico City for a categorical stand on the note.[84]

The State Department remained opposed to any departure from neutrality and nonintervention. The continuity of policy emerged clearly in a lengthy memo on the Mexican situation composed in October by J. R. Clark in response to Senator Fall's continuing attacks on the administration.[85] Clark summarized the conditions facing Americans in Mexico and pointed out that from the beginning of the Madero revolution they had been vulnerable to attacks by mobs, guerrillas, and bandits. The American government had two choices: it could help them either by employing the army and navy against Mexico or by looking to the Mexican government for their protection and holding it responsible for any failures. Clark repeated his earlier arguments against intervention stressing, in the words of a subheading, "PROTECTION BY INTERVENTION MEANS IN THE FIRST PLACE THE NEEDLESS SLAUGHTER OF HUNDREDS, PERHAPS THOUSANDS OF INNOCENT NON-BELLIGERENT, AMERICAN CITIZENS, AND IN THE SECOND PLACE, WAR WITH ALL ITS ACCOMPANYING SACRIFICES OF LIFE AND TREASURE."[86] The possibility of withdrawing American citizens prior to intervention had been considered and rejected for a number of reasons. Thousands of Americans were probably too poor to leave immedi-

---

[83] *Foreign Relations, 1912,* p. 872.
[84] See his Memo to the Chargé in Mexico City, December 21, 1912, *Foreign Relations, 1912,* p. 985.
[85] "The Mexican Situation," October 1, 1912, Knox Papers, Correspondence, 19: 3106–3207.
[86] *Ibid.,* p. 3110.

ately; they would be victimized if forced to sell out, their journey out would expose them to great danger, and they would emerge penniless.[87] Clark pointed out that these observations had nothing to do with the ability of the United States to overrun and conquer Mexico. "That we are big enough and strong enough to do this if we so determine obviously admits of no question."[88] Nor was it feasible to issue an ultimatum to the Mexican government unless the United States was prepared to enforce it by arms. The use of force, Clark pointed out, had been shown as most likely to bring about the destruction rather than the preservation of American lives and property.

Because the use of force would have backfired, because it was impossible for Americans to withdraw from Mexico, and because an ultimatum was infeasible, the American government had chosen to seek protection for its citizens "through the ordinary, well established and clearly recognized methods of diplomacy."[89] Americans in Mexico had suffered death, hardship, and loss and had been victims of atrocities. But all of these, including the atrocities, accompanied war. On balance, few Americans had died, and of these most had been killed by rebel forces. Heavy property losses had occurred, but they in no way approached Senator Fall's figure of $500 million, which appeared to exceed the total value of all American property in Mexico.[90] Clark closed with a strong defense of the president's policy:

The constant problem which has confronted the President has been to secure the maximum amount of protection for American life and property with the minimum amount of danger thereto. So far no one with any adequate understanding of the situation believes that we should have intervened in Mexico or that we should intervene now. There will probably never come a time to intervene if we exercise the forbearance with [Mexico] that we should desire for ourselves. But, however that may be, it is clear that the time to intervene will be when we can save more American lives by going into Mexico than by staying out of Mexico. At present we seem to be a long distance from that contingency.[91]

---

[87] *Ibid.*, p. 3112.
[88] *Ibid.*, p. 3113.
[89] *Ibid.*, p. 3114.
[90] On the basis of consular reports Clark estimated American interests in Mexico to be worth about $330 million, or one-third the generally accepted figure of $1 billion. See *ibid.*, pp. 3106–3107.
[91] *Ibid.*, p. 3207.

The Díaz Rebellion

The Taft administration's policy received another test barely
two weeks after Clark had completed his memo. On October
16 troops loyal to Félix Díaz, nephew of the ousted dictator,
seized the city of Veracruz. The American chargé d'affaires,
Montgomery Schuyler, greeted the attempt as the "most cheerful
news for a long time concerning the revolutionary situation as
that movement now has a certain element of respectability attached to it with the consequent responsibility as to lives and
property of foreigners."[92] The Madero government easily defeated the uprising. Díaz was captured and condemned to death,
but his sentence was commuted to life imprisonment, and he
lived to take part in Madero's overthrow. Schuyler obviously
shared Ambassador Wilson's dislike of Madero and could not
keep his initial warm feelings toward Díaz and the attempted
coup out of his official reports. Like Schuyler, the American
consul at Veracruz, William Canada, also believed that Díaz
would succeed or would be defeated only after bloody and destructive fighting.

The State Department, relying on prejudiced official reporting
and "unconfirmed rumors,"[93] took the rebellion seriously and
sent two warships, the *Des Moines* to Veracruz and the *Tacoma*
to Tampico, to observe and report on the situation and to protect
Americans and their interests.[94] The president was told that "developments will be rapid and important."[95] It must have been
with regret that Chargé Schuyler reported Díaz's failure. On
October 21 Schuyler forwarded this firsthand account of the
situation at Veracruz:

The German Minister, Rear Admiral von Hintze, has just called.
He passed through Vera Cruz Saturday. Díaz supplied him with
a special train to this city which he reached this morning. He
said that in view of his military training I might like to have
his ideas of the situation in Vera Cruz which he had examined
with great care. The loyal war vessels had no guns of any size
and very little ammunition. Díaz troops, whose numbers had been
exaggerated, were concentrated in a barracks at some distance from
the city with only a few outposts in the city. His entrenchments

---

[92] Schuyler to Secretary of State, October 16, 1912, 812.00/5253.
[93] Confidential report from Alvey A. Adee to President Taft, October
19, 1912, 812.00/5290.
[94] *Ibid.*
[95] *Ibid.*

were stupidly made and showed little military knowledge. There was no probability of a bombardment. . . . Troops had little ammunition and no artillery except machine guns. He thought each side would prefer not to fight and that the Díaz uprising had been premature. He found [the foreign] consuls panic stricken although there was no reason for such fear.[96]

Madero's forces squashed the uprising two days later. Yet in the same report in which he confirmed the defeat and capture of Díaz, Schuyler incredibly added: "We should have warships in every Mexican port and they should be prepared to remain indefinitely. The United States must be ready for any eventuality as the Madero Administration is absolutely impotent to bring about even a semblance of peace and order. The above views seem pessimistic but I am unable to find a single encouraging feature in the outlook."[97]

This judgment found little support at the State Department. Reassured by the quick defeat of Díaz and by encouraging reports from the American naval officers now on the scene, the department rejected Schuyler's advice. The reply to Schuyler's request for warships in every Mexican port stated that two vessels in addition to the *Des Moines* and *Tacoma* were being held ready in case of need on the east coast. One of the additional ships was of light draft for service in the shallow waters of the Yucatán peninsula. Four vessels were ready to cover the west coast ports of Guaymas, Mazatlán, Manzanillo, and Salina Cruz. Huntington Wilson advised Schuyler: "The Department does not feel justified in requesting the Navy Department to order these vessels at once to Mexico as there would appear to be nothing in the local situation at any of the ports named to warrant the sending of vessels there for the protection of Americans and American interests and they could not plausibly be sent for any other purpose."[98] The American government was ready to act but it would act only to protect American lives and property, and these did not appear to be threatened.

---

[96] Schuyler to Secretary of State, October 21, 1912, 812.00/5305.
[97] Schuyler to Secretary of State, October 23, 1912, 812.00/5333.
[98] Huntington Wilson to American Embassy, Mexico, October 26, 1912, *ibid.*

3 The Overthrow of Madero

The collapse of the abortive Díaz uprising left the Madero administration as strong (and as weak) as ever. Greater tranquillity existed in Mexico than at almost any time since the overthrow of Porfirio Díaz, and the new year seemed to promise a further consolidation of the government's control over the nation. At a New Year's Day reception, President Madero took the American chargé aside. He spoke with great earnestness and asked the chargé to send a "competent and disinterested agent" to investigate the situation in Chihuahua, in his opinion the only remaining danger point.[1] Reports of American losses had been greatly exaggerated, he said. The few who had lost some thousands of pesos received great attention, yet hundreds had not been molested and were making more money than ever before. His administration was doing its utmost to defeat the rebels and end the disorders. The army was loyal and the government was working hard, though Mexico's basic problems and a lack of popular support hindered its progress. The Mexican president's evident desire to normalize relations with the United States received additional emphasis during discussions in Washington beginning January 2, 1913, between Taft, Knox, and the Mexican foreign minister, Pedro Lascuráin. The talks in Washington proved inconclusive, but an amicable exchange of views had occurred and chances seemed good for the settlement of a number of claims for damages and other problems. The president and Secretary Knox desired to work with the Mexican government and thought it feasible to do so, while safeguarding their "case" pending the creation of a claims commission or other means to reach a general settlement. Their assessment that conditions in Mexico were improving and their maintenance of an unruffled approach through normal diplomatic channels left them unprepared for the flood of alarming reports from Ambassador Wilson that began arriving after the first of the year.

THE STATE DEPARTMENT VERSUS AMBASSADOR WILSON

Early in January, Ambassador Wilson returned to the embassy after two months in the United States. On January 7 he said The area of armed revolution against the Government has for

---

[1] Schuyler to Secretary of State, January 2, 1913, 812.00/5802.

1. President Francisco I. Madero, ca. June 1911 (Prints and Photographs
Division, Library of Congress)

the moment sensibly diminished with possibilities that at any time
one or more revolutionary movements maybe more [will erupt],
all in a greater or less degree, dangerous to the Government which
is already suffering from universal unpopularity mixed with certain
elements of fear and contempt. . . . All over Mexico there is political unrest and dissatisfaction which may culminate at any moment
in the overthrow of the Government which will not be able to
resist a formidable and respectable movement.

The economic situation continues to grow worse. . . . The economic fruits of the revolution and bad government are now becoming more strikingly apparent each day and unless an unexpected
change occurs a crisis will be inevitable. . . . I regard the entire
situation as gloomy if not hopeless.[2]

Even for Ambassador Wilson this report and those that followed it expressed extreme pessimism and represented a drastic
shift in interpretation that bewildered the State Department.
Finally, on January 21, Secretary Knox asked for an explanation
of the abrupt change.[3] Knox's query fell short of a direct challenge to Wilson's analysis, but it pointed to the change in the
tenor of his reports and stated that without a general statement
of the reasons for the change the department felt unsure both
of the actual state of affairs in Mexico and of what it should
do to meet the situation. This sort of communication implies
a rebuke, of course. Though Knox carefully avoided saying so
in precise terms, he seemed to be warning Ambassador Wilson
not to exaggerate the seriousness of conditions in Mexico. The
ambassador took the message as an unjustified reprimand. He
replied that his reports were "plain narratives of facts occurring
from day to day" and that he reported firsthand only about
those states without American consuls.[4] All other reports were
based on information from accredited American representatives.
He denied that he had ever exaggerated the gravity of the situation and petulantly announced he would suspend his political
reporting pending receipt of further instructions from the department. Secretary Knox immediately instructed him to continue
his reports, "being guided by the merely cautionary intent of
the telegram of January 21," and regretted that a misunder-

---

[2] H. L. Wilson to Secretary of State, January 7, 1913, 812.00/5823;
see also Ambassador Wilson's, January 14, 1913, 812.00/5867; January
17, 1913, 812.00/5889; January 18, 1913, 812.00/5891; January 20, 1913,
812.00/5904.
[3] Knox to American Embassy, Mexico, January 21, 1913, 812.00/5913A.
[4] H. L. Wilson to Secretary of State, January 22, 1913, 812.00/5916.

standing had occurred.[5] Many consular reports during this time
contradicted the ambassador's reports of disorder and impending
disaster, but a few mentioned an atmosphere of anxiety and
expectancy, as though something could happen soon.[6]

On January 27, Fred Dearing attached a written observation
to one of Ambassador Wilson's telegrams that disclosed what
lay behind Knox's cautionary note to the ambassador:

Please keep this newspaper attached to this telegram from the
Embassy at Mexico City. It bears the same date as the Embassy's
telegram and was probably delivered to the Embassy early in the
morning. It would seem likely therefore that the Embassy's telegram
had been made up solely on the newspaper accounts of various
happenings; that no effort was made on the part of the Embassy
to verify the news transmitted to the Department; that the newspaper's information was vague at best and apt to be played up
in a more or less sensational way. It may be observed in this connection that almost all of the pessimistic reports from the Embassy
during the recent past seem to have been made up in the same
way,—i.e., wholly from a cursory reading of this one newspaper
printed in Mexico City.[7]

---

[5] H. L. Wilson to Secretary of State, January 24, 1913, 812.00/5916.
[6] See, for example, Guyant (Ensenada) to Secretary of State, January
23, 1913, 812.00/5924; Lespina (Frontera) to Secretary of State, January
10, 1913, 812.00/5925; Edwards (Acapulco) to Secretary of State, January 23, 1913, 812.00/5926; Hamm (Durango) to Secretary of State,
January 30, 1913, 812.00/5930; Bowman (Nogales) to Secretary of State,
January 25, 1913, 812.00/5941; Canada (Tampico) to Secretary of State,
January 26, 1913, 812.00/5942; Kirk (Manzanillo) to Secretary of State,
January 16, 1913, 812.00/5945; Schmutz (Aguascalientes) to Secretary
of State, January 20, 1913, 812.00/5946; Alger (Mazatlán) to Secretary
of State, January 18, 1913, 812.00/5947.
[7] Dearing to Buck, January 27, 1913, 812.00/5904. Ambassador Wilson's
telegram (of the same number) was dated January 20, 1913, and reported
in part as follows: "There was general activity in the south yesterday
and many small towns and haciendas were attacked. Quijingo, in the
State of Mexico, was taken after the garrison was destroyed, and five
women were carried off. Numerous trains have been attacked and railway
property destroyed. Railway service between here and Toluca has been
abandoned. Revolutionists approached to within fifteen miles of the capital at a point between San Angel and Contreras. In this instance also
women were carried off. The troops which were dispatched by the Government to the relief of Acapulco arrived there with one-third missing
and without guns and practically without clothing. The American
hacienda and mills owned by J. M. Gleason in the State of Tlaxcala
were attacked yesterday. All of his employees were butchered, the hacienda looted and women carried off. His son and wife escaped
miraculously."

In a letter dated January 27, Secretary Knox brought the matter officially before the president. Knox discussed three aspects of Ambassador Wilson's conduct. He mentioned first the reports of pessimism about the political situation, which appeared to the department to be "unjustified, if not, indeed, misleading."[8] Second, Knox pointed to evidence that the ambassador had taken a position of his own in regard to claims against the Mexican government, "his expression in this regard amounting almost to a criticism of the actions of the Department with regard to claims, and seeming to show a disposition to drive the Department to action along the lines which he, for reasons of his own, seems set upon."[9]

Third, Knox advised the president that some of the ambassador's recent reports appeared to reveal "an intention on the part of the Ambassador to force this Government's hand in its dealing with the Mexican situation as a whole, the apparent disagreement between the Ambassador and the Department being so fundamental and serious that the Department feels it would err if it did not bring the matter pointedly to your notice."[10] As evidence, Knox cited a telegraphic exchange between Washington and Mexico City. On January 9, Ambassador Wilson had referred to the severe protest of September 15, 1912, and had suggested that the complaints raised at that time should be treated "collectively not independently."[11] He added, "We owe it to our own dignity to make the requirement that promises clear and specific be given of satisfaction for all the items of complaint outlined in our note."[12] The secretary had then asked

---

[8] Knox to Taft, January 27, 1913, 812.00/7229A. Knox had attached, among others, the ambassador's "gloomy if not hopeless" report of January 7 and the department's cautionary note of January 21.
[9] *Ibid.*
[10] *Ibid.*
[11] Wilson was objecting to the administration's willingness to discuss individual cases pending a general settlement with Mexico. Wilson favored an arbitral commission appointed by both presidents (see *Foreign Relations, 1912*, p. 985). Knox thought arbitration inappropriate for the settlement of damage claims. During a visit by the Mexican Foreign Minister Pedro Lascuráin to Washington in early January 1913, Knox and Taft showed a willingness to settle as many problems in Mexican-American relations as possible. See U.S., National Archives, General Records of the Department of State, Record Group 59, Protection of American Interests in Mexico, 312.11/1031c, 312.11/1032a, 312.11/1041a (hereinafter cited by number and date only).
[12] H. L. Wilson to Secretary of State, January 9, 1913, 5 P.M., 812.00/7229A.

Ambassador Wilson to submit a draft note verbale.[13] Wilson's
reply amounted to a plea in favor of abandoning the policy
of neutrality and compensation through diplomacy and of forcing matters to a head with the Mexican government. Wilson
based his case for a change of policy on the protest of September
15, 1912, which in his view "marked a distinctly new departure
in our dealings with [the Mexican] Government."[14] He described
the note as differing from an ultimatum only in the absence
of a prescribed time limit for the performance of the demands
made. That was, of course, a great difference. He added:
Having assumed this position and having stated clearly to the Mexican Government that unless compliance with the demands made
therein was forthcoming we would feel compelled to take such
steps for the protection of our rights as might seem proper to
us, we cannot with due regard for our dignity, prestige and consistency retrace our steps, ignore the formal diplomatic exchanges
and reappear before the Mexican Government in the light of an
humble supplicant. Our note of September 15th was undoubtedly
carefully considered in all of its bearings by the Department before
its transmission to the Mexican Government and it must have
been understood at that time that there could only be one of two
conclusions resulting therefrom viz., either the Mexican Government must yield, repair the damages it has done to us and give
clear guarantees for the future or we must take some vigorous
and drastic action with the purpose of securing redress for our
wrongs, an abatement of the situation, and perhaps, incidentally,
the downfall of a government which is hateful to a vast majority
of the people of this country and which has given us innumerable
evidences of its bad faith, inefficiency, hostility and insincerity.[15]
Wilson denied advocating the occupation of Mexico or the
seizure of Mexican territory. But he argued that the avoidance
of drastic action would bring disaster "and forfeit to us in the
estimation of [Latin American] peoples the respect and awe with
which they have been taught to regard us."[16] The draft note
verbale offered by Wilson condemned the Mexican government's
response to the earlier protest and its incompetency in allowing
armed revolution to continue, brigandage to grow, and the economic situation to become a menace. The note warned the Mexi-

---

[13] Knox to American Embassy, Mexico, January 11, 1913, 1 P.M.,
812.00/7229A.
[14] H. L. Wilson to Secretary of State, January 18, 1913, 312.11/1048.
[15] *Ibid.*
[16] *Ibid.*

can government to adjust the grievances named in the earlier
note and to guarantee American lives and property against violence, intrigue, antiforeign sentiment, and injustice.[17] Without
actually saying it, the ambassador strongly implied that he
favored military intervention if the Mexican government failed
to respond:
Of course the Department will understand that unless the delivery
of this proposed Note should obtain satisfaction from the Mexican
Government we must then adopt one of the several drastic courses
which have been under consideration by the Department and which
in my judgment though perhaps necessarily delayed by patience,
a repugnance to extreme measures, a reluctance to engage in adven-
turous sallies and a natural fear of misinterpretation of our motives,
must finally be adopted in the interest of peace in America and
the protection of our own interests.[18]

Wilson's arguments, based as they were on considerations of
prestige and a patronizing, almost colonial, attitude toward Latin
America, fail to persuade. More important to Taft, Knox, and
Huntington Wilson, the ambassador had not demonstrated that
conditions in Mexico had deteriorated sufficiently to warrant
abandoning a long-standing and relatively successful policy. Taft
and Huntington Wilson had not been entirely candid with the
ambassador about their true motives for sending the protest of
September 15, and it is perhaps understandable that the ambassador had perceived a turning point in Mexican-American relations where none actually existed. The crucial point was that
in a highly delicate political situation the ambassador differed
profoundly with the administration, both over political facts and
over basic policy. The ambassador's exaggerated pessimism and
his advocacy of "drastic action," at a time when neither appeared reasonable or desirable in Washington, signaled an alarming divergence of viewpoint that threatened the Taft administration's entire Mexican policy. As evidence accumulated challenging the reliability of Wilson's political reporting, Knox acted
to close the gap, cautioning the ambassador to maintain perspective and taking the matter up with the president. But time was
running out. Less than two weeks remained from the time that
Knox wrote the President until the attack that began the *Decena
Tragica* ("Ten Tragic Days," February 9–18, 1913), the tragic

---

[17] *Ibid.*, Enclosure 1, p. 6.
[18] *Ibid.*

2. Presidential candidate William Howard Taft, ca. June 1908 (Prints and Photographs Division, Library of Congress)

days of street fighting in Mexico City that culminated in the overthrow of Madero.

COUP D'ETAT

Ambassador Wilson's report of February 4 proved to be his last important political summary before fighting broke out in Mexico City. Wilson omitted the sort of prescriptions for drastic action that had alarmed his superiors and, though he could not resist castigating Madero, gave a convincing account of the forces working against the existing Mexican government. The army, he reported, was demoralized, "torn by intrigues and dissensions and united only in its contempt and dislike for the present government."[19] The disorders had forced mines to stop operating, while strikes added to unemployment and disrupted production. Food was scarce, prices were high, and the general economic situation was bad. Madero's cabinet was split into factions and was absorbed in "liliputian politics which have little to do with the salvation of the country or the restoration of national prestige at home or abroad."[20]

The coup against Madero began with the rescue from jail of two old enemies of the president, Bernardo Reyes and Félix Díaz. Once free, these men led their followers in an unsuccessful assault against the National Palace. In the ensuing battle General Reyes was killed and General Lauro Villar, commander of the federal forces, was wounded. Madero's fateful choice as Villar's successor was Victoriano Huerta.

Under Huerta's command, the federal attempts to drive the rebels from the Ciudadela, an ancient fortress, were grotesquely and needlessly mismanaged, and probably designed to destroy as many loyal troops as possible. For nine days, artillery and small arms fire raked the city indiscriminately and took the lives of helpless noncombatants whose decomposing corpses had to be left where they fell. Finally on February 18, General Huerta openly joined forces with Díaz and ordered the arrest and imprisonment of President Madero, his brother Gustavo, the Vice-

---

[19] H. L. Wilson to Secretary of State, February 4, 1913, 812.00/6068.
[20] The ambassador's analysis finds support from friendly biographers of Madero who are hostile to Ambassador Wilson and all he did and represented. Cf. Stanley R. Ross, *Francisco I. Madero: Apostle of Mexican Democracy* (New York: Columbia University Press, 1955), pp. 276–280.

President, Pino Suárez, and the cabinet.[21] Late in the evening of February 22, Madero and Suárez were taken from their cells and shot. The official version of their deaths asserted that they had been killed during an attack while being transferred to a different prison, but there is no reason to doubt that they were murdered in cold blood.[22] Madero fell victim to treason at the highest military and civilian levels.

Ambassador Wilson's reports exaggerated the successes of the rebels, and his actions, such as the mobilization of the most important members of the diplomatic corps to demand Madero's resignation, often exceeded both his instructions and his legitimate role as a foreign ambassador. There is considerable evidence that he knew in advance of Huerta's treason. Wilson was in close communication with Huerta, who advised him the day before the coup that Madero would soon be forced from power.[23] Wilson was not a man to leave loose ends hanging, especially if a word or two from him promising to work for the early

---

[21] Ambassador Wilson secured the release of the cabinet during a meeting with Huerta and Díaz at the American embassy on the evening of February 18. See H. L. Wilson to Secretary of State, February 19, 1913, 812.00/6264.

[22] Among the numerous works that deal with the overthrow, Ross, *Madero,* has a detailed account. See also Parkes, *History of Mexico;* Charles C. Cumberland, *Mexican Revolution: Genesis under Madero* (Austin: University of Texas Press, 1952); and Ernest H. Gruening, *Mexico and Its Heritage* (New York: Appleton-Century-Crofts, 1928).

[23] See the ambassador's reports of February 16, 1913, 812.00/6180; February 16, 1913, 812.00/6186; and February 17, 1913, 812.00/6225. On March 12, 1913, Ambassador Wilson made a lengthy report to the new administration explaining the events that surrounded Madero's overthrow and murder. He stated that his communications with Huerta had led him to expect action against Madero: "In my own mind I anticipated a mild form of *coup d'état,* which would lead to the resignation of Madero after a refusal on the part of the Federal troops further to engage the troops of Diaz, might be undertaken. But I had no reason to think that violence would occur and that the President and his ministers would be made prisoners. . . ." Of his own role in securing an agreement between the victorious generals, Huerta and Díaz, Ambassador Wilson stated: "The consummation of this arrangement I regard as the most successful and far-reaching of all the difficult work I was called upon to perform during the revolution in that it stopped further effusion of blood, allowed the population of the city to resume their ordinary peaceful occupations, and led finally to the creation of a provisional government which is rapidly establishing peace throughout the Republic." H. L. Wilson to W. J. Bryan, March 12, 1913, 812.00/6840.

3. Deposed dictator Victoriano Huerta, ca. June 1915 (Prints and Photographs Division, Library of Congress)

recognition of a new government, for example, would have precipitated the overthrow of a man and a regime he despised. On the other hand, he needed to say or do very little. He was notoriously out of sympathy with the Madero government, and his actions during the days of fighting spoke eloquently his desire to see Madero overthrown. Moreover, even if he had followed the intent of Taft and Knox and been entirely noncommittal throughout, it is hard to imagine Victoriano Huerta allowing so perfect an opportunity to slip through his fingers. In the effort to determine Wilson's complicity, the other actors and the fragility of Madero's regime must not be forgotten. Without a strong party behind him, with the revolutionary army long since disbanded, Madero depended more and more on the federal army for survival. When its loyalty cracked there was nothing left to save him. Ambassador Wilson's conduct was improper and instrumental in the coup. Ironically, despite his idealization of action and men of action, Wilson was more often manipulated than manipulator, more often prisoner than executioner.

INTERVENTION?

The same day the rebellion began in Mexico City, Ambassador Wilson took up with the State Department the question of intervention. Explaining a request for protection of foreigners that he had made of both Madero and Díaz, he added: "Our Government . . . should take prompt and effective action to meet the obligations which rest upon it."[24] Knox replied the next day, asking the Ambassador to make "a specific statement of the obligations which you think now rest upon this Government and outline precisely the prompt and effective action to meet these obligations which you say this Government should now take."[25] The ambassador declined to comment on how protection might be extended to Americans in Mexico City, but he strongly recommended dispatching warships and marines to Mexican ports and displaying alertness along the border.[26] The following day four American warships were ordered to proceed to Mexican ports. On the east coast the *Virginia* was ordered to Veracruz, and the *Georgia* to Tampico; on the west coast the *South Dakota* was sent to Acapulco, and the *Colorado* was ordered to divide

---

[24] H. L. Wilson to Secretary of State, February 9, 1913, 812.00/6058.
[25] Knox to American Embassy, Mexico, February 10, 1913, 812.00/6058.
[26] H. L. Wilson to Secretary of State, February 10, 1913, 812.00/6076.

its time between Mazatlán and Manzanillo. By February 12,
four ships had been ordered to the Tampico-Veracruz area:
the *Vermont, Nebraska, Georgia,* and *Virginia.*[27]

On Tuesday, February 11, Ambassador Wilson, on grounds
of the indiscriminate firing in the city and the menace to foreign
lives and property, requested "instructions of a firm, drastic,
and perhaps menacing character to be transmitted personally
to the Government of President Madero, and to the leaders
of the revolutionary movement."[28] Wilson believed that these
powers would enable him to bring the fighting to an end and
to bring about negotiations between the combatants. Secretary
Knox refused Wilson's request for two reasons. He pointed out
that drastic representations might influence the issue of military
supremacy in the capital, a responsibility the Administration
refused to assume. Moreover, Knox stated,

if the Embassy's representations under such instructions should be
disregarded the enforcement of such representation with the accompanying message to Congress looking to authority for measures
of actual war might precipitate intervention, which should not
be considered except as a last resort and if found justified after
deliberate consideration of the whole Mexican question including
the situation of foreigners throughout the Republic. Just now action
looking to intervention might moreover precipitate many of the
evils of actual intervention and might indeed subject American
interests in the City of Mexico to increased dangers under the
cloak of the present turmoil.[29]

Without waiting for this refusal, Ambassador Wilson proceeded
to act as if he had received the powers he had requested. Wednesday morning, February 12, with the consent of the Austrian,
Spanish, and British ministers he protested to President Madero
against a continuation of hostilities and issued an intimidating
warning: "I desire to say that the President of the United States

---

[27] For the assignment of the various vessels, see the following: 812.00/6529,
812.00/6915A, 812.00/6947, 812.00/6085A, 812.00/6085B, 812.00/6085C,
812.00/6095, 812.00/6995C, 812.00/6127, 812.00/6127B, 812.00/6127D,
812.00/6172A.
[28] H. L. Wilson to Secretary of State, February 11, 1913, 812.00/6092.
[29] Knox to American Embassy, Mexico, February 12, 1913, 812.00/6092.
See also a memo of the same number by the Latin American division
which added the consideration that if the Taft administration began
a war it could not finish before leaving office, the new administration
could not be held responsible for the state of affairs existing on its
coming to power.

is much concerned over the situation; that vessels have been ordered to the various seaports, as well as transports with marines which *will* be landed if necessary and brought to this city to maintain order and afford protection to the lives and property of foreigners."[30] (Italics added.) Ambassador Wilson made an identical protest to Díaz, but under the circumstances and given the ambassador's known dislike for Madero, it hardly carried the same force. On Friday, February 14, the ambassador revealed more about his desire to move events with threats if possible and with force if necessary by requesting complete discretionary authority over the American ships and marines heading for Mexican ports.[31] Then from one to three o'clock in the morning on February 14, the Ambassador met with the British, German, and Spanish ministers. Their little group agreed to advise President Madero to resign. The Spanish minister conveyed their proposal later the same day and received Madero's indignant refusal.[32]

Wilson had outrun his superiors who, instead of issuing binding instructions, contented themselves with rejecting after the fact each of the ambassador's progressively more martial requests. Thus on February 15, Secretary Knox refused to put Wilson in command of the ships and marines being sent to the Mexican coast, and told him: "The sending of the vessels represents no change whatever in the policy of the President, but responds merely to the necessity of great caution made necessary by the uncertainty of the new conditions caused by the uprising at Mexico City, and the effect of these conditions upon Americans and American property both locally and throughout Mexico."[33]

Nothing in the conduct of the administration in Washington suggested a change in policy toward the Mexican government. In fact, Knox believed on February 15 that conditions had improved.[34] Control over policy had slipped from Knox's hands, however, for Ambassador Wilson in Mexico City had threatened invasion and had asked for Madero's resignation. Alarmed and confused, Madero telegraphed the American president on Febru-

---

[30] H. L. Wilson to Secretary of State, February 12, 1913, 812.00/6112. The ambassador's warning has been changed from the past tense of his official report to present tense.
[31] H. L. Wilson to Secretary of State, February 14, 1913, 812.00/6149.
[32] H. L. Wilson to Secretary of State, February 15, 1913, 812.00/6175.
[33] Knox to American Embassy, Mexico, February 15, 1913, 812.00/6149.
[34] *Ibid.*

4. Ambassador Henry Lane Wilson, ca. 1911
(Prints and Photographs Division, Library of Congress)

ary 14 that he had been told of the dispatch of warships to Mexican ports carrying troops to be disembarked for Mexico City. He assured Taft that no Americans need suffer from the fighting in the capital if they would withdraw from the danger zone, and he stressed the willingness of the Mexican government to accept responsibility for all damages. He appealed to Taft not to land troops in Mexico.[35] A similar request reached the State Department the same day in a note from the Mexican embassy. The embassy's note mentioned specifically that Ambassador Wilson had inspired a request for Madero's resignation and that he might try to disembark troops.[36] Somewhat bewildered himself, Secretary Knox told Ambassador Wilson that the president desired to know "just what the Embassy has said to the Mexican Government and what part the Embassy had in the reported request made by part of the Diplomatic Corps that Madero resign."[37] Taft in his reply to Madero denied any intention to intervene,[38] but Madero feared the worst and sent the text of his note to Taft to the governors of all the Mexican states.[39] To prove his goodwill Madero agreed to a twenty-four hour armistice and to certain other restrictions on military activities proposed by Ambassador Wilson.[40]

Rumors of intervention spread rapidly, alarming Washington in turn, but Knox was unwilling to deny the rumors too emphatically and to weaken their deterrent effect on the Mexican people and government. Instead, he advised Ambassador Wilson, "With your full knowledge of the President's policy and your intimate knowledge of the local situation it is left to you to deal with this whole matter of keeping Mexican opinion, both official and unofficial in a salutary equilibrium between a proper degree of wholesome fear and a dangerous and exaggerated apprehension."[41]

Two days prior to Madero's arrest, the Taft administration decided to take the additional steps of assembling at Guan-

---

[35] Knox sent Ambassador Wilson a copy of Madero's telegram. See Knox to American Embassy, Mexico, February 15, 1913, 12 midnight, 812.00/6172.

[36] Ibid.

[37] Ibid. For Wilson's reply see H. L. Wilson to Secretary of State, February 17, 1913, 812.00/6208 and February 17, 1913, 812.00/6224.

[38] Taft to Madero, February 16, 1913, 812.00/6219A.

[39] See 812.00/6183, 812.00/6181, 812.00/6429, 812.00/6223a.

[40] H. L. Wilson to Secretary of State, February 15, 1913, 812.00/6178.

[41] Knox to American Ambassador, February 17, 1913, 812.00/6223a.

tanamo a force of 2,000 marines on transports.[42] Nor did
Madero's overthrow end the military precautions. On February
21, without consulting the State Department, Taft directed that
the Fifth Army Brigade, about 5,000 men, and four transport
ships be sent to Galveston, Texas.[43] And on February 25, Knox
wrote the secretary of navy suggesting that many more ships
should visit Mexican ports:

In the opinion of this Department, few things will work so successfully towards the reestablishment of peace and order in Mexico
as an effective but unoffensive display of the great naval power
of this nation. Not only will the local population be left with a
wholesome regard for the might of the United States Government,
but the central government at Mexico City will be kept in a state
of careful regard; watchful to prevent any incident which might
provoke the use of this great power and, by pointing out the likelihood that it will be used in certain contingencies, be materially
strengthened and braced in dealing with any recalcitrant elements
in the country.[44]

TAFTIAN NONRECOGNITION

Just as the fighting in Mexico City had raised the question of
intervention, Huerta's success against Madero posed the question
of recognition of the new government. From the moment of
Madero's overthrow, Ambassador Wilson openly associated himself with the coconspirators, Díaz and Huerta. Only a few hours
after Madero's arrest, the ambassador was conveying messages
between the usurpers.[45] A few hours later, fearing that the two
would disagree and the fighting would begin again, he invited

---

[42] 812.00/6245C, February 18, 1913.
[43] See Huntington Wilson to Rudolph Forster, February 22, 1913,
812.00/6418A, for Huntington Wilson's communication to the President's
private secretary that he had "heard casually this afternoon" about the
dispatch of the brigade. Taft's announcement to the press mentioned
two brigades at Galveston. Huntington Wilson to American Embassy,
Mexico, February 22, 1913, 812.00/6294B.
[44] Knox to Secretary of the Navy, February 25, 1913, 812.00/6274. These
steps were certainly taken with an eye to controlling domestic criticism
of the president's policy. On February 26, Secretary of War Stimson,
at the urging of Senator Elihu Root, met with the members of the
Senate Foreign Relations Committee "to prevent the rushing through
in Congress of some sort of a drastic and inopportune resolution at
the instance of the Senators from Texas upon whom a great deal of
pressure is being brought by people along the Texas border." F. M.
Dearing, Memorandum, February 26, 1913, 812.00/6558.
[45] H. L. Wilson to Secretary of State, February 18, 1913, 812.00/6244.

them to the embassy. After a three-hour meeting and "enormous difficulties," Díaz and Huerta agreed that Huerta would be provisional president and that Díaz would name the cabinet and have Huerta's support for the permanent presidency.[46] Wilson also secured the release of Madero's cabinet and a promise of an uncensored press and telegraph service and joint action between Díaz and Huerta to maintain order in the city.[47] On the day after Madero's overthrow, the ambassador advised: "Our position here is stronger than it has ever been and I would suggest that I have general instructions immediately to bring to the attention of whatever Government may be created here the complaints set forth in our note of September fifteenth and urge for at least an arrangement to settle them all."[48] Then, on February 20, just two days after the coup, Wilson reported that the new provisional government had been securely established and asked to be instructed about recognition. Wilson stated that the provisional government had taken office "in accordance with the constitution and precedents."[49] His attribution of legality to Huerta's presidency represented a meaningless formalism. While under arrest Madero and Pino Suárez resigned, apparently in exchange for Huerta's promise to allow them to leave the country. The presidency then passed, according to the Constitution, to the Foreign Minister, Lascuráin, who obligingly resigned in favor of Huerta whom he had just appointed minister of government, next in line for the presidency. The State Department accepted the fiction of legality.[50]

In the United States, a widespread revulsion of feeling developed toward Huerta's government following the deaths of Madero and Suárez. On February 21, Knox informed Ambassador Wilson that although the new government appeared to be legally established and apparently intended to reestablish peace and order in Mexico,

---

[46] H. L. Wilson to Secretary of State, February 18, 1913, 12 midnight, 812.00/6246.
[47] H. L. Wilson to Secretary of State, February 19, 1913, 5 P.M., 812.00/6264.
[48] Ibid.
[49] H. L. Wilson to Secretary of State, February 20, 1913, 812.00/6287.
[50] Knox to American Embassy, Mexico, February 21, 1913, 812.00/6325A, stated that "the Department is disposed from the statements and tenor of your recent telegrams to consider the new Provisional Government as being legally established. . . ."

5. Secretary of State designate Philander C. Knox, ca. 1908
(Prints and Photographs Division, Library of Congress)

especially in view of the situation which has prevailed for the past two years or more this Government must very carefully consider the question of [the Provisional Government's] ability and earnest disposition to comply with the rules of international law and comity, the obligations of treaties, and the general duties to foreigners and foreign governments incidental to international intercourse. Under these circumstances you are instructed to say to those seeking recognition as the new Provisional Government that the Government of the United States will be glad to receive assurances that the outstanding questions between this country and Mexico . . . will be dealt with in a satisfactory manner.[51]

The questions the United States wanted to have "dealt with and got out of the way" included the Chamizal controversy, to be settled by direct agreement; the equitable distribution of the waters of the Colorado River, to be settled by a convention; the border claims arising from the battles of Agua Prieta and Juárez in 1911, to be settled by payment of the American demands; the improvement of Mexican justice for foreigners; and most important, all claims resulting from loss of American lives and property, to be settled by a mixed international commission which would award damages.[52]

Ambassador Wilson, again acting without instructions, assembled the diplomatic corps to discuss recognition of the new government. He reported that all of his colleagues were without instructions, but that all agreed on the imperative need to recognize the new government "to the end of enabling it to impose its authority and reestablish order."[53] Wilson also stated he was sending a circular telegram to all consuls instructing them to do all possible to bring about a general acceptance of the provisional government. His telegram to the consuls contained a flat lie. Though he knew that he and all of his colleagues were without instructions, he advised the consuls to "urge general submission and adhesion to the new Government which will be recognized by all foreign Governments today."[54]

Actually, the other foreign governments intended for the immediate future to follow the American lead.[55] Taft and Knox

---

[51] *Ibid.*
[52] *Ibid.*
[53] H. L. Wilson to Secretary of State, February 21, 1913, 812.00/6319.
[54] H. L. Wilson to Secretary of State, February 21, 1913, 812.00/6325.
[55] This was true for Brazil, Norway, Chile, Austria, Britain, Germany, and Spain. See H. L. Wilson to Secretary of State, March 3, 1913, 812.00/6489. For the last correspondence of the Taft administration,

continued to refuse recognition without binding assurances from Huerta, and the latter continued to try to outwait the American government, hoping to gain recognition without committing himself. With Ambassador Wilson working diligently to strengthen Huerta and with the Mexican and American governments deadlocked, the Taft administration expired.

see H. L. Wilson to Secretary of State, February 22, 1913, 812.00/6326; Knox to American Embassy, February 23, 1913, 812.00/6326; H. L. Wilson to Secretary of State, February 25, 1913, 812.00/6373; H. L. Wilson to Secretary of State, February 25, 1913, 812.00/6374; Knox to American Embassy, February 25, 1913, 812.00/6379A; H. L. Wilson to Secretary of State, February 26, 1913, 812.00/6394; and H. L. Wilson to Secretary of State, March 3, 1913, 812.00/6491.

II. Controlling Revolution:
The Response of the Wilson Administration, 1913–1917

4 The Development of the Mexican Revolution

In retrospect, Madero's brief term as President of Mexico appears as a pause in the movement toward a final struggle between conservatives and revolutionaries that began after the collapse of the Díaz regime in 1911. The initial declarations against Huerta embodied in the Plan of Guadaloupe adopted in March 1913 emphasized the political and legal tasks of ousting the tyrant Huerta and of reestablishing constitutional government in Mexico. *Constitucionalista*, the name adopted by the anti-Huerta movement, fitted these aims perfectly. The movement attracted many of the most capable men in northern Mexico. Though Venustiano Carranza, ex-Governor of Sonora, asserted his primacy as first chief of the Constitutionalist army, the revolutionary forces remained grouped around men like Alvaro Obregón in the northwest and Francisco Villa in the northeast.

Opposition to Huerta proved an insufficient bond, and the unity of the anti-Huerta movement broke down even before Huerta's resignation and flight in July 1914. During the meeting of the victorious revolutionary leaders at Aguascalientes in October and November 1914 the factions of Villa and Zapata joined in a loose alliance.[1] Forcing a split, they elected a provisional "conventionist" government unacceptable to Carranza. Fortunately for Carranza, many of the most able military chiefs followed him to the state of Veracruz to form the core of what became the triumphant revolutionary movement.[2]

The fortunes of the Constitutionalists reached their lowest ebb in the last months of 1914. To rally desperately needed popular support for the impending military campaigns against Villa, Carranza on January 6, 1915, issued a first cautious decree on agrarian reform. Though the decree may have been a "counsel of despair,"[3] it complemented Obregón's military effort against Villa and signaled a new direction for the Mexican Revolution.

The crucial steps toward radical social and economic reform

---

[1] For an account of this meeting see Robert E. Quirk, *The Mexican Revolution, 1914–1915: The Convention of Aguascalientes* (Bloomington, Ind.: Indiana University Press, 1960).

[2] Among the most important leaders who decided to accept Carranza's political leadership were Generals Álvaro Obregón, Luis Blanco, Cándido Aguilar, and Pablo González.

[3] Frank Tannenbaum, *Peace by Revolution: An Interpretation of Mexico*

occurred at the constitutional convention that opened in Querétaro in December 1916. During the convention it became clear that profound differences existed within the triumphant Constitutionalist movement. A radical group, led by General Francisco Múgica and Andrés Molina Enríquez and backed by General Obregón, succeeded in winning approval for the most far-reaching reforms. Article 27 of the new constitution, covering land and natural resources, reached to the roots of the unrest in Mexico. It envisioned the enforced breakup of the hacienda system and the restoration of communal lands taken from the villages during the Díaz regime. In addition, Article 27 vested subsoil rights in the nation and thus struck directly at foreign monopoly of Mexico's natural resources. Under the new constitution the Mexican government might grant concessions for the exploitation of minerals but ownership remained inalienably Mexican, and the government enjoyed the right of total regulation. Article 123 of the new constitution protected wage earners by guaranteeing decent working conditions, the eight-hour day, a minimum wage, and right to organize unions and strike.[4]

Carranza had desired only political reforms. These were enacted, including the establishment of universal male suffrage and a bicameral legislature, and the prohibition of reelection to the presidency. The constitution promised profound economic and social reform as well, but it remained more pragmatic and nationalist than dogmatic and ideological. The federal and state governments were empowered to improve the lives of the Mexican people through management of the national wealth and regulation and elimination if necessary of foreign investment.

At the time of the revolution, Mexico was overwhelmingly rural, and the revolutionaries understandably emphasized agrarian reform. As early as July 1913 Francisco Escudero, Constitutionalist agent in Washington, gave as the aims of his movement justice, the improvement of the lot of the farmer, the removal of the burden of taxation from the poor, the return of illegally confiscated lands to those who owned them, division of the enormous estates, the creation of a new financial system to enable the farmer to borrow at low interest rates, the establishment

---

(New York: Columbia University Press, 1933), p. 201. I have relied on Tannenbaum and on Parkes's *History of Mexico* for this interpretation of the radicalization of the Mexican Revolution.

[4] For text of 1917 Constitution, see *Foreign Relations, 1917*, pp. 950–981.

of agricultural schools, increased irrigation, improvement of the
lot of the worker, and "protection, education, and redemption
of the neglected Indians." The priorities were those of the Constitutionalists, and the preoccupation with agrarian problems
is obvious.

Despite great loss of life to disease and civil war, the Mexican
people and particularly the peasant remained the subject rather
than the object of the revolutionary destruction. The changes
accomplished by the Mexican Revolution anticipated less the
Russian and Chinese Communist experiments than the subsequent welfare-state reforms in Britain, France, Germany, and
the United States. The Mexican constitution protected the right
to strike, for example, and the right to strike is not "proletarian
and peasant" in the sense those terms are used by Marxist-Lenin-
ists or Maoists. Great power was given to the government as
the agent of the people, not as the agent of a party acting for
history. The Mexican revolutionaries replied to the complaints
of the American government against confiscation and radical
reforms by saying that what was done had to be done and done
quickly *because the people wanted it done*. The sentiments and
philosophy behind that position differ profoundly from the dogmatic faith in rational man common to another stream of Western revolutionary thought represented by Rousseau, the Jacobins,
and the Bolsheviks.

On the other hand, neither Carranza nor Obregón made good
the promises of the Querétaro constitution. Within the Mexican
domestic context each appeared as a conservative implementing
a radical program. Foreign governments held a different view,
and the constitutional alterations in property rights immediately
brought the Mexican government into conflict with American
interests and their defender the American government. For six
years, first Carranza and then Obregón sought to implement
the reforms of the constitution of 1917 against the opposition
of the United States. When a modus vivendi was finally achieved
in 1923, the Mexican government had yielded more than it
had won, but the ideals of the constitution remained alive and
were finally carried to their logical conclusion under Cárdenas.

In responding to the constitution of 1917, the United States
followed a policy of requiring "just treatment" of American
interests. In practice, this meant that the American government
insisted that interests legally acquired before the official promul-
gation of the constitution (May 1, 1917) were not subject to

expropriation or reduction except with compensation and through due process of law.

The outbreak of World War 1 and the eventual intervention of the United States as an ally of Britain, France, and Russia profoundly affected America's response to the Mexican Revolution. In some respects, Mexican leaders must have welcomed the war. The American government and people, engrossed by the "Great Cause," had little time or inclination to worry about occurrences in Mexico, and Mexico gained a welcome respite from her overzealous neighbor. In addition, the Mexican government affected a stance of reluctant neutrality, and America's desire for this to continue gave Mexico some much-needed diplomatic leverage.

On balance, the war seems to have been more of a loss than a gain for Mexico. Above all, it effectively eliminated Germany as a partner for Mexico and a counterweight to American influence. Pro-German sentiment in Mexico was strong, and the Zimmermann telegram created a sense of alarm and urgency in the United States. But an alliance with Germany was never a real option for Mexico. Mexican leaders feared that the United States would seize on war with Germany as a pretext to invade Mexico. To prevent his country from becoming the first victim of the American war effort against Germany, Carranza launched a peace plan in February 1917 and, less than two weeks after the United States declared war on Germany, the first chief announced Mexico's neutrality in the war. The German navy could not escape from the North Sea, let alone enter and operate in the Gulf of Mexico. Even the American ambassador to Mexico, Henry P. Fletcher, was inclined to regard German activities in Mexico, including the Zimmermann note as a part of a long-range plan "to lay the foundations for an economic position after the war."[5] Pro-German sentiment in Mexico rose and fell with Germany's fortunes on the battlefield, and Germany's defeat ended hopes for external support against the United States.

Even without an external ally hostile to the United States, Mexico paid dearly during the war. The emergency controls adopted by the United States hurt Mexico and altered the course

---

[5] U.S., National Archives, General Records of the Department of State. Record Group 59, Internal Affairs of Germany, German Military Activities in Mexico, Fletcher to Secretary of State, May 8, 1917, 862.20212/331 (hereinafter cited by number and date only).

of the revolution. Understandably, the United States put the war effort in Europe ahead of all other priorities, and this disrupted prewar commercial patterns. The Allies were determined to prevent Germany from acquiring food and war materials through willing neutrals. Tragically, the wartime controls were also harnessed to force the Mexican government to provide "protection" and "just treatment" for American interests. Through a combination of inhumanity, indifference, inefficiency, and calculation, thousands of Mexicans were allowed to starve when the United States refused to export corn and pork to Mexico, even though American stocks had surpassed even wartime requirements. The Carranza government was denied arms and munitions it desperately needed to pacify the country, and the relatively insignificant Mexican gold reserves were frozen as hostages to Mexico's good conduct.

During the war American leaders tried to put problems between Mexico and the United States on the shelf. If the Mexican government refused to agree to American demands and would not yield to diplomatic pressure, American policy was to maintain the status quo until the war ended and the difficulties could receive full attention. The situation in and around the Tampico oil fields exemplifies this. There the federal Mexican government occupied the cities and a rebel guerrilla leader, General Manuel Peláez, in the pay of the oil companies, controlled the oil fields and the countryside. The federal government received income from the export of the oil, but wished to assert full control of the area and to implement its revolutionary program, particularly Article 27 of the new constitution. At the same time, the Mexican government realized that if it pressed a military campaign against Peláez, the threat of damage to the oil fields might bring American intervention to protect the flow of Mexican oil for war purposes. President Wilson decided before the United States entered the war that if necessary he would send troops to occupy the oil fields in order to forestall European intervention. The Mexican government acted with great caution and the necessity never arose. Throughout the war the oil companies demanded diplomatic protection from the United States, plotted and dreamed of an "Oil Republic" on the east coast of Mexico, continued to buy "protection" from Peláez, and hoped that the United States would occupy all of Mexico and restore the situation to its prerevolutionary tidiness. The American government forcefully protested every decree altering subsoil and property rights and managed to maintain the status quo by winning delays and postponements in the implementation of the reforms. Though this failed to settle the status of American interests in Mexico, it enabled them to keep what they had. The overall effect in America and on the American war effort was negligible in any case. This was not true for Mexico. The wartime freeze imposed on land and petroleum reforms profoundly influenced the course of the Mexican Revolution.

Last, the very success of the United States in the war created problems for Mexico. At the end of World War I, the power, prestige, and influence of President Wilson and the United States had increased enormously. The discrepancies in strength and influence had been greatly disadvantageous to Mexico before World War I. After the war they were overwhelming.

During the first two weeks of his administration, President Wilson dramatically served notice of a new departure in American foreign policy. In statements to the press about Latin America and China, Wilson attempted to disassociate the United States from the foreign policies of the Taft administration, and in particular from "dollar diplomacy." With regard to China, Wilson announced the withdrawal of the American government's support for the participation of American bankers in a six-power loan to the Chinese government. Wilson observed: "The conditions of the loan seem to us to touch very nearly the Administrative independence of China itself; and this administration does not feel that it ought, even by implication, to be a party to those conditions."[1]

A week earlier the president had made a similar disclaimer of mercenary interest in Latin America and had attempted, as in the statement on China, to identify the aims of the American government and people with the aspirations of colonial and undeveloped peoples: "The United States has nothing to seek in Central and South America except the lasting interests of the peoples of the two continents, the security of governments intended for the people and for no special group or interest, and the development of personal and trade relationships between the two continents which shall redound to the profit and advantage of both and interfere with the rights and liberties of neither."[2]

Wilson had implied that the United States would act only as a sympathetic example in China, but he committed the

---

[1] March 18, 1913, The Papers of Woodrow Wilson, The Library of Congress, Ser. 3, 2: 21 (hereinafter cited as Wilson Papers). This was too much for Assistant Secretary of State Huntington Wilson, a holdover from the Taft administration, who promptly resigned. In his bitter letter of resignation, Huntington Wilson pointed out that "precisely because of the ultimate possibility of a measure of foreign control of China's finances, which may be inferred from a study of other countries which have found themselves in a similar situation, it was deemed imperative that there should be American participation in the rehabilitation of China's finances, in order to make sure of the presence of the potent, friendly and disinterested influence of the United States. The only practicable method of such participation was by the use of reliable American bankers." H. Wilson to Woodrow Wilson, March 19, 1913, Wilson Papers, Ser. 4, casefile 245.

[2] March 12, 1913, Wilson Papers, Ser. 3, 2: 20.

United States to a far-reaching, activist, and specifically political role in Latin America:

We hold, as I am sure all thoughtful leaders of republican government everywhere hold, that just governments rest always upon the consent of the governed, and that there can be no freedom without order based upon law and upon the public conscience and approval. *We shall lend our influence of every kind to the realization of these principles in fact and practice,* knowing that disorder, personal intrigue and defiance of constitutional rights weaken and discredit government and injure none so much as the people who are unfortunate enough to have their common life and their common affairs so tainted and disturbed. We can have no sympathy with those who seek to seize the power of government to advance their own personal interests or ambition. We are the friends of peace, but we know that there can be no lasting or stable peace in such circumstances. As friends, therefore, we shall prefer those who act in the interest of peace and honor, who protect private rights and respect the restraints of constitutional provision.[3] (Italics added.)

In retrospect, this brash, unannounced press release explains much of Wilson's Latin American policy and supplies most of the motives for the frequent Caribbean interventions undertaken during his administration. In addition to charting a general course, Wilson intended the statement to signal his opposition to Victoriano Huerta and to the manner in which the Mexican dictator had come to power.

The president's unmistakable reservation about Huerta failed to diminish Ambassador Wilson's enthusiasm for the dictator and his government. On March 5, 1913, the ambassador stated: "I expect at any moment to have news of the submission or the annihilation of the rebels."[4] Only five days later the consul at Ciudad Juárez reported: "Every indication justifies the claim of the anti-Government faction and they are daily growing in number. It is also becoming apparent that the struggle now augmenting will prove to be a real war and that the opposing forces will be enemies."[5] The view was equally good from Mexico City for all but the ambassador. On April 7, Captain W. A. Burnside, the American military attaché, observed: "From a military point of view the situation of the Mexican Government is at the present time desperate." He added what proved to be a sound estimate of the course of the civil war: "Few

---

[3] *Ibid.*
[4] H. L. Wilson to Secretary of State, March 5, 1913, 812.00/6505.
[5] Edwards to Secretary of State, March 10, 1913, 812.00/6611.

hopeful signs for the pacification of the country can be seen. The one circumstance in favor of the Government is that the revolutionists are as deficient in funds and military initiative as is the Government itself. Neither the Government nor the revolutionists have obtained any positively decisive results, and no such results are to be expected in the near future."[6] The ambassador continued to work for recognition. In his report to Bryan about Huerta's coup and the murder of Madero, he urged recognition on grounds of the new regime's legality and of the need to"strengthen and sustain" Huerta's government. Ambassador Wilson advised that recognition should follow proof of the regime's ability to pacify Mexico, to protect the lives and property of foreigners, and to satisfy the claims raised in the United States government's note of September 15, 1912.[7] Not surprisingly, the Ambassador reported the next day that Huerta had agreed to accept in principle all of the American claims. This included Chamizal, claims for damages, and the establishment of a general claims commission.[8] The ambassador had already reported that Huerta could and would pacify Mexico and protect foreigners and their property. In the ambassador's mind, the Huerta government deserved recognition. The administration in Washington left Ambassador Wilson uninstructed while it searched for a way to impose its will on Huerta.

THE SEARCH FOR A MEXICAN POLICY

The president's statement on Latin America in March had set forth general principles; it still remained to translate these principles into an effective policy. The most important early initiatives in Washington came from American industrialists and financiers with interests in Mexico. In early May, James Speyer, whose firm held a $10 million Mexican loan, urged that the United States recognize Huerta.[9] On May 6, Colonel House forwarded

[6] Captain W. A. Burnside, April 7, 1913, 812.00/7349.
[7] H. L. Wilson to Secretary of State, March 12, 1913, 812.00/6840.
[8] H. L. Wilson to Secretary of State, March 13, 1913, 812.00/6681. This offer was withdrawn on May 7, 1913, as a result of the American government's delay in granting recognition. H. L. Wilson to Secretary of State, May 8, 1913, 812.00/7431.
[9] W. G. McAdoo to W. W., May 7, 1913, 812.00/7473, forwarding Speyer's memorandum; J. B. Moore to W. W., May, 3, 1913, Wilson Papers, Ser. 4, casefile 471; Speyer to Moore, May 1, 1913, 812.00/7545; Speyer to Moore, May 19, 1913, 812.00/7546. Speyer met with Bryan at Bryan's home on June 4, 1913; see 812.00/7651 and 812.00/7706.

to the president three letters about Mexico from the president
of the board of the Southern Pacific Railroad, J. R. Kruttschnitt,
from James Speyer, and from a Mr. Ludlow, a long-time resident in Mexico. House advised the president: "The situation
has about reached a point where it seems advisable for you
to take a hand."[10] Kruttschnitt endorsed a plan drawn up by
D. J. Haff and approved by Phelps, Dodge and Company, the
Greene Cananea Copper Company, Edward L. Doheny of the
Mexican Petroleum Company, and "others."[11] In Haff's view,
the situation in Mexico favored action by the United States
government to bring about a cease-fire in Mexico and an agreement between the Constitutionalists and the Huerta regime. Haff
pointed out that, while the Constitutionalists actually controlled
the northern states, they were without funds and therefore might
accept American mediation. If left alone, he added, the Constitutionalists would never treat with Huerta. Haff proposed that
the United States recognize Huerta if Huerta agreed to call
an election before October 26, the date he had set, and to guarantee a fair election in the states he controlled. The United
States would ask the Constitutionalists to participate in the election, to guarantee its fairness in the areas they controlled, and
to agree to suspend hostilities and support whatever President
was chosen in the election.

It is difficult to say whether this was a disingenuous plan. Kruttschnitt and the others may have been committed to Huerta,
but above all else they desired stability and a maintenance of
the status quo and were willing to accept any Mexican government that could guarantee good business conditions. The plan's
disadvantages for the Constitutionalists are obvious. They were
to be asked to abandon their insurgency in exchange for Huerta's
promise to hold fair elections which, because he still controlled
most of Mexico, he would certainly arrange to win by whatever
means necessary. The only sure results likely to flow from the
plan would be detrimental to the Constitutionalists, including
the recognition of Huerta by the United States and the flow
of loans and investments that would follow recognition, the holding of elections that were certain to be rigged and which they
would lose, and the suspension of military operations with the
accompanying erosion of revolutionary morale and momentum.

---

[10] E. M. House to W.W., May 6, 1913, Wilson Papers, Ser. 2.
[11] Kruttschnitt to House, May 6, 1913, Wilson Papers, Ser. 2.

A more important consideration dictated against acceptance of
the plan by the Constitutionalists. To accept American mediation
in Mexico's revolutionary civil war would be to recognize the
United States as the arbiter of Mexico's future, and this the
Constitutionalists rejected out of hand. Haff believed that both
sides would agree to his plan:
We feel certain, from our knowledge of the temper of both sides,
that both the Federalists and the Constitutionalists would welcome
the friendly intervention of the Department of State of our Government. . . . Our Ambassador in Mexico is, in my opinion, the man
to attempt this work. It might be found necessary to send a special
envoy to treat with the Constitutionalists, while entrusting our
Ambassador in Mexico to treat with the Huerta Government. But
in any event, it should be an easy task for the Department of
State, because neither side will for one minute repudiate an official
suggestion of the United States Government and its powerful influence presented in the form of a wish and backed, as it necessarily
is, with the moral right to demand that it shall be accepted and
complied with, when it is considered that the interests of the United
States in Mexico represent practically every industry of that country, excepting that of agriculture, and that the commerce of Mexico
with the United States represents more than 75% of her total
foreign trade, all of which, so important to both countries is now
imperilled.[12]

A week later, the counselor of the State Department, John
Bassett Moore, made the international lawyer's case for recognition of Huerta: "The Government of the United States having
originally set itself up by revolution has always acted upon the
de facto principle. We regard governments as existing or as not
existing. We do not require them to be chosen by popular vote.
We look simply to the fact of the existence of the government
and to its ability and inclination to discharge the national obligations." Moore argued that, regardless of the condition of
Huerta's rise to the presidency, the United States still had to
deal with the Mexican government and this necessitated recognition: "The government of the United States once recognized
five governments in Mexico within a few months, and did not
injure its own interests or commit itself to any responsibilities
by so doing. Recognition is purely and simply the avowal of
an apparent state of fact, and the advantage gained by it is

---

[12] *Ibid.* Haff also wrote to Wilson directly about his plan, Haff to W.W.,
May 12, 1913, Wilson Papers, Ser. 2.

that the country is held responsible for the acts of the authority so acknowledged."[13]

In the abstract, Moore's position is unassailable. For the United States to have recognized Huerta in 1913, however, would have involved much more than the "avowal of an apparent state of fact" and would have provided extensive, perhaps determining, advantages to Huerta in his struggle against the Constitutionalists. Money that was frozen by nonrecognition would have become available to Huerta, and with that money he might have been able to launch a successful military campaign against the revolutionaries. European and American bankers were reluctant to accept Mexican loans until the United States recognized the Huerta government. Moreover, when the Wilson administration recognized a government in Mexico it became responsible for that government's conduct, for President Wilson had not repudiated the policeman's responsibilities that accompanied the Roosevelt corollary to the Monroe Doctrine. The president believed that early recognition of Huerta would wrongly prejudge the Constitutionalists' chances of success against Huerta. To recognize Huerta would defeat his hopes to align the United States on the side of democratic, constitutional government in Latin America. In Latin America the president's dramatic March announcement would have been discounted, and there would have appeared little reason to distinguish Wilson from Taft or Theodore Roosevelt.

Moore condemned the introduction of political or moral considerations into the recognition of a foreign government. He failed to comprehend that political, social, and economic conditions may be implicit in the recognition of a government capable of discharging its "international obligations." The major European powers construed "international obligations" to include the protection of exploitative foreign activities in Asia, Africa, Latin America, and Mexico. Recognition was granted to those regimes that were willing to play along or were too weak and narrowly based to resist European gunboat diplomacy. Those regimes that resisted European demands usually found themselves at war with the Europeans and, in China, the Japanese. The Taft administration had refused to recognize Huerta largely because Huerta would not give binding promises to protect

---

[13] Moore to W.W., May 15, 1913, Wilson Papers, Ser. 2. The memorandum was prepared by Moore for Bryan and dated May 14, 1913.

American lives and property, promises that obviously carried the most far-reaching political, economic, and moral significance for Mexican society.

President Wilson's doctrine of recognition represented less a departure from earlier methods than a change in the conditions for recognition that the major powers had come to apply to undeveloped and colonial countries. The Chinese and Mexican Revolutions, by raising up first movements and later governments unwilling to sacrifice their people to foreign economic exploitation, posed the question of recognition in an unprecedented way. President Wilson's actions were closer in spirit to the actions and ideals of the Mexican and Chinese revolutionaries than they were to the standards of the imperialist powers.

President Wilson was sufficiently impressed by Haff's proposal to make it the basis of a tentative plan for achieving a Mexican settlement. Lifting phrases from Haff's memorandum, the president drafted instructions to be sent to Ambassador Wilson in Mexico City. The draft stated that the United States government would recognize Huerta:

on condition that all hostilities cease, that he call an election at an early date, the twenty-sixth of October now mentioned being, in our judgment much too remote, and that he absolutely pledge himself as a condition of our action in his behalf that a free and fair election be secured by all proper machinery and safeguards. Upon this understanding this Government will undertake the friendly office of securing from the officials of the states which are now refusing to acknowledge the authority of Huerta's government an agreement to cease hostilities, maintain the status quo until the election shall have been held, and abide by the result of the election if it be held freely and without arbitrary interference of any kind as we have suggested.[14]

These instructions were not sent, however, and on May 26 the Kruttschnitt group took up with Secretary Bryan its plea for action by the United States that would help reestablish peace

---

[14] Confidential Instructions to H. L. Wilson, n.d., Wilson Papers, Ser. 2, filed in folder for May 27–c. May 1913. Arthur S. Link put the date of this draft as a "short time" after May 12, 1913, the date of Haff's memo to the president. *Wilson: The New Freedom* (Princeton, N.J.: Princeton University Press, 1956), p. 351. An outline marked "Mexico. Settlement," making the same points as Haff's plan is in Wilson Papers, Ser. 2, n.d. [May 12, 1913?], in the folder for May 27–c. May 1913.

and stable government in Mexico.[15] Bryan was particularly impressed by a proposal submitted by Edward Brush and S. W. Eccles, which assigned to the Mexican congress the task of calling and supervising elections.[16] Bryan advised the president: "This seems to me to offer a way out."[17] The president replied enigmatically that the suggestions of the two men were "most interesting and, I think, important," and agreed to discuss them with Bryan at an early date.[18]

The president kept his own counsel, however, and perhaps as a result of the uncertainty of information about conditions in Mexico and the popular outrage against Ambassador Wilson's role in the coup against Madero, decided to send William Bayard Hale to Mexico to investigate as his personal representative.[19] Hale knew nothing about Mexico, but he was an able journalist, had edited a collection of the president's campaign speeches, *The New Freedom,* and, most important, had the confidence of the president. Ambassador Wilson's inaccurate, partial political reporting and rash conduct had lost him the confidence of the Taft administration. His urgent pleas for recognition of Huerta made the gap between ambassador and president even greater after the Wilson administration took office. Hale filed his first report from Mexico City on June 3. A week later Ambassador Wilson, acting as he had in the last months of the Taft administration, moved to force the administration's hand.

Ambassador Wilson's Last Efforts

On June 10, Ambassador Wilson filed a despatch that implicitly condemned the president's refusal to recognize Huerta:
    The increasing difficulty and embarrassment attending the transac-

---

[15] Kruttschnitt to Bryan, May 26, 1913, Wilson Papers, Ser. 4, casefile 471.
[16] Brush and Eccles to Bryan, May 26, 1913, *ibid.*
[17] Bryan to W.W., May 27, 1913, *ibid.*
[18] W.W. to Bryan, May 28, 1913, *ibid.*
[19] Ambassador Wilson was under heavy attack and sought to clear himself in every way possible. See, for example, his request of ex-President Taft for a statement approving his conduct as ambassador, H. L. Wilson to Taft, June 3, 1913, Knox Papers, Correspondence, 20: 3356. Taft referred the request to Knox. Taft to Knox, June 19, 1913, *ibid.,* p. 3357. Knox replied cautiously, suggesting that Taft give only "general approval" and commend the ambassador for his efforts to protect American lives and property: "A wholesale approval of his course would transfer the attack from him to you." Knox to Taft, n.d., handwritten, *ibid.,* p. 3359.

tions of this Embassy with the Mexican Government; the vast
injury which is being inflicted upon American interests and American lives; the freedom and persistence with which the rebel forces
are claiming our attitude to be a signal of encouragement and
support; the hostility of a rapidly growing Mexican opinion supported by an almost unanimous resident American opinion; the
great and permanent advantages which European nations are securing as a result of our forced inactivity, are making such a disheart-
ening impression on me that, at the risk of being considered intru-
sive and insistent, I must again urge upon the President that on
the highest grounds of policy, which in this case I understand
to be the conserving and the extension of our material interests
in Mexico, the restoration of peace and the cultivation of sentiments
of friendship and respect with a neighboring and friendly nation,
that we should without further delay, following the example of
all governments accredited here but two, accord official recognition
to the present provisional Government.[20]

The president's reply to this veiled indictment of his policy
came on June 15. Ambassador Wilson was advised for his own
information and not for communication to the Mexican
government:

This Government does not feel that the provisional government
of Mexico is moving towards conditions of settled peace, authority,
and justice, because it is convinced that within Mexico itself there
is a fundamental lack of confidence in the good faith of those
in control at Mexico City and in their intention to safeguard constitutional rights and methods of action. This Government awaits
satisfactory proof of their plans and purposes. If the present provisional government of Mexico will give the Government of the
United States satisfactory assurances that an early election will
be held, free from coercion or restraint, that Huerta will observe
his original promise and will not be a candidate at that election,
and that an absolute amnesty will follow, the Government of the
United States will be glad to exercise its good offices to secure
a genuine armistice and an acquiescence of all parties in the program. It would be glad, also, to be instrumental in bringing about

---

[20] H. L. Wilson to Secretary of State, June 9, 1913, 812.00/7743. The
original despatch was sent to the president on June 10; Wilson Papers,
Ser. 4, casefile 502. Spain recognized Huerta on April 1, 1913, Great
Britain on May 3, France and Austria-Hungary on May 12, Japan on
May 13, Italy and Germany on May 17, Russia on June 1, and the
Netherlands on June 13. See "Chronology of Important Political Events
in Mexico from the Overthrow of Porfirio Diaz down to the Present
Time (July 1, 1914)," compiled by Calvin M. Hitch, Department of
State Division of Latin American Affairs, 812.00/24267.

any sort of conference among the leaders of the several parties in Mexico that might promise peace and accommodation. The interests of the United States are vitally involved with conditions of peace, justice, and recognized authority in Mexico, and the Government of the United States can acquiesce in nothing which does not definitely promise these things.[21]

The president had settled on a policy, compounded of Haff's proposal, opposition to Huerta, and a desire to force events in Mexico into peaceful, constitutional channels. Ultimately, the president decided to send yet another special agent to Mexico to carry out this policy, and chose the former Governor of Minnesota John Lind.[22] Lind was instructed to seek the same objectives described in the note sent to Ambassador Wilson: peace between the factions, the resignation of Huerta, and an honest election. For the next two years, in fact, the Wilson administration pursued these objectives consistently and, with the exception of the downfall of Huerta, unsuccessfully.

Ambassador Wilson reacted to the statement of the president's policy by continuing his efforts to prompt recognition and, when that proved impossible, by attempting to persuade the administration to choose between recognizing Huerta and breaking off diplomatic relations with Huerta. He continued to forward encouraging reports of the progress of the Mexican government's campaigns against the Constitutionalists.[23] On July 8 he submitted a vague dispatch stating that the other governments represented at Mexico might ask the United States either to recognize Huerta or to intervene to restore order and implicitly raising the issue of European intervention in Mexico.[24] The next day the ambassador confronted the administration with his view of the practical alternatives: recognize Huerta or get out of Mexico:

---

[21] Secretary of State to H. L. Wilson, June 15, 1913, 812.00/7743. A draft in Wilson Papers, Ser. 2, dated June 14, 1913, is marked "To be sent in cipher by the State Department to Henry Lane Wilson at Mexico," and carries revisions in the President's handwriting. The President was mistaken about Huerta's promise not to be a candidate. After the overthrow of Madero, Huerta had promised to support Félix Díaz for the presidency but had never declined to run himself.

[22] Lind was preceded into Mexico by Hale and by two agents commissioned by Secretary Bryan, W. H. Sawtells, and Reginald F. del Valle. Lind's mission, unlike the others, was primarily diplomatic.

[23] See, for example, H. L. Wilson to Secretary of State, June 12, 1913, 812.00/7769; June 30, 1913, 812.00/7933; and July 13, 1913, 812.00/8036.

[24] H. L. Wilson to Secretary of State, July 8, 1913, 812.00/7992.

Deeply impressed with the situation which is being developed
by the constantly increasing bitterness and resentment against the
Government of the United States on account of its policy and
attitude toward the present Administration, I am obliged on behalf
of our great trade and commercial interests with this country which
have been practically wiped out; for the preservation of those
harmonious relations which should exist between contiguous and
friendly nations; on behalf of the some thirty thousand suffering
Americans who are still left in Mexico, the subjects of public hatred
and without any guarantees of protection for their lives and property; and also because of the more than one hundred thousand
Mexicans whose lives have now been sacrificed in the struggle
to restore order and peace in Mexico, to again urge upon the
President the urgent necessity for some action of a drastic and
convincing kind that will convince this government and this people
that our Nationals must be protected in life and property, and
that the barbarous and inhuman warfare which has now been
waged for three years shall cease. This may be brought about in
two ways. First, by the official recognition of this Government
coupled with a demand for guarantees not only for the settlement
of the existing questions between Mexico and the United States
which have already been agreed to in principle, but also for a
clear and defined policy of protection to American lives and to
American interests . . . second, by the closing of our diplomatic
establishment . . . and the withdrawal of the Ambassador and
First Secretary as a protest against existing conditions. . . .

I submit these two courses as the only ones by which our interests
may be conserved, our people protected, and a bloody war
arrested.[25]

In a subsequent dispatch, Ambassador Wilson reiterated his
proposal and advised that "the President should understand that
in dealing with this situation he is now face to face with grave
responsibilities which cannot be evaded by a halting or uncertain
policy but only by an action of a firm, formidable and impressive
character."[26] And on July 12 the ambassador warned that "a
strong and aggressive attitude should be assumed at Washington." Four days later he was recalled, ostensibly for consultations
but actually to be dismissed from the diplomatic service.[27] Am-

[25] H. L. Wilson to Secretary of State, July 9, 1913. This despatch was
forwarded to the president, J. B. Moore to W.W., July 10, 1913, Wilson
Papers, Ser. 2.
[26] H. L. Wilson to Secretary of State, July 11, 1913, 812.00/8027.
[27] Secretary Bryan interviewed Ambassador Wilson in Washington and
forwarded the ambassador's views to the president, Bryan to W.W., n.d.
[July 26, 1913?], Wilson Papers, Ser. 2.

bassador Wilson desired the recognition of Huerta as a first and necessary step in protecting American lives and property and sustaining America's economic domination of Mexico. President Wilson desired the elimination of Huerta as the first step in restoring peace to Mexico and in establishing a constitutional government that would attack the social and economic injustices that sparked revolution in Mexico. Given this divergence in viewpoint, the ambassador's recall was only a matter of time. The precise moment of his recall was largely determined by Hale's reports from Mexico City about Ambassador Wilson's role in the overthrow of Madero.

The First Hale Mission

Hale's presence in Mexico City through June, July, and August provided President Wilson with a source of information against which to judge Ambassador Wilson's reports and, more importantly, a source the president trusted as he did not trust the ambassador. Hale reported on general political conditions and on Ambassador Wilson's role in the coup against Madero. Hale's reports about the ambassador's role in the coup persuaded the president to recall and to dismiss Henry Lane Wilson. The reports on general political conditions could only have confirmed in the president a belief in the instability of Huerta's rule, the formidable yet inconclusive nature of the anti-Huerta movement, and, consequently, in the need for American mediation.

Shortly after his arrival in Mexico City, Hale wired that Ambassador Wilson had sympathized with the conspiracy against Madero, that he had misrepresented the views of the diplomatic corps, the majority of whom had favored upholding the Madero government, and that he gratuitously interfered in Mexico's domestic affairs.[28] In his full report on Madero's overthrow, Hale established that the ambassador was privy to the treasonous agreement between Félix Díaz and Huerta and had either welcomed it or, by not disapproving and opposing it, had tacitly signaled his willingness to aid the usurpers. Hale's summation was measured and damning. Pointing out that Ambassador Wilson sincerely believed that Madero would ruin Mexico and American interests in Mexico, Hale added:

None the less, however sincere may have been his motives, it is impossible not to conclude that Mr. Wilson's course was utterly mistaken, mischievous and tragically unhappy in its results.

[28] Hale to Ben G. Davis, June 12, 1913, copy in Wilson Papers, Ser. 2.

It is hardly a matter of conjecture—it is a conclusion to which all facts point—that without the countenance of the American Ambassador given to Huerta's proposal to betray the President, the revolt would have failed. . . .

There was not a moment during the "Decena Tragica" when it would not have been possible to "end the distressing situation," [and] "put a stop to this unnecessary bloodshed" by stern warning from the American Embassy to the traitorous army officers that the United States would countenance no methods but peaceful constitutional ones and recognize no government set up by force. . . .

It must be a cause of grief that what is probably the most dramatic story in which an American diplomatic officer has ever been involved should be a story of sympathy with treason, perfidy and assassination in an assault on constitutional government.[29]

This report arrived by mail or diplomatic pouch late in June and convinced the president of the need to recall Ambassador Wilson.[30] Hale's political reports contradicted the ambassador's optimistic accounts of Huerta's success in pacifying Mexico, and there can be little doubt that the president accepted Hale's views which, in retrospect, seem to have been well informed. Four days before the ambassador reported the elimination of virtually all rebels and bandits, for example, Hale reported:

The general picture is that of a country "on the loose"; "out of hand"; with a Government which may be said actually to be in control of perhaps one third of its territory, conditions in that third being disorderly; and utterly unable to maintain anything approaching order, except along a few railroad lines—unable, indeed, to send its troops, except in large bodies, prepared to fight their way through constant harrassing guerrillas.

It is hardly necessary to dwell on the hard lot of the unfortunates who inhabit the ravaged regions. There is no security for any sort of property or life. Lands are going out of cultivation; mines are closed down; only the most necessary labor and trade is carried on. . . . Prisoners are shot by both sides.[31]

The president received the views of the Constitutionalists through their special agent in Washington, Francisco Escudero,

[29] W. B. Hale [no indication of to whom it was sent], Mexico City, June 18, 1913, 812.00/7798-½, filed on roll 26, "Documents not Bound in Volumes 1–34."
[30] W.W. to Bryan, July 1 and July 3, 1913, Wilson Papers, Ser. 4, casefile 502.
[31] W. B. Hale, "Memoranda on Affairs in Mexico," July 9, 1913, 812.00/8203.

later Constitutionalist minister of foreign affairs. The information supplied by Escudero inclined the president toward the Constitutionalists. Escudero, for example, identified the cause of the Constitutionalists with the aims of the 1910 Revolution against Díaz and cited agrarian reform, relief of the poor and the workers, and expansion of education as Constitutionalist objectives.[32] Escudero also warned the president that the Constitutionalists would reject any attempt by a foreign country to promote a compromise settlement. Compromise, he pointed out, had led to Madero's overthrow and murder. The Constitutionalists would never negotiate with Díaz or Huerta and would keep the revolutionary army under arms to deal with enemies of the revolution. "No compromise would insure peace." With regard to foreign interference, he stated:

The intervention of any foreign power in our internal affairs would only favor the interest of Huerta and the reactionary party. The interests of the people would be greatly prejudiced, inasmuch as it would compel them to enter into some unjust compromise with their oppressors. Furthermore, the idea of intervention is highly unpopular among the people, and it would surely originate evils far greater than those it intended to remedy.

Among the people at large there is no anti-American feeling; on the contrary there is a feeling of true friendship. The great majority, as heretofore stated, have their sympathies with the Constitutionalists, and, therefore, the failure to recognize Huerta has been considered by them as a justification of their attitude, and has been regarded as an indirect help to them which has been greatly appreciated. . . .

The Constitutionalists have never asked, and never will ask, any help from foreign powers. All they desire is that these powers consider their cause with justice and calmness. The lives and property of foreign subjects and citizens have been protected by every possible means within their jurisdiction, and it is fair to say that no honest man need have fear.[33]

The president ignored this and other warnings that the Constitutionalists and Huerta would reject mediation.[34] Wilson acted

---

[32] See, for example, a memo by Escudero dated July 24, 1913, forwarded to the president's secretary, Thomas Hopkins to Rudolph Forster, July 25, 1913, Wilson Papers, Ser. 2.

[33] *Ibid.*

[34] J. B. Moore had warned in May that "in the first place we know not only that in most cases of civil strife such proposals from the outside are unwelcome, but also that they are usually repulsed with more or less heat by both sides in order to conciliate popular feeling. In the

on the basis of what he thought was best for Mexico and what
he thought he could accomplish. In this case he undoubtedly
believed that he could compel Huerta to accept his plans and,
once Huerta had accepted, that the Constitutionalists could not
refuse. He was wrong on both counts.

THE LIND MISSION

In late July the President decided to send John Lind to Mexico
as his special envoy to negotiate with Huerta. Lind stayed in
Mexico traveling between Mexico City and Veracruz until
April 1914, and his mission is of singular importance to the
Mexican Revolution. Since the details of Lind's mission are
treated elsewhere,[35] it is possible to concentrate here on those
aspects of the mission most helpful in understanding the Wilson
administration's response to the Mexican Revolution.

Lind's Instructions

President Wilson had asked Lind on June 11 to serve as American Ambassador to Sweden. Lind had declined on grounds that
he thought it unwise to go as ambassador to the country of
his birth and that he preferred working in politics at home and
on behalf of the administration's policies. He said he would
gladly serve in another capacity if the president needed him.[36]
When appointed as the president's special envoy to Mexico,
Lind, like Hale, was totally without expertise in Mexican affairs
but, again like Hale, he had the trust of the president. He left
Washington on August 4 in possession of a detailed plan drafted
by the president for a political settlement in Mexico. In his
instructions to Lind the president drew together the various principles and specifics about Latin American policy that had been
advanced by him and by those close to him. He stressed the
special responsibilities and disinterestedness of the United States
in its dealings with Mexico and added:

---

second place, if such a proposal were made by the United States and
declined by the Mexicans, it might be thought that we had tried the
last peaceful expedient and that nothing but intervention remained."
J. B. Moore to W.W., May 15, 1913, Wilson Papers, Ser. 2. Moore's
memo was intended originally for Secretary Bryan and was dated May
14, 1913.
[35] See Link, *Wilson: The New Freedom,* pp. 357ff. and George M.
Stephenson, *John Lind of Minnesota* (Minneapolis: University of Minnesota Press, 1935).
[36] Wilson Papers, Ser. 4, casefile 579.

A satisfactory settlement seems to us to be conditioned on—

(a) An immediate cessation of fighting throughout Mexico, a definite armistice solemnly entered into and scrupulously observed;

(b) Security given for an early and free election in which all agree to take part;

(c) The consent of General Huerta to bind himself not to be a candidate for election as President of the Republic at this election; and

(d) The agreement of all parties to abide by the results of the election and cooperate in the most loyal way in organizing and supporting the new administration.

The Government of the United States will be glad to play any part in this settlement or in its carrying out which it can play honorably and consistently with international right. It pledges itself to recognize and in every way possible and proper to assist the administration chosen and set up in Mexico in the way and on the conditions suggested.

Taking all the existing conditions into consideration, the Government of the United States can conceive of no reasons sufficient to justify those who are now attempting to shape the policy or exercise the authority of Mexico in declining the offices of friendship thus offered. Can Mexico give the civilized world a satisfactory reason for rejecting our good offices? If Mexico can suggest any better way in which to show our friendship, serve the people of Mexico, and meet our international obligations, we are more than willing to consider the suggestion.[37]

When Lind's instructions leaked to the press, Huerta bluffed publicly that he would go to war rather than submit to American intervention.[38] His official reaction was far more cautious, requiring only that Lind possess proper credentials.[39] Lind met with Federico Gamboa, the minister of foreign affairs, on August 12, and next day recommended that his instructions be sent

---

[37] *Foreign Relations, 1913*, p. 822. Original draft on Wilson's typewriter with revisions in his handwriting marked "Instructions (Mexico)," July 30, 1913, Wilson Papers, Ser. 2.

[38] The *New York Times*, August 9, 1913.

[39] Nelson O'Shaughnessy to Secretary of State, August 9, 1913, 812.00/8573. O'Shaughnessy, first secretary of the embassy in Mexico City, had become chargé on the recall of Henry Lane Wilson. The Wilson administration took Huerta's threats seriously enough to take a look at its naval forces in Mexican waters. A memo from the secretary of the navy, Josephus Daniels, to the president on August 8, disclosed that twelve American warships would be in Mexican waters by August 9. Daniels added that "we can get plenty of transports when desired." Wilson Papers, Ser. 2.

to the major foreign governments.[40] Bryan took his suggestion up with the president, proposing that the entire instructions be communicated to the European powers, Argentina, Brazil, Chile, and Peru, and that the proposal alone be communicated to the other governments represented at Mexico City.[41] The president approved the idea and instructed Lind to put the proposal before the Mexican government.[42]

Huerta's Refusal

Gamboa replied on August 16, rejecting the request that Huerta drop his candidacy and mischievously taking up Wilson's request for suggestions as to how to serve Mexico by proposing the prompt exchange of ambassadors "without previous conditions."[43] Lind thought Huerta was convinced that the United States would not resort to force unless provoked by a Mexican equivalent of the sinking of the *Maine*.[44] Accordingly he tried to increase the pressure on Huerta by suggesting personally and without instructions that unless Huerta accepted the president's plan, "one of three courses would be forced on the administration in spite of any less drastic policy that the president might wish to pursue. First, the modification of our neutrality laws in those respects in which they are more strict than international law; second, granting the rebels belligerency; third intervention."[45] The next day Bryan wired Lind to ask if Gamboa's rejection were final. "Has there been no sober second thought?" he asked.[46]

Apparently there had been some second thoughts and, stalling for time, Gamboa asked on August 21 if he might come to

[40] Lind to Secretary of State, August 13, 1913, 812.00/8334.
[41] Bryan to W.W., August 14, 1913, 812.00/8334.
[42] Bryan to Lind, August 14, 1913, 812.00/8334. Bryan suggested to the president that he seek Congressional approval for his plan in the form of a joint resolution. Bryan supported mediation and opposed intervention, but he realized mediation might fail. Bryan to W.W., August 10, 1913, Wilson Papers, Ser. 2.
[43] Gamboa to Lind, August 16, 1913, Wilson Papers, Ser. 2.
[44] Lind to Secretary of State, August 17, 1913, forwarded to the president by J. B. Moore, Wilson Papers, Ser. 2.
[45] Lind to Secretary of State, August 18, 1913, Wilson Papers, Ser. 2.
[46] Bryan to Lind, August 19, 1913, 812.00/10641A. Hale agreed with Lind that Huerta doubted the United States would use force. "Mr. Lind exhausted the possibilities of politeness," Hale reported. "I suggest an object lesson of a different character." Hale to Secretary of State, August 20, 1913, Wilson Papers, Ser. 2.

Washington for talks with the president and secretary of state.[47] On the same day Lind softened his terms and tried to sweeten them with American dollars. Lind proposed to Gamboa that if Huerta would hold honest elections on October 26 and agree not to stand for the presidency, then the president would continue to forestall action in the American Congress, would delay an impending message to Congress on Mexico, and would favor a loan by American bankers to the Mexican government. Lind had been acting on his own again, but he felt confident the President would approve the plan to buy off the Mexican government.[48] Bryan wired the president's approval of the loan proposition on August 24.[49]

The president thought that Gamboa's request for talks in Washington might signify that Huerta had reconsidered. Accordingly, Lind was instructed to tell Gamboa that if the Mexican government would withdraw its first rejection of the proposals, still with the understanding that the United States would never recognize Huerta, then Gamboa would be welcome in Washington.[50]

"Watchful Waiting"

Wilson waited five days before delivering his message to Congress, and as he spoke he knew the Mexican government had just replied to Lind's second set of proposals. His message to Congress thus left open the possibility for further negotiations and announced two decisions intended to maintain and even to strengthen the position of the United States as a disinterested mediator.

In his message, the president reported on Lind's unsuccessful mission and, though the attempt at peacemaking had failed, declared:

We can afford to exercise the self-restraint of a really great nation, which realizes its own strength and scorns to misuse it. It was our duty to offer our active assistance. It is now our duty to show what true neutrality will do to enable the people of Mexico to set their affairs in order again and wait for a further opportunity to offer our friendly counsels. The door is not closed against the resumption, either upon the initiative of Mexico or upon our own,

[47] Lind to Secretary of State, August 21, 1913, 812.00/10642.
[48] Lind to Secretary of State, August 22, 1913, Wilson Papers, Ser. 2.
[49] Bryan to Lind, August 24, 1913, 812.00/8526, and Wilson Papers, Ser. 2.
[50] Bryan to Lind, August 22, 1913, 812.00/10642.

of the effort to bring order out of the confusion by friendly co-operative action, should fortunate occasion offer.[51]

Wilson then urged all Americans to leave Mexico and announced his intention to forbid the export of arms to any part of Mexico. This resounding if anticlimactic message seemed to signal a substantive change in policy, as doubtless it was intended to do. Actually, the president had gained time at home without significantly altering his policy. From the outset he had intended to accomplish his ends in Mexico through "the steady pressure of moral force." His message to Congress merely reaffirmed that intention. American policy remained, as carelessly defined in Lind's instructions and as restricted in the course of the negotiations at Mexico City, dedicated not to Huerta's elimination but to his elimination from candidacy in the coming elections. Huerta soon taught Wilson a lesson in how far an unscrupulous dictator could go to satisfy the form of such a demand through manipulation of the very democratic processes Wilson cherished.

Gamboa's reply reached Washington on August 27. After launching another diatribe against the president's policy and declining the loan deal, Gamboa seemed to yield on the crucial point. "We are compelled to acknowledge that we have made a mistake," he declared.[52] A provision of the Constitution had been overlooked, and Huerta could not be a candidate after all.

Lind jubilantly reported: "Every point contended for in the first note is accepted in fact, though not in form. From a diplomatic standpoint the mission is a success. . . ."[53] He advised that it was now time to approach the Constitutionalists:

I have already requested Burnside [American military attaché] to be prepared to advise me as to the character of the revolutionary forces that should be entitled to our good offices in considering measures for the cessation of hostilities. Some good man or men should [undertake] that in the north. The lesson of non-recognition is our weapon [;] it can be wielded effectively in the north, I believe. The real work commences now. I cannot prophesy success but the possibility of it is worth our best efforts.[54]

---

[51] *Public Papers: The New Democracy* 1: 49.
[52] See text of translation of the note, O'Shaughnessy to Secretary of State, August 27, 1913, 9 p.m., Wilson Papers, Ser. 2; and Lind to Secretary of State, August 27, 1913, 4 p.m., Wilson Papers, Ser. 2.
[53] Lind to Secretary of State, August 27, 1913, 11 p.m., Wilson Papers, Ser. 2.
[54] *Ibid.*

Bryan responded immediately. "Accept my hearty congratulations. Huerta's announcement that he will not be a candidate is the one thing necessary to restoration of peace."[55] Next day he wired the president's congratulations, and advised Lind to be ready for further negotiations.[56] O'Shaughnessy reported that Gamboa had reiterated to him that Huerta would not be a candidate. But O'Shaughnessy had his doubts and suggested that if the president would take steps to convince the Huerta government that armed intervention would follow a continuation of the present unsettled conditions, then his proposals would be accepted.[57]

Instead of following Lind's advice to approach the Constitutionalists immediately about a cease-fire and elections, President Wilson allowed a month to pass in futile expectation of further concessions from Huerta. Turning down a request by Huerta to send an envoy to Washington, Bryan told Lind there was nothing to discuss,

unless it is desired to renew negotiations with a view to securing first, an armistice, and, second, the insuring of free elections. While the tone of the second note of Señor Gamboa was not what might have been hoped for, or expected, we understand from it that General Huerta withdraws his request for recognition and excludes the possibility of his candidacy for President at the coming election. These things being understood, it is now possible to confer in regard to carrying out of the proposals of the President looking for the restoration of permanent peace.[58]

Why Wilson allowed his Mexican policy to drift through September is unclear. He had apparently swallowed Huerta's baited noncandidacy and believed subsequent events could be easily channeled into constitutional forms. He continued to ignore the Constitutionalists. As Arthur S. Link observed, "Wilson and Bryan proceeded throughout the summer and early autumn of 1913 very much as if the Constitutionalists did not exist."[59] It may well be that Wilson and Bryan intended from the start to work only through the formal governmental structure in Mexico. Perhaps the administration had been intoxicated by the president's rhetoric and the prospect of moral forces producing

[55] Bryan to Lind, August 27, 1913, 812.00/8593.
[56] Bryan to Lind, August 28, 1913, 812.00/8593.
[57] O'Shaughnessy to Secretary of State, August 28, 1913, 812.00/8606.
[58] Bryan to Lind, September 8, 1913, Wilson Papers, Ser. 3, 6: 314.
[59] *Wilson: The New Freedom,* p. 364.

a Mexican settlement. In any event the morning after began
to dawn in September as reports flowed in describing Huerta's
success in gathering money at home and abroad and in using
some of his new wealth to buy arms.[60] The embargo on arms
shipments from the United States to Mexico favored Huerta
because the Constitutionalists were landlocked. Lind had warned
against this unequal effect three days after the president's message to Congress:

The [Huerta] Government hails with great satisfaction the announced attitude of the United States to prohibit effectively the
shipment of munitions to Mexico, its wants can be and are being
supplied from Europe. In view of situation would it not be wisdom
to consider whether or not the United States is justified in regarding
munitions of war destined for Mexico as contraband irrespective
of origin. In my judgment no policy will solve the situation that
is not equally effective against all combatants.[61]

On September 10, acting secretary of war Henry Breckinridge
reported that since the president's message to Congress the
Huerta government had made final arrangements to receive
77,000 rifles and 24 million cartridges from Europe and Japan,
as well as shrapnel in unknown quantities from France and
England.[62]

When O'Shaughnessy reported his personal interpretation, his
views were pessimistic and prescient. On September 10, he reported, "If Congress becomes uncontrollable Huerta will dissolve
it."[63] Some days later he commented, "In my opinion, the situation is very serious and if the Chamber of Deputies continues
to oppose the President there will be a dissolution of the Chamber of Deputies and a military dictatorship established."[64]
Huerta, of course, denied all such allegations and enigmatically
told O'Shaughnessy that he had made but two political promises: "to pacify the country and to enforce the laws."[65]

---

[60] Lind to Secretary of State, September 1, 1913, 812.00/8635, reporting
loans by Mexican landowners to Huerta. O'Shaughnessy to Secretary
of State, September 1, 1913, Wilson Papers, Ser. 2, reporting a 200
million peso (?) loan by the Speyer interests to Huerta.
[61] Lind to Secretary of State, August 30, 1913, 812.00/10494.
[62] Breckinridge to W.W., September 10, 1913, Wilson Papers, Ser. 2.
[63] O'Shaughnessy to Secretary of State, September 10, 1913, 812.00/8768
and Wilson Papers, Ser. 2, forwarded to the president on September 18.
[64] O'Shaughnessy to Secretary of State, September 19, 1913, Wilson
Papers, Ser. 2.
[65] O'Shaughnessy to Secretary of State, September 24, 1913, Wilson
Papers, Ser. 2.

The nomination by the hollow Catholic party of Gamboa and General Ugenio Rascón as its candidates for the elections and Huerta's apparent acquiescence in their candidacy convinced Secretary Bryan that the end was in sight. "I feel that we are nearly at the end of our trouble," he wrote to the president on September 25.[66] Wiring Lind the good news the next day, he at last indicated that the administration had consulted the Constitutionalists: "We are hoping that the Constitutionalists will join in the election and have so intimated to those who are in touch with them."[67]

A memorandum from Hale to the president on September 28 underlined the need to take account of the Constitutionalists. Hale suggested that the United States should move to implement its original propositions of an armistice and a nationwide election. "I believe that consent to this could now be secured, both from the Mexican Congress and from the Revolutionists; and that a stable basis of peace could thus be established. . . ."[68] Hale admitted that Huerta had probably been eliminated and that an election would be held in October, but he warned that the Constitutionalists would never participate in the election and would continue their struggle. Hale proposed that the United States should "induce" the revolutionaries to participate in an election. It was the one chance for peace, the only chance in sight:

True, the Revolutionists declare that they will take part in no election so long as Huerta remains in the presidential chair. Even that may be arranged, if only once the Mexico City Government and the Revolutionists could be brought into negotiations. . . .

We could open physical channels of communication between them. We could set negotiations going. By means of suggestions, privately made, we could probably bring about an armistice and a real election [and] accomplish, not merely such a "vindication" of the Administration's policy as the crowding out of Huerta would be, but the complete success of restoring peace in Mexico.[69]

The administration had already asked the Constitutionalists if they would participate in the October elections. Now it returned to the original plan, as Hale had proposed. Lind was ordered to advise Huerta:

---

[66] Bryan to W.W., September 25, 1913, Wilson Papers, Ser. 2.
[67] Bryan to Lind, September 26, 1913, 812.00/10645B.
[68] Hale to W.W., September 28, 1913, Wilson Papers, Ser. 2.
[69] *Ibid.*

The Government of the United States will not feel that a satisfactory constitutional settlement has been made unless an earnest and sincere effort is made to secure the participation and cooperation of the leaders in the north. This government *hopes* that its good offices may now be made use of for this purpose. It is as necessary in our view that this participation and cooperation should be striven for and secured as that a free election be held at which General Huerta shall not be a candidate.[70] (Italics added.)

O'Shaughnessy continued to suspect Huerta's good faith, and in early October Lind joined him, reporting that the impression "is gaining ground that the promise of fair elections is mere subterfuge."[71] Both men remained convinced that Huerta discounted any chance of American military intervention in Mexico. Acting on his own again, Lind approached Huerta around the first of October with a plan to arrange negotiations between the provisional government in Mexico City and the Constitutionalists. Lind proposed that Huerta, the United States, and the Constitutionalists appoint commissioners with plenary powers who would meet to work out a plan for a cease-fire and an election in which all Mexicans could participate.[72] On the same day that Lind reported Huerta's rejection of the proposed commission, the Constitutionalists communicated to Secretary Bryan their intention to fight on and their flat refusal to participate in the October elections.[73]

From this time on Lind became an increasingly ardent champion of the Constitutionalist cause. They would not have welcomed his support. Underlying his endorsement of the revolution lay an assumption of America's right to interfere in and to supervise the course of events in Mexico. On October 9 he declared: I become more and more convinced that if order and pacification can be accomplished by Mexican means it will be necessary to utilize the rebel organization in part at least for the work. . . .

[70] Bryan to Lind, October 1, 1913, 812.00/10645C. For the original draft, composed by the president, see W.W. to Bryan, October 1, 1913, 812.00/9583.
[71] Lind to Secretary of State, October 2, 1913, 812.00/10646. See also O'Shaughnessy to Secretary of State, October 1, 1913, Wilson Papers, Ser. 2.
[72] Lind to Secretary of State, October 7, 1913, 812.00/9192. See also Lind to Secretary of State, October 4, 1913, Wilson Papers, Ser. 2, and Bryan to Lind, October 5, 1913, 812.00/10646B, approving Lind's activities.
[73] Escudero to Bryan, "Aide Memoire," October 7, 1913, Wilson Papers, Ser. 2.

Recognition of the rebels may become a vital question as one of the instruments for establishing a semblance of law and order. If recognition were deemed expedient for that purpose, would it not be feasible to arrive at an understanding with the rebels that recognition is granted on condition that the rebels shall not regard the entrance of United States troops at points where there is no adequate protection for life and property as an invasion or in any other light than as a friendly act to Mexico. Once recognized and afforded a fair opportunity to contend, the rebels will easily prevail. The Huerta Government will crumble like a house of cards. The reason I venture above suggestion is because it would not surprise me to learn any morning that all means of communication between Mexico City and outside world have been severed. In such an event a relief expedition would have to be started from the coast; [it] should have good will of rebels.[74]

On October 8, the day before Lind sent this dispatch, the Constitutionalists had won an important victory, capturing the northen city of Torreón. On October 10, Huerta moved against the increasingly unmanageable Mexican congress, arrested 110 members of the chamber of deputies, and sent them to the penitentiary. The congress had been elected during the Madero period and had remained a center of opposition to Huerta. When Senator Belisario Domínguez disappeared, apparently a victim of Huerta's police, the chamber directed an investigation and passed a resolution warning Huerta that if another deputy or senator were arrested congress would seek a place where it could convene in safety, implicitly, of course, behind Constitutionalist lines. Huerta ordered the arrest of the members when they refused to withdraw the resolution, and on October 11 assumed dictatorial powers. O'Shaughnessy wired on October 11: "Huerta has his back to the wall and may now be considered an absolute military dictator."[75]

---

[74] Lind to Secretary of State, October 9, 1913, Wilson Papers, Ser. 2, forwarded to the president on October 10. See also Lind to Secretary of State, October 10, 1913, Wilson Papers, Ser. 2.
[75] O'Shaughnessy to Secretary of State, October 11, 1913, Wilson Papers, Ser. 2.

President Wilson's attempt to mediate in the Mexican Revolution had fallen flat before Huerta dropped his disguise as Mexico's constitutional caretaker in favor of the image of the nation's military guardian. Neither the Constitutionalists nor the provisional government in Mexico City had ever shown the slightest inclination to accept the good offices of the United States. Still, the arrest of the deputies came as a slap in the face. Wilson responded to the changed situation by intensifying American diplomatic pressure against Huerta and by launching a campaign to deprive his government of foreign support.[1] For several more months he held on to his hope for American mediation, and not for another two years did he abandon the hope to oversee a compromise settlement among the factions and an immediate return to peace and constitutional government in Mexico. As the end of 1913 approached, the president altered his policy from mediation to, first, aiding the Constitutionalists and, ultimately, to using force to facilitate the overthrow of the Huerta government.

DIPLOMATIC PRESSURE

The president regarded Huerta's actions as a demonstration of "bad faith" toward the United States and instructed O'Shaughnessy to inform the Mexican government that under the circumstances the United States could neither regard the pending elections as valid nor recognize whoever was elected president.[2]

The imprisonment of constitutionally elected representatives offended Wilson as little else could. All lines of policy came furiously alive. The president and secretary of state attempted to formulate a new policy toward Huerta. Hale, on his own suggestion, was dispatched to the Mexican border near the Constitutionalists and told to await instructions.[3] On October 24,

---

[1] For Wilson's efforts to obtain foreign, especially British, support for his Mexican policy, see Philip H. Lowry, "The Mexican Policy of Woodrow Wilson," unpublished Ph.D. dissertation, Yale University, 1949, pp. 64–87; Link, *Wilson: The New Freedom*, pp. 369–377; and Wilson Papers, Ser. 2, October 1913–January 1914.

[2] Bryan to American Embassy, Mexico, October 13, 1913, 812.00/9180a.

[3] Bryan to W.W., October 24, 1913; W.W. to Hale, October 24, 1913, Wilson Papers, Ser. 2.

Bryan asked the powers not to recognize the government elected in Mexico on October 26 until the United States had made known its position.[4] The British agreed to this on October 27, and their acceptance was crucial because the other powers tended to follow their lead in Mexico.[5] The Russians also agreed on October 27. In what was probably meant as a friendly gesture the Russian foreign minister added: "In my opinion the only satisfactory solution is annexation, and this action Russia would see with approval."[6]

Wilson's Mexican policy had consistently reflected two serious shortcomings: an insensitivity to Mexican nationalism and an unwillingness to wield convincingly the threat of armed intervention. Unable to perceive that his policy had failed because of its own inadequacies, Wilson lashed out at European imperialism as the culprit in Huerta's continuation in power.[7] The reports of Lind and O'Shaughnessy about British financial intrigues caused the president to suspect that the British government was sustaining Huerta in power for purely commercial reasons.[8] On October 25, for example, Lind reported: "The control and monopoly of the oil fields and oil business in Mexico is not only the aim of the Lord Cowdray interests but also of the English Government. England's Mexican policy for some time past has been shaped and exerted with this sole aim in view."[9]

The British were attempting to protect their interests in Mexico against the operation of an American policy they considered unwise.[10] But the president saw a sordid commercial diplomacy

---

[4] Bryan to W.W., October 24, 1913, Wilson Papers, Ser. 2. Bryan mentioned specifically Great Britain, Germany, France, Austria, Russia, Italy, Spain, and Japan. For the replies to Bryan's notes to the powers, see *Foreign Relations, 1913*, pp. 846–852.

[5] W. H. Page to Secretary of State, October 27, 1913, Wilson Papers, Ser. 2.

[6] American Ambassador to Secretary of State, October 27, 1913, Wilson Papers, Ser. 2.

[7] Secretary of State to American Embassy, Mexico, October 24, 1913, Wilson Papers, Ser. 2. This is marked "Not Sent."

[8] See Acting Secretary of State to W. H. Page, October 11, 1913, Wilson Papers, Ser. 2; Lind to Secretary of State, October 15, 1913, Wilson Papers, Ser. 2; O'Shaughnessy to Secretary of State, October 20, 1913, Wilson Papers, Ser. 2; O'Shaughnessy to Secretary of State, October 22, 1913, Wilson Papers, Ser. 2.

[9] Lind to Secretary of State, October 25, 1913, Wilson Papers, Ser. 2.

[10] See W. H. Page to Secretary of State, October 21, October 25, November 2, November 8, 1913, Wilson Papers, Ser. 2; and Page to Secretary of State, October 28, 1913, 812.00/9442.

and determined to strike directly at Huerta's foreign support
by accusing the powers of sustaining a usurping military dictator.
He directed the State Department to prepare a strong circular
note to this effect singling out Great Britain for special criticism
and at Mobile, Alabama, on October 27, delivered a bitter attack against foreign economic exploitation of Latin America.
In his address Wilson sought to identify the struggle within the
United States to free the government and the lives of the people
from control by "material interests" with the struggle of the
Latin American countries to free themselves from foreign and
domestic exploitation. He contrasted the "investments" made
by American capitalists with the "concessions" granted to other
foreign capitalists and said he was glad that the subordination
to foreign interests was ending. Last, he renewed the commitment of the United States to foster democracy in the world,
a note he had struck in March with regard to Latin America:
There is a reason and a compulsion lying behind all this which
is dearer than anything else to the thoughtful men of America.
I mean the development of constitutional liberty in the world.
Human rights, national integrity, and opportunity as against material interests—That . . . is the issue which we now have to face.
I want to take this occasion to say that the United States will
never again seek one additional foot of territory by conquest. She
will devote herself to showing that she knows how to make honorable and fruitful use of the territory she has, and she must regard
it as one of the duties of friendship to see that from no quarter
are material interests made superior to human liberty and national
opportunity. . . . What is at the heart of all of our national problems? It is that we have seen the hand of material interest sometimes about to close upon our dearest rights and possessions. We
have seen material interests threaten constitutional freedom in
the United States. Therefore we will now know how to sympathize
with those in the rest of America who have to contend with such
powers not only within their borders but from outside their borders
also.[11]
   Secretary Bryan had assigned to J. B. Moore the task of draft-
ing the circular note requested by the president. Moore sent
a draft of the note to the president on October 28 along with
a closely reasoned memorandum arguing against impugning the
motives of the other powers in recognizing Huerta. Moore's proposed circular telegram followed the president's instructions
closely. He wrote:

---

[11] *Public Papers: The New Democracy*, 1: 67–68.

The interests of other Governments in Mexico are chiefly commercial, but conditions in that country affect not only the material interests of the United States but also the life, the happiness, the liberty and the essential welfare of all peoples of this hemisphere, and particularly of the peoples of Central America. The interest and responsibility of the United States as an American nation stand therefore in a case by themselves. It is the belief of the President that the Government of Huerta, based upon usurpation and force, would long ago have broken down but for the encouragement and financial aid derived directly or indirectly from its recognition by other nations.[12]

The powers were asked to act in harmony with American policy.

Another draft circular was prepared, much less judiciously cast than Moore's,[13] that accused "European financiers" and "European governments" of supplying Huerta the means to perpetuate his power and asked all governments that had recognized Huerta to withdraw their recognition so that the Mexican people could reestablish constitutional government. Neither draft was sent, perhaps because of the cooling of tempers and the arguments Moore advanced in the memorandum that accompanied his draft. Moore argued against invoking the Monroe Doctrine in connection with the recognition of Huerta by the European states. Moore also challenged the inference that just because the European governments had recognized Huerta, they had acted under the influence of material interests: "There is nothing on the record to show that the governments that recognized the Administration at the City of Mexico in May, June, and July last felt that they were actuated by any other design than that of recognizing, in conformity with practice, what appeared to them to be the only governmental authority holding out the prospect of being able to re-establish order in the country. Nor had the United States said anything to indicate to them that it entertained a different view of their conduct."[14]

Moore observed that the statement of the president's position sent to Ambassador Wilson on June 15 had not been communicated to any foreign governments; their first insight into his policy came through his message to Congress on August 27.

---

[12] Moore to W.W., October 28, 1913, enclosure 1, Wilson Papers, Ser. 2.
[13] See Link, *Wilson: The New Freedom*, pp. 367–368.
[14] Moore to W.W., October 28, 1913, Wilson Papers, Ser. 2, and 812.00/11321a.

As for singling out Great Britain for condemnation, Moore suggested that there were at least five reasons other than "improper or sordid motives" why the British might resist the president's Mexican policy. These were (1) the decision under the Taft administration to exempt the American coastal trade from Panama Canal tolls, (2) the delay in the renewal of the arbitration treaty with Britain which, of course, would make possible the arbitration of the Panama tolls question, (3) the introduction of a seaman's bill touching the rights of other countries on the eve of an international conference on seamen's rights, (4) difficulties with Canada over fishing rights, and (5) a new tariff that provided a five percent discount on goods shipped in American vessels.

While the president was attempting to formulate a statement of his Mexican policy, Bryan renewed his proposal that the United States fund the debt of bankrupt Latin American countries. In keeping with the Monroe Doctrine and to win the trust of the Latin American peoples, Bryan suggested the United States should announce its willingness to buy the bonds of constitutional governments, including, of course, the one to be established in Mexico.[15] The president seemed to favor more drastic action, and he discussed military measures with Colonel House, including blockading Mexico's ports and sending troops across the border into the northern states to protect American lives and property. But these were more indicative of the trend of Wilson's thoughts than of his immediate intentions.

On November 1, he turned again to diplomatic pressure. Wilson instructed O'Shaughnessy to say that Huerta's coup against the Mexican congress contravened the assurances already conveyed to the United States government:

(2) That, unless General Huerta now voluntarily and as if of his own notion retires from authority and from all attempt to control the organization of the government and the course of affairs, it will be necessary for the President of the United States to insist upon the terms of an ultimatum, the rejection of which would render it necessary for him to propose very serious practical measures to the Congress of the United States. (Suggest here as if from your own mind the countenance and active assistance of the Constitutionalists by the United States.)

---

[15] Bryan to W.W., October 28, 1913, 812.00/9469a, original in Wilson Papers, Ser. 2.

(3) That the Government of the United States is anxious to avoid extreme measures, for Mexico's sake no less than for the sake of the peace of America, and is therefore willing to do anything within reason to spare General Huerta's feelings and dignity and afford him personal protection;

(4) That it, therefore, suggests the following course: The choice of some man or small group of men, as little as possible identified with the recent troubles (elderly men now in retirement, for example, who enjoy the general public confidence) to constitute a provisional government and arrange for early general elections at which both a new Congress and a new executive shall be chosen, and the government put upon a constitutional footing;

(5) That some such course, approved by the Government of the United States, is now absolutely necessary, that government being firmly and irrevocably resolved, by one method or another, to cut the government of Huerta off, if he persists, from all outside aid or countenance, and Huerta will only for a very few days longer be free to act with apparent freedom of choice in the matter. His retirement and an absolutely free field for a constitutional rehabilitation being the least the United States can accept. This Government cannot too earnestly urge him to make the inevitable choice wisely and in full view of the terrible consequences of hesitation or refusal.[16]

This represented not an ultimatum but the promise of an ultimatum. Moreover, the ultimatum when delivered was to carry not the usual threat of the initiation of hostilities but a threat to aid the enemies of Huerta. Wilson had not eliminated the possibility of American intervention, but he plainly desired to accomplish his purpose without the use of force, through the revolutionaries, if necessary, but so as to leave intact the formal, constitutional structure in Mexico. The near-ultimatum to Huerta indicated that the president intended to follow a course of gradual "escalation" in his efforts to overthrow Huerta and to preserve constitutional government in Mexico. First would come diplomatic pressure and isolation from foreign support. If this failed, the United States would aid the Constitutionalists. If Huerta still remained in power, the United States would use force, though how and under what circumstances force would be used remained unclear and perhaps so vague as to seem improbable.

O'Shaughnessy tried desperately to persuade Huerta to capitu-

---

[16] Bryan to American Embassy, Mexico, November 1, 1913, 812.00/10143a, drafted on Wilson's personal typewriter with his handwritten revision.

late,[17] but despite initial encouraging signs, he refused. On November 5, O'Shaughnessy reported: "In short, Huerta's answer to your demands is practically: 'I would like to come to an understanding but I cannot.' "[18] Huerta told O'Shaughnessy that publication of stories in the press about an American ultimatum had deterred him from reaching an understanding,[19] but it seems most likely that his doubts that the United States would use force and his hopes for money from Europe were determining factors. Lind desired the president to issue an ultimatum, and O'Shaughnessy believed that the time had come for intervention.[20]

But the president was on another track. First, he informed the nations represented at Mexico City of his intention to "require" the elimination of Huerta by whatever means were necessary, and asked them to advise Huerta to retire.[21] He then dispatched Hale to meet with the Constitutionalists to discover their reaction to a proposal to lift the arms embargo.

BARGAINING WITH REVOLUTIONARIES AND REACTIONARIES

The president knew the Constitutionalists fervently wanted him to lift the arms embargo. On November 1, Carranza had proposed to the State Department that if the department would receive his proposition he would set forth a way for the restoration of peace in Mexico. Three days later the message arrived:

---

[17] O'Shaughnessy's wife wrote that he "tried to convince him of the complete impossibility of standing up against the United States, and urged him again and again to give way." Edith O'Shaughnessy, *A Diplomat's Wife in Mexico* (New York: Harper, 1916), p. 32. See also O'Shaughnessy to Secretary of State, November 3 and November 5, 1913, Wilson Papers, Ser. 2.
[18] O'Shaughnessy to Secretary of State, November 5, 1913, 9 P.M., Wilson Papers, Ser. 2.
[19] O'Shaughnessy to Secretary of State, November 6, 1913, Wilson Papers, Ser. 2. To strengthen O'Shaughnessy's position, Bryan publicly denied that an ultimatum had been issued. Statement by the secretary of state to the press denying that an ultimatum had been sent to Mexico, November 4, 1913, 812.00/9594a.
[20] Lind to Secretary of State, November 7, 1913, 812.00/9611, and O'Shaughnessy to Secretary of State, November 5, 1913, 9 P.M., Wilson Papers, Ser. 2.
[21] In a note revised by the president, Bryan so instructed the American diplomatic representatives in Britain, France, Germany, Japan, Norway, Italy, Brazil, Argentina, Chile, Belgium, Spain, Guatemala, Salvador, Costa Rica, Honduras, Panama, and Nicaragua. See 812.00/9625A.

"Carranza makes only this request: that our Government permit free importation of equipments of war. He gives positive assurance under these circumstances of speedy peace and stable constitutional Government but he would deplore intervention as grave and disastrous mistake."[22]

One week later the president sent Hale instructions to meet with the Constitutionalists: "Confer with northern leaders and inform [them] that we contemplate permitting shipments of arms but before doing so we desire you to make the following statement. We desire above all things else to avoid intervention. If the lives and properties of Americans and all other foreigners are safeguarded we believe intervention may be avoided. If not we foresee we shall be forced to it. We rely upon them to see to it that there is no occasion for it in their territory."[23]

Bryan informed Lind that the president was considering withdrawing all diplomatic representatives from Mexico and removing the embargo on arms shipments. He told Lind: "Other steps will follow as they are found necessary but these will come first."[24] The next day Lind, acting on his own again, tried to increase the pressure on Huerta and in the process stiffened the American terms for a settlement. On November 12, Lind had O'Shaughnessy inform Huerta that unless the congress elected on October 26 was disposed of by some means—by declaring it illegal or by dissolving it—he would break off negotiations. No answer came and Lind departed for Veracruz: "I left word with O'Shaughnessy that the United States would entertain no proposition from Huerta Government until officially advised that the Congressional elections had been denounced and the Congress non-existing. I trust this action meets the approval of the President. Was above hasty on my part[?] If approved and if it is not followed by immediate action by Huerta

---

[22] Henry Allen Tupper to Secretary of State, November 4, 1913, Wilson Papers, Ser. 2.

[23] Bryan to Hale, n.d. [November 11, 1913?], Wilson Papers, Ser. 2. The original note in Wilson's handwriting is filed under November 28–c. November 1913. Wilson was also considering recognizing the belligerency of the Constitutionalists. Sometime in November he requested copies of Grant's and Cleveland's special messages on recognition of Cuban belligerency against Spain. See Wilson Papers, Series 2, c. November 1913. Marked "From State Department by my request. W.W."

[24] Bryan to Lind, November 11, 1913, Wilson Papers, Ser. 2.

then I trust it will be followed up by early action by the United States. . . ."[25]

Lind's initiative provoked a response from Huerta. The dictator's private secretary called on O'Shaughnessy and proposed a three point plan. The Mexican congress would annul the October elections because an insufficient number of polls had been in operation. Congress would then confirm Huerta's extraordinary powers, call new elections, and dissolve itself. If the United States would support the interim administration thus created, the federal government would suppress the revolutionaries without help.[26] The president replied that Lind would return to Mexico City and reopen negotiations if the newly elected congress was not permitted to assemble and if "General Huerta will absolutely eliminate himself from the situation immediately upon the constitution of an *ad interim* government acceptable to the United States the character and personnel of such a government to be agreed upon by negotiation."[27]

Only in Wilson's concept of the teacher-pupil relationship of the United States and the Philippines does one find an analogy for the role Wilson sought for the United States in Mexico, for he went on to require: "Such a provisional government having been agreed upon, we will arrange for its prompt recognition by the Government of the United States and will at once come to an understanding with it with regard to the complete reconstitution of the government of Mexico under the constitution of 1858 by means of free elections to be held at as early a date as possible."[28]

While O'Shaughnessy approached Huerta with these new conditions, Hale met with the Constitutionalists and delivered the president's message. The Mexicans manifested "great eagerness" to be allowed to import arms but were perplexed by the president's reference to intervention. Carranza, however, made a

---

[25] Lind to Secretary of State, November 13, 1913, Wilson Papers, Ser. 2. See also Lind to Secretary of State, November 12, 1913, 812.00/9677 for Lind's report of his action and Bryan to Lind, 812.00/9677, approving Lind's initiative.
[26] O'Shaughnessy to Secretary of State, November 13, 1913, 812.00/9705.
[27] Bryan to American Embassy, Mexico, November 14, 1913, 812.00/9705, drafted on Wilson's personal typewriter.
[28] *Ibid.*

strong declaration of purpose to protect foreign lives and property.[29]

Acting on instructions, Hale also raised the president's plan for a settlement between the Mexican factions and a return to constitutional government through agreement on a neutral interim regime and early elections.[30] The Constitutionalists refused to consider the idea:

Carranza and his cabinet strongly insist that they will go into no negotiations with Huerta or any remnant of his Government. They require its total extinction and then elimination from Mexican politics of the element that have made a Huerta possible. These men are plainly bent on a complete political and social revolution for Mexico. They are taciturn of speech but their moral enthusiasm is evident. They describe themselves as citizens in arms and declare their abhorence of militarism. . . . They say they have resorted to arms as a result of intolerable conditions. Having done so they propose to stop at nothing short of possession of Mexico City and the Government. They declare they will destroy the taste [sic] of military element and landed aristocracy, restore peace thence as soon as possible hold a free, general election and hand over the Government to officials named by the people.[31]

The Constitutionalists distrusted the United States and feared that the president was only playing them off against Huerta and would not lift the arms embargo.[32] After a period for reflection the Constitutionalists took up a decidedly unreceptive position. When Carranza had revised his initial reply to the president, for example, Hale found an entirely different emphasis:

Today's version dwells much more strongly on their uncompromising objection to intervention. In addition to presenting this revised version General Carranza made a formal speech which was interpreted phrase by phrase and taken down by a stenographer in which he stated that he took occasion solemnly to reiterate and emphasize anew that the Constitutionalists refused to admit the right of any nation on this continent acting alone or in conjunction with European Powers to interfere in the domestic affairs of the Mexican Republic; that they held the idea of armed intervention from outside as unconceivable and inadmissable upon any grounds

---

[29] Hale to Secretary of State, November 12, 1913, 812.00/9685; and Hale to Secretary of State, November 14, 1913, 812.00/9733 and Wilson Papers, Ser. 2.

[30] See Hale to Secretary of State, November 18, 1913, 812.00/9814 and Wilson Papers, Ser. 2.

[31] Hale to Secretary of State, November 14, 1913, 2 p.m., 812.00/9735.

[32] Hale to Secretary of State, November 14, 1913, 812.00/9736.

or upon any pretext. . . . General Carranza feared that the Constitutionalists' attitude on this point was not clearly understood at Washington and charged me to make the representation of it emphatic. . . . Underneath their uneasiness on the subject of possible intervention is the suspicion which they strongly entertain, but have not expressed, that Washington is using the threat of lifting the arms embargo merely to unseat Huerta and to set up another President in Mexico City. This they would never forgive.[33]

Carranza and his colleagues convinced Hale they would never negotiate with Huerta. Hale reported this to the president and stressed, as he had in Washington, that the mere elimination of Huerta would not bring peace to Mexico. Hale implied that the president should concentrate on the Constitutionalists instead of the government in Mexico City:

They appreciate it highly that the thought of the United States has turned in their direction and they will be deeply grateful for permission to import munitions of war. But they are absolutely set on the total destruction of the old regime and their own unencumbered triumph. There is no limit to their detestation of the whole predatory aggregation at Mexico City. . . . The Constitutionalists know their own minds perfectly, their program is definite, their pertinacity is intense and their prospects bright. Do they not thus constitute the most powerful, single factor in the whole problem and is not any attempted solution which forgets that fact certain to fail to give Mexico peace?[34]

The same day that Hale reported the Constitutionalists had rejected negotiations and American good offices, Huerta rejected the proposal submitted to him through O'Shaughnessy.[35] Once again, both Mexican factions had spurned the president's proposals.

The president's reply to Hale on November 16 showed considerable agony of spirit, but gave no indication that Wilson had altered his tutelary approach. He desired only to assist in restoring constitutional government in Mexico, the telegram read. He would not use force unless compelled to, and if he resorted to force he would issue guarantees against seeking territory or in-

---

[33] Hale to Secretary of State, November 14, 1913, 812.00/9738. For Carranza's formal reply, see Hale to Secretary of State, November 16, 1913, 812.00/9768 and Wilson Papers, Ser. 2.
[34] Hale to Secretary of State, November 15, 1913, 812.00/9759 and Wilson Papers, Ser. 2.
[35] O'Shaughnessy to Secretary of State, November 15, 1913, 812.00/9757 and Wilson Papers, Ser. 2.

demnities. But the president desired answers to a number of questions before going further.

Are the Constitutionalists willing to have Constitutional Government restored by peaceable means or do they prefer force? If assured of a free and fair election would they submit their cause to the ballot or do they still insist on the sword as the only available weapon? Are there any men outside of their army in whose wisdom and patriotism they have confidence, if so secure as many names as possible? [sic] If the Constitutionalists succeed in setting up a Government by force do they intend to give the people an early opportunity to elect a president and congress at a free and fair election? If so would they be willing to surrender the government into the hands of those selected by the people at such an election even though the persons elected were not the ones preferred by those in power? These questions are suggested that the President may be informed as to the views and plans of the leaders of the Constitutionalists. He is deeply disturbed by the impression he gets from your last telegram that the leaders of the Constitutionalists would trust no one but themselves. He would not be willing, even indirectly, to assist them if they took so narrow and selfish a view. It would show that they do not understand Constitutional processes.[36]

Hale spent hours attempting to persuade the Constitutionalists to acquiesce in the president's plans, but without success. "They do not swerve from their position that no triumph will be secure which is not secured by arms. They are unwilling to accept the idea of Provisional Government even though its personnel were believed by Washington to be unconnected and unsympathetic with Huerta or Huerta methods."[37] Following the example of Benito Juárez, the Constitutionalists intended to appoint an interim president who would enact the necessary social and political reforms, and only then would they hold an election.

The next day Carranza broke off the direct talks.[38] The intransigence of the Constitutionalists came as a a disappointment to Wilson. There were grounds for encouragement, however, for the Constitutionalists had pledged themselves to hold early elections: "Their answer to your question as to their intention to give the people an early opportunity to elect President and

---

[36] Bryan to Hale, November 16, 1913, 812.00/9759, original in Bryan's handwriting.
[37] Hale to Secretary of State, November 17, 1913, 812.00/9789 and Wilson Papers, Ser. 2.
[38] Hale to Secretary of State, November 18, 1913, 812.00/9814 and Wilson Papers, Ser. 2.

Congress at free and fair election is an earnest affirmative and
they further affirm that they will surrender the Government
into hands of those selected by [the] people at such election
even though persons elected were not preferred by them."[39]
     The Constitutionalists dealt so firmly with the president for
several reasons. They resented outside, particularly American,
interference. They knew that if they accepted any assistance
from the United States they would sacrifice their integrity in
the eyes of the Mexican people and find it difficult to draw
the line once the principle was breached against American domination of their affairs. Equally important, they were confident
of achieving a military victory against Huerta with or without
American assistance. Wilson shared their confidence and ignorance, for he too believed he could achieve his purposes with
or without the cooperation of the Constitutionalists; at least he
was determined to try.
     Hale, like Lind, had paternalistically embraced the cause of
the Constitutionalists. The president soon began to share their
view of the Constitutionalists. But he, like his special agents,
favored the revolutionary cause with the silent assumption that
its success would surely leave ample opportunity for American
supervision and guidance of Mexican affairs.

"QUID PRO QUO" WITH GREAT BRITAIN

While Hale was meeting with the Constitutionalists on the border, President Wilson met in Washington with Sir William Tyrrell, private secretary to the British foreign minister, Sir Edward
Grey. Tyrrell had left Britain on October 25 when the president
seemed about to launch an anti-British Mexican policy. By the
time Tyrrell arrived in Washington and conferred with the president on November 13, the crisis in Anglo-American relations
had passed. Some nice diplomatic work was done on both sides,[40]
but in the end both Wilson and Grey acted as they had intended to act. Wilson's meeting with Tyrrell offers a good example of "summit" diplomacy that was successful because neither
side had to sacrifice anything vitally important. The British

---

[39] Hale to Secretary of State, November 17, 1913, 812.00/9789 and Wilson
Papers, Ser. 2.
[40] See Charles Seymour, ed., *The Intimate Papers of Colonel House,*
2 vols. (Boston: Houghton Mifflin Company, 1926), Vol. 1, *Behind the
Political Curtain, 1912–1915*, pp. 197–202, and Lowry, "Wilson's Mexican
Policy," pp. 78–81.

wanted Wilson to promise to protect foreign lives and property in Mexico and to work for repeal of the exception from Panama Canal tolls of American coastal ships. Wilson had already demanded protection for foreigners of both Mexican factions. As for the Panama tolls, Wilson had decided that the British were right nearly two months before taking office.[41] Mexican oil and investments were important to Britain; they were certainly important to politically influential Britons. On the other hand, good relations with the United States were infinitely more important to Great Britain than all of Mexico's oil and foreign investments.[42] It was not a matter of whether the British would follow Wilson's lead in Mexico but of how hard a bargain they would drive for their support. W. H. Page, American ambassador in London, understood this and advised the president: "to put it to Sir Edward Grey as squarely and as hard as may be prudent that one way lies a friendly act to us and that the other way lies an unfriendly. . . . This Government will not risk our good will—if they are forced to choose & if it seems wise to you to put them to a square test. I don't think they will. Our good will is a club they are afraid of. . . ."[43] The British sought to protect themselves in Mexico against the operation of an American policy they considered imprudent and unwise.[44] When Wilson insisted on his Mexican policy, however, there should have been less doubt and alarm in Washington than apparently existed about what Britain would do. The British really had no choice but to go along with the United States, and on November 11, two days before Tyrrell's conference with Wilson, Page reported Britain's acquiescence:

In giving his answer . . . as to the British Government's attitude

[41] Link, *Wilson: The New Freedom*, p. 306.
[42] The importance of Mexican oil to Great Britain has been exaggerated. Throughout World War I, for example, the United States exported ten times more petroleum to the United Kingdom than did Mexico. Harold F. Williamson *et al.*, *The American Petroleum Industry*, 2 vols. (Evanston, Ill.: Northwestern University Press, 1963), Vol. 2, *The Age of energy, 1899–1959*, p. 267.
[43] Page to W.W., October 25, 1913, Wilson Papers, Ser. 2.
[44] For Grey's scepticism of the president's policy, see W. H. Page to Secretary of State, October 21, 1913, Wilson Papers, Ser. 2; W. H. Page to W.W., October 25, 1913, Wilson Papers, Ser. 2; W. H. Page to Secretary of State, October 28, 1913, 812.00/9442; W. H. Page to W.W., November 2, 1913, Wilson Papers, Ser. 2; and W. H. Page to W.W., November 8, 1913, Wilson Papers, Ser. 2.

toward Huerta, Sir Edward made the unhesitating declaration that
they would lend no support to Huerta as against the United States.
I repeat the dialogue:
Question:
What do you mean by support?
Answer:
Aid of any sort as against the United States.
Question:
How would that be made effective?
Answer:
If Huerta asked for our aid we shall tell him we cannot lend it.
Question:
Will you declare that to Huerta?
Answer:
I will instruct Carden that if Huerta asks for aid or shows by act that
he expects it he (Carden) is to inform him that he shall not have
it.[45]

Two days later O'Shaughnessy reported that the British ambassador in Mexico had called to express his willingness to help
accomplish the president's objectives in Mexico.[46] The British
may have thought they had driven a hard bargain, and it was
to Wilson's advantage to encourage them to be satisfied with
the result. He wrote to Tyrrell after their meeting:

I am more than willing to comply with Sir Edward Grey's suggestions as conveyed to me in your letter of yesterday, which has
just been placed before me. My only embarrassment is this, whenever I make any public announcement, it is met by some form
of defiance or some indication of irritation on the part of either
the Huerta people or the Constitutionalists in Mexico, and the
things which are in course of being handled are put back a little
and embarrassed.

I beg that you will assure Sir Edward Grey that the United States
Government intends not merely to force Huerta from power, but
also to exert every influence it can exert to secure Mexico a better
government under which all contracts and business and concession
will be safer than they have been.

It has taken every possible step, also, to see that property is protected. Again and again every consul of the United States in
Mexico has been instructed to warn the authorities, whether at
Mexico City or in the North, on this score, and as often it has
received assurances that the property of all foreigners would be

---

[45] W. H. Page to Secretary of State, November 11, 1913, 812.00/10438,
and Wilson Papers, Ser. 2.
[46] O'Shaughnessy to Secretary of State, November 13, 1913, Wilson
Papers, Ser. 2.

protected as far as military operations made it possible. . . .

We have also instructed our naval commanders on the coast to render every possible assistance not only to our own citizens but to the nationals of other countries.

I hope that Sir Edward Grey will feel free to convey the contents of this letter to those British and Canadian investors for whom he, naturally, feels a sympathetic anxiety.[47]

But the president continued on his own course and continued to despise "European" diplomacy. Replying to one of Page's eulogies of America's moral diplomacy, Wilson wrote: "It is fine the way you are pounding elementary doctrine into them. Perhaps after while they will believe we are really convinced democrats."[48]

---

[47] W.W. to Tyrrell, November 22, 1913, Wilson Papers, Ser. 3, 7: 234.
[48] W.W. to W. H. Page, December 6, 1913, Wilson Papers, Ser. 3, 8: 347.

Both Huerta and the Constitutionalists had rejected Wilson's efforts in mid-November to fashion a Mexican settlement. Though the president remained convinced that his policy was correct, as 1914 approached he began more and more to favor the Constitutionalists. The failures of his policy forced him to concentrate on the means by which he could at least secure Huerta's downfall. Bryan wrote to Page on November 19:
The President feels it his duty to force Huerta's retirement, peaceably if possible but forcibly if necessary. The steps which he has in mind are (A) withdrawing of diplomatic representatives (B) raising of embargo on arms shipped to Constitutionalists (C) blockading of ports (D) use of army. This is the order contemplated but subject to change to meet new conditions. He still hopes Huerta can be induced to retire or, if not, that Consitutionalists can compel his retirement without necessity for employment of force by us.[1]

With the British supporting his policy or at least not actively opposing and with the Mexicans adamant against American mediation, the president returned to "watchful waiting." He signaled the change in approach in a circular note sent on November 24. "The purpose of the United States," the note read, "is solely and singly to secure peace and order in Central America by seeing to it that the processes of self-government there are not interrupted or set aside."[2] The note stressed the American government's preference for peaceful means to accomplish the overthrow of Huerta and indicated that it was not necessary for the present to use force. The note also revealed that the president hoped that a "domino" effect would follow the restoration of peace and constitutional government in Mexico: "Each conspicuous instance in which usurpations of this kind are prevented will render their recurrence less likely, and in the end a state of affairs will be secured in Mexico and elsewhere upon this continent which will assure the peace of America and the untrammeled development of its economic and social relations with the rest of the world."[3]

[1] Bryan to W. H. Page, November 19, 1913, 812.00/9817a.
[2] Secretary of State to all embassies except Turkey and Mexico and to legations in Belgium, Netherlands, Norway, Sweden, Denmark, and Portugal, November 24, 1913, 812.00/11443b.
[3] *Ibid.*

The president's first annual message to Congress on December 2 provides an interesting example of the tension between his desire to allow the Mexicans to settle their own affairs—which promised at that moment an early victory for the Constitutionalists—and his desire to promote constitutional government in Mexico and the world. He told Congress:

There can be no certain prospect of peace in America until General Huerta has surrendered his usurped authority in Mexico; until it is understood on all hands, indeed, that such pretended governments will not be countenanced or dealt with by the Government of the United States. We are the friends of constitutional government in America; we are more than its friends, we are its champions; because in no other way can our neighbors, to whom we would wish in every way to make proof of our friendship, work out their own development in peace and liberty.[4]

Mexico had no government, Wilson said. Huerta had laid aside all pretense and was a dictator. The fundamental rights of the Mexican people were imperiled, but Huerta had failed in his efforts to set up a permanent government:

He has forfeited the respect and the vocal support even of those who were at one time willing to see him succeed. Little by little he has been completely isolated. By a little every day his power and prestige are crumbling and the collapse is not far away. We shall not, I believe, be obliged to alter our policy of watchful waiting. And then, when the end comes, we shall hope to see constitutional order restored in distressed Mexico by the concert and energy of such of her leaders as prefer the liberty of their people to their own ambitions.[5]

Wilson decided to abstain from active involvement in Mexico for a number of reasons. First, both sides had again rejected his overtures. To have kept pressing Huerta or the Constitutionalists to accept American mediation would have brought on military intervention, which Wilson desired to avoid. During his abstention, the Constitutionalists seemed likely to triumph, and the president now welcomed the prospect of a Constitutionalist victory.

The increased warmth in Wilson's attitude toward the Constitutionalists became apparent in mid-December. On December 12, Lind asked Bryan about the attitude of the Wilson administration toward the revolutionaries of the north. Bryan replied: "President's sympathy entirely with Constitutionalists but their attitude makes it impossible at present to give any open manifes-

[4] *Public Papers: The New Democracy* 1: 71.
[5] *Ibid.*, p. 72.

tation of that sympathy. We are expecting Constitutionalists to push their successes South to the capital but are hoping by urgent warnings to reduce cruelty and destruction of property to a minimum."[6]

On one other occasion at least the president told Lind of his sympathy for the Constitutionalists' cause. In mid-January a group of German businessmen approached Lind to complain that Huerta had suspended the payment of interest on outstanding obligations. Lind reported this and added that Admiral von Hintze, the German ambassador, was coming to lunch. Lind regarded von Hintze as "shrewd, prudent, and strong" and wanted to have something to tell him about American policy. Bryan obliged:

Answering your enquiry you may say that suspension of interest payments by Huerta was inevitable and would have come sooner but for the support which he was led to expect. Suspension of payments was a step toward his final elimination. Other steps will follow. We shall let him fall. He must go, there is no doubt about that but the President prefers that he shall be overcome by domestic forces rather than by us. Let your visitors know that the men of the north have our sympathy and will have our active support if necessary.[7]

The president carried his support for a Constitutionalist victory to the extent of allowing shipments of arms to "slip through" customs. On January 13, Hale wrote Wilson that there were 10,000 Krag-Jorgenson rifles and a quantity of ammunition at San Francisco which, with "a little lenience" shown by San Francisco port authorities, could be cleared for China and landed at Topolobampo for the Constitutionalists. "They could get carloads of ammunition through at Douglas, Arizona with a little indulgence."[8] Wilson forwarded Hale's memo to the secretary of the treasury, William Gibbs McAdoo, with a request that Hale's suggestions be carried out: "Here are memoranda from Hale upon which I based what I said to you last night. May I not suggest that in some confidential way the arrangements be made at San Francisco and Douglas, Arizona which Hale suggests?"[9]

The president conferred with Lind on January 2, 1914, on board the U.S.S. *Chester* off Gulfport, Mississippi. Lind came

[6] Bryan to Lind, December 13, 1913, 812.00/10152.
[7] Bryan to Lind, January 17, 1914, 812.00/10580a.
[8] Hale to W.W., January 13, 1914, Wilson Papers, Ser. 2.
[9] W.W. to McAdoo, January 15, 1914, Wilson Papers, Ser. 2.

away from the meeting with the impression that the president agreed with him about the Mexican situation. If Lind correctly interpreted the president's views, his reports should furnish helpful insights into Wilson's thoughts as the new year began. Lind's reports in December and January tended to stress two aspects of the Mexican situation. First, he emphasized the need to end the civil war in order to avoid American intervention and to cut short the suffering of the Mexican people.[10] Second, he described Huerta's ability to hang on to power: "If given time he will extricate himself from his present embarrassment sufficiently at least to prolong his rule indefinitely."[11] Each of these observations was given in turn as a reason why the United States should help the Constitutionalists. On January 14 he reported:

I am more and more convinced . . . that the time has arrived for active support of the revolutionists. Revolutionary success or armed intervention is the alternative we face. If the revolutionists succeed I believe we may escape intervention. We make no mistake in aiding them in breaking the old regime, it is an incubus that must be removed before there can be any constructive work. *Under our guidance* I think the revolutionists if successful will be able to enter upon the constructive work with a fair prospect of success.[12] (Italics added.)

Late in January he referred to his conference with the president and recommended lifting the arms embargo: "If it is still within your plan to raise the embargo then I am clear that now is the time to take such action. The psychological effect of the step at this juncture would be peculiarly effective. It would shut off all voluntary contributions of funds and Huerta would be remitted to such resources as he can compel by absolute force.

---

[10] See Lind to Secretary of State, December 13, 1913, Wilson Papers, Ser. 2; Lind to Secretary of State, December 14, 1913, 812.00/10185, and Wilson Papers, Ser. 2; Lind to Secretary of State, December 22, 1913, 812.00/10291; Lind to Secretary of State, January 14, 1914, Wilson Papers, Ser. 2.
[11] Lind to Secretary of State, January 26, 1914, 812.00/10688.
[12] Lind to Secretary of State, January 14, 1914, Wilson Papers, Ser. 2. Lind had adopted many of the attitudes and rationales of the Mexican revolutionaries. A month earlier after reporting an especially barbarous act by Huerta's forces, he declared: "With such provocation can we expect the rebels to act as saints? My only hope is that they will kill in an orderly way; the killing must be done if this country is ever to have decent Government and I am grateful for any instrumentality that saves us the horrible task." Lind to Secretary of State, December 13, 1913, Wilson Papers, Ser. 2.

It ought to encourage the revolutionist campaign and it would tend to demoralize the federal forces."[13]

ARMS FOR THE REVOLUTIONARIES

Late in January a stalemate appeared to have developed in Mexico. Neither Huerta nor the Constitutionalists seemed able to defeat the other. The president decided to lift the arms embargo. Before he could act, the British offered to request Huerta to resign on condition that the president present a definite plan for the pacification of Mexico after Huerta had been eliminated.[14] The president's reply showed how far his position had advanced toward the Constitutionalists and communicated the decision to raise the embargo:

The President warmly appreciates the suggestion of Sir Edward Grey but fears that the revolution in Mexico has reached such a stage that the sort of settlement proposed, namely the elimination of General Huerta and the substitution of others in authority at Mexico City, would now be without the desired effect of bringing peace and order. The men in the north, who are conducting a revolution with a program which goes to the very root of the causes which have made constitutional government in Mexico impossible, and who are not mere rebels would still have to be reckoned with. No plan which could be carried out at Mexico City at the present juncture could be made the basis of a satisfactory settlement with them. No plan which does not include them can now result in anything more than a change in the personnel of an irrepressible contest.[15]

The section of the president's note to the British that dealt with lifting the arms embargo was subsequently included in a communication on January 31 to all American embassies and legations. The section read:

No one outside Mexico can now accommodate her affairs. The withdrawal of all moral and material support from without is the indispensable first step to a solution from within. From many sources which it deems trustworthy the Government of the United States has received information which convinces it that there is

---

[13] Lind to Secretary of State, January 26, 1914, Wilson Papers, Ser. 2. On January 28 he asked if the president still intended to act along the lines discussed during their conference: "Are the plans the same as then indicated and are any positive steps contemplated in the near future?" Lind to Secretary of State, January 28, 1914, 812.00/10713.
[14] W. H. Page to Secretary of State, January 28, 1914, 812.00/10712.
[15] Bryan to W. H. Page, January 29, 1914, 812.00/10712, and Wilson Papers, Ser. 2, drafted on Wilson's personal typewriter.

a more hopeful prospect of peace, of the security of property and
of the early payment of foreign obligations if Mexico is left to
the forces now reckoning with one another there than there would
be if anything by way of a mere change of personnel were effected
at Mexico City. There are no influences that can be counted on
at Mexico City to do anything more than try to perpetuate and
strengthen the selfish oligarchical and military interests which it
is clear the rest of the country can be made to endure only by
constant warfare, and a pitiless harrying of the north. The President
is so fully convinced of this, after months of the most careful study
of the situation at close range, that he no longer feels justified
in maintaining an irregular position as regards the contending
parties in the matter of neutrality. He intends therefore, almost
immediately, to remove the inhibition on the exportation of arms
and ammunition from the United States. Settlement by civil war
carried to its bitter conclusion is a terrible thing, but it must come
now, whether we wish it or not, unless some outside power is to
undertake to sweep Mexico with its armed forces from end to
end, which would be the mere beginning of a still more difficult
problem.[16]

Apparently for domestic consumption the president put a gloss
of neutrality on his act, an act that was decidedly unneutral
and meant to be so. The note to the powers declared that the
United States was putting itself "in the same position as other
nations whose citizens have all along been at liberty to sell what
they pleased to Mexico. The Government of the United States
deems it essential to the settlement of her present difficulties
that Mexico should be treated as any other country would be
which was torn by civil war."[17] The president signed the proclamation on February 3, revoking the restraints on arms shipments
imposed by President Taft two years earlier.[18]

Wilson spoke confidently about the purposes of the Constitutionalists because in late January he had been communicating
through Assistant Secretary of State William Phillips with Luis
Cabrera, a special agent for the revolutionaries in Washington.
Cabrera gave Wilson a persuasive account of the causes of the
Mexican Revolution and the reforms the Constitutionalists intended to enact and discussed the lifting of the arms embargo.
Though Cabrera gave sweeping guarantees that the Constitutionalists would preserve the rights of property and oppose con-

---

[16] *Ibid.*
[17] Bryan to Lind, and to all embassies and legations, January 31, 1914,
812.00/10735a.
[18] *Foreign Relations, 1914,* pp. 447–448.

fiscation,[19] the president apparently tried to extract promises for the protection of foreigners that the Constitutionalists were unwilling to make. The president believed that the Constitutionalists would triumph very soon and was anxious to secure protection for Mexico City with its large diplomatic and foreign colonies. In reply Carranza ordered Cabrera to limit himself to a discussion of lifting the arms embargo, and though Cabrera reassured the president about Mexico City and tried to smooth over the situation, his orders represented yet another example of the sensitivity of the revolutionaries and their determination to prevent all foreign meddling in Mexican affairs.[20]

THE OCCUPATION OF VERACRUZ

During the two months that followed the president's proclamation the Constitutionalists failed to achieve victory. If anything Huerta seemed to have strengthened his position. Lind continued to plead for more assistance to the Constitutionalists.[21] Most important from the president's viewpoint were the reports that Huerta's tenure promised to become permanent. On February 3, for example, Lind wired: "Huerta is resourceful in devising ways for raising money. Financial pressure alone will never terminate his rule so long as there are resources left in Mexico."[22]

As days became weeks without an end to the civil war in Mexico, Lind's recommendations became more and more drastic. Late in February he described Mexico in extremely pessimistic terms—the suffering and losses of Mexicans and foreigners, the inactivity of the revolutionaries, the plotting among foreigners to bring about American intervention—and declared: "I believe, and I say this after serious reflection, that if the revolutionists fail to take active and efficient action by the middle of March it will be incumbent on the United States to put an end to Huerta's saturnalia of crime and oppression. I think our position before the world, our responsibility in the premises, and our interests demand that it be done."[23]

---

[19] Phillips to W.W., January 28, 1914, Wilson Papers, Ser. 2.
[20] Cabrera to Phillips, January 30, 1914, Wilson Papers, Ser. 2.
[21] Lind to Secretary of State, January 30, 1914, Wilson Papers, Ser. 2. On February 7 he urged that the United States supply the Constitutionalists with an American naval officer and the "means" to capture a Mexican gunboat. On February 21 he urged that the United States secure artillerists for the Constitutionalists.
[22] Lind to Secretary of State, February 3, 1914, 812.00/10778.
[23] Lind to Secretary of State, February 24, 1914, Wilson Papers, Ser. 2.

On March 8, Lind reported that Huerta had arranged a bond issue and that he had every intention of continuing to float similar loans for whatever speculators would pick them up. To Lind, the time had come to act: "In my judgment the situation is too serious to permit Huerta to continue any longer. He is not only ruining Mexico but he is involving us. If there is no decided change by the fifteenth I believe he should be eliminated within forty-eight hours after that date. It can be done and our preparations at this end are so complete that I believe it can be accomplished without the military loss of an American."[24] With the support of the senior American naval officer in Mexican waters, Admiral Frank F. Fletcher, Lind advocated sending a force of American marines to capture Mexico City and overthrow Huerta. "No formal orders are needed or wanted except the President's authority to proceed, and such directions as he may give for my guidance."[25]

To quiet opinion at home the president in a newspaper interview at the White House stated:

A country of the size and power of the United States can afford to wait just as long as it pleases. Nobody doubts its power, and nobody doubts that Mr. Huerta is eventually to retire. There need be no hesitation in forming the judgment that what we wish to accomplish in Mexico will be accomplished. But these people who are in haste to have things done, as they say, forget that they will have to do them themselves. They will have to contribute brothers and sons and sweethearts to do it if they want something done right away. If they are willing to wait, that may not be necessary.[26]

But events in Mexico made it difficult for the president to keep to his course of indirect assistance to the Constitutionalists. A week after his interview with the press he learned that Germany would consider drastic action if any of their nationals were harmed in Mexico.[27] On March 11 and 19, Lind reported

---

[24] Lind to Secretary of State, March 8, 1914, 812.00/11098.
[25] *Ibid.* See also Lind to Secretary of State, March 12, 1914, 812.00/11227: ". . . I wish to make it plain that the sole purpose I have in suggesting the Mexico City expedition is to place before you a positive method for eliminating Huerta in case the plan now followed proves too slow for the prevention of international complications."
[26] March 2, 1914, Wilson Papers, Ser. 2.
[27] American Ambassador James W. Gerard to Secretary of State, March 9, 1914, 812.00/11097, copied to the president on March 9. The German government apparently was emulating the great concern voiced in Britain

the arrival of large arms shipments from Europe and Japan. O'Shaughnessy had concluded that Huerta was going to win, reported Lind, as had the secretary of the British embassy.[28] On March 24, Lind reported that the foreign banking concerns had agreed to loan Huerta 54 million pesos in return for his abandonment of a scheme to deprive them of the privilege to issue currency. Three days later Lind described the situation as "utterly hopeless" unless the president either gave decisive assistance to the Constitutionalists or intervened militarily.[29] And on April 1, Lind recommended that the United States seize Tampico, the major oil center on the east coast, and protect it until order had been restored to Mexico. "This would be [a] peaceful measure and could be accomplished, Admiral Fletcher assures me, without the loss of a single life."[30]

The moment seemed to have arrived for Wilson to act. But he had foreseen this eventuality for months and had, since at least November, included in his plans the possibility of using force to accomplish the overthrow of Huerta. Thus it is hard to imagine the extent to which he felt "surprised" or "trapped" by developments in Mexico. He was reluctant to use force and deeply disturbed over the loss of American and Mexican lives when the time came. But he was more ready in early April to use force than at any other time in the preceding months. What was lacking was some pretext or incident that would justify intensified opposition to Heurta and, if necessary, military action. That incident occurred on Thursday, April 9, at Tampico when Huertista soldiers arrested the paymaster and whaleboat crew from the U.S.S. *Dolphin*. The American commander of the squadron at Tampico, Admiral Henry T. Mayo, regarded the proffered verbal apology as inadequate and gave the Mexican officer in charge twenty-four hours to come up with a formal disavowal of the act, an official apology, punishment of the officer

---

over the murder by Villa of a British subject, William J. Benton. For an account of the Benton affair and its embarrassment of the president, see Clarence C. Clendenen, *The United States and Pancho Villa: A Study in Unconventional Diplomacy* (Ithaca, N.Y.: Cornell University Press, 1961), pp. 65–70.

[28] Lind to Secretary of State, March 22, 1914, 812.00/11237; and Lind to Secretary of State, March 22, 1914, Wilson Papers, Ser. 2.

[29] Lind to Secretary of State, March 27, 1914, 812.00/11313; and Wilson Papers, Ser. 2.

[30] Lind to Secretary of State, April 1, 1914, Wilson Papers, Ser. 2.

responsible, and a salute to the American flag. Bryan wired the president, "I do not see that Mayo could have done otherwise."[31] Wilson approved Mayo's ultimatum,[32] seizing the incident as an opportunity further to undermine Huerta. During the next few days several additional incidents occurred involving American officials. An inexperienced Mexican telegraph clerk delayed a cipher message to Mexico City and, on April 11, a mail orderly from the U.S.S. *Minnesota* was arrested and taken to jail. Though these events were unrelated, the president made them, together with the incident at Tampico, into a conspiracy against Americans in Mexico.

The details of the events leading up to the occupation need not be recounted here.[33] It is necessary only to note that the president had found an issue on which to base new and more drastic opposition to Huerta. In a sense the president could not lose however Huerta responded. If the dictator backed down and apologized, he would have humiliated himself in Mexico and strengthened the appeal of the Constitutionalists. If, on the other hand, Huerta stood firm, the president would present his case to the American Congress and people and then help the Constitutionalists by occupying and denying to Huerta one or more of the vital eastern ports. Either way Huerta would be weakened and, as it appeared to the president, the way cleared for a settlement in Mexico on American terms. The Atlantic fleet sailed for Mexico on April 16, without, however, having received definite orders to land troops.[34] Meanwhile O'Shaughnessy worked desperately to persuade Huerta to fire the salute, even offering to sign a protocol promising that the United States would return the salute.[35] Wilson refused this ploy and instructed Bryan that "in no case should any concession of any kind in detail or otherwise be made."[36]

Wilson went before Congress on April 20 and asked approval for using the armed forces to enforce his demands on General

---

[31] Bryan to W.W., n.d. [April 9, 1913?], Wilson Papers, Ser. 2.
[32] Bryan to American Embassy, Mexico, April 11, 1914, *Foreign Relations, 1914,* p. 452.
[33] See Robert E. Quirk, *An Affair of Honor: Woodrow Wilson and the Occupation of Vera Cruz* (Lexington: University of Kentucky Press, 1962); Lowry, "Wilson's Mexican Policy," pp. 112–124; and Link, *Wilson: The New Freedom,* pp. 395–400.
[34] Josephus Daniels to W.W., April 16, 1914, Wilson Papers, Ser. 2.
[35] Bryan to W.W., April 19, 1914, Wilson Papers, Ser. 2.
[36] W.W. to Bryan, April 19, 1914, Wilson Papers, Ser. 2.

Huerta.[37] Objectively, the president failed to make a persuasive
case that "a series of incidents" had occurred which indicated
an intention on the part of the Huerta government to attack
the dignity and interests of the United States. A president's appeal to Congress to defend the national honor was hard to oppose, however, and the House passed the required resolution
by a vote of 337 to 37 on the same day.

The president had given a preview of his speech and resolution
to senior Democratic and Republican members of the Senate
Foreign Relations Committee at a meeting in the White House.
The conference had not been a success. Henry Cabot Lodge
in particular objected to intervening on the grounds of an
affront to national honor. Lodge wanted the United States to
intervene to protect American lives and property, while the
president feared that this would lead to the full-scale war he
desired to avoid.[38] Lodge carried his disagreement to the Senate
where, thanks to a coincidental Republican majority on the
Foreign Relations Committee, he led a temporarily successful
effort to block the president's resolution until amended to require
intervention on behalf of American lives and property.

While the Senate deliberated, the president acted. A German
steamer, the *Ypiranga,* carrying 200 machine guns and 15 million rounds of ammunition, was due to arrive in Veracruz. The
president and his cabinet decided to take Veracruz when the
exact hour of the *Ypiranga*'s arrival was known.[39] Admiral
Fletcher was ordered to prepare to land on short notice. Early
in the morning of April 21 the State Department learned that
the *Ypiranga* would arrive that very morning. At 11:30 A.M.,
April 21, American marines landed at Veracruz and seized the
customs houses and wharf to prevent the landing of the
Ypiranga's cargo. The next day, in order to overcome the opposition of those Mexicans who had chosen to fight the invaders,
American forces advanced and occupied the entire city.
Ironically, because the United States had not declared war on
Mexico it could only honor the protest of the German govern-
ment and allow the *Ypiranga* to land its entire cargo in late
May at Puerto México.

---

[37] U.S., Congress, House, Document No. 910, 63rd Cong., 2d sess., April 20,
1914.
[38] Henry Cabot Lodge, *The Senate and the League of Nations* (New
York: C. Scribner's Sons, 1925), pp. 13–14.
[39] Lowry, "Wilson's Mexican Policy," p. 118.

The occupation of Veracruz was unpopular and misunderstood by most Americans and Europeans, and by the Constitutionalists as well. The president withheld his true motives and objectives from Congress and the public, and thus he had only himself to blame for the revulsion of opinion that followed the landing. The real question lay in whether the landing was necessary to overthrow Huerta. The Constitutionalists had recaptured Torreón early in April, and this success could have put them firmly on the road to Mexico City. On the other hand, Huerta, with the money and arms that he had begun to receive, might have managed to suppress the revolutionaries, or at least to prolong his rule indefinitely. Even in retrospect, the trend of the civil war in the spring of 1914 seems unclear. The view from the White House must have been very depressing. Every report the president received from Lind and O'Shaughnessy indicated stalemate or, worse, progress for Huerta. Money and arms were flowing to the dictator in increasing amounts. Given the president's objectives and sources of information, only one course seemed open to him. When the American sailors were arrested, he seized on the incident and acted.

It is possible to find fault with the landing at Veracruz as a useless half measure that failed even to stop the *Ypiranga* from delivering its cargo of arms. But the president wanted the Constitutionalists to win in Mexico, and taking Veracruz away from Huerta seemed to the president to be vital to a Constitutionalist victory. The occupation of Veracruz undoubtedly weakened Huerta and contributed to the victory of the Constitutionalists. The debate should be joined then over the question whether the United States should assist revolutionary movements to overthrow corrupt, dictatorial regimes. If the answer is affirmative, then the president's decision to occupy Veracruz gains a different perspective. From this standpoint one is impressed by the effectiveness of the Veracruz occupation and by the extent to which President Wilson controlled the use of force and made military power serve his policy objectives. The president, for example, made every effort in word and deed to prevent the landing from growing into war. In his message to Congress he declared that "if armed conflict should unhappily come as a result of [Huerta's] attitude of personal resentment toward this Government, we should be fighting only General Huerta and those who adhere to him. . . ." Wilson made a similarly qualified declaration of intent to the Constitutionalists.[40] He immediately shelved all plans to march on Mexico City or to expand the area of occupation beyond the city of Veracruz.[41] In short, Wilson desired to use only that force necessary to overthrow Huerta and no more. This is not to deny his intention to supervise the outcome of the Mexican Revolution but to say that, as the passage of time proved, the president acted in one way toward Huerta and in an entirely different way toward the Mexican revolutionaries.

Whatever trust the president had accumulated among the more militant Constitutionalists became an early casualty of the landing at Veracruz. In reply to the president's communication Carranza stated that Huerta could never involve Mexico in a war with the United States. He asked with dignity and firmness that the president withdraw American troops from Mexico and take up its complaints against Huerta with the Constitutionalist government.[42]

The president's objectives in Mexico included more than the elimination of Huerta, and this emerged again in an exchange of notes with Carranza. Two days after the landing at Veracruz Carranza proposed that the Constitutionalists and the American government appoint high commissioners to treat "upon the state of affairs."[43] The president turned down the offer:

If General Carranza could make it clear by another public statement that he stands neutral in respect of every matter that has arisen or may arise between the United States and General Huerta, that he will not assist Huerta or resist the United States in its efforts to enforce specific redress for indignities which the officers of General Huerta have put upon the Government of the United

---

[40] Bryan to Special Agent George C. Carothers, April 21, 1914, Wilson Papers, Ser. 2.

[41] For the nature of these plans see Garrison to W.W., April 18, 1914, Wilson Papers, Ser. 2.

[42] Carothers to Secretary of State, April 22, 1914, Wilson Papers, Ser. 2. Foreshadowing the split between Villa and Carranza, Villa reacted warmly to the American occupation: "As far as he was concerned we could keep Vera Cruz and hold it so tight that not even water could get in to Huerta and . . . he could not feel any resentment." Carothers to Secretary of State, April 23, 1914, Wilson Papers, Ser. 2. Villa's friendly response undoubtedly accounts for the favor Villa enjoyed in Washington long after he had separated himself from the constructive aspects of the revolution. See W.W. to W. H. Page, June 4, 1914, Wilson Papers, Ser. 2.

[43] Marion Letcher to Secretary of State, April 23, 1914, 812.00/11651.

States, such a statement will undoubtedly hasten General Huerta's elimination, which all parties desire. General Huerta evidently is being encouraged to believe that the Constitutionalists will join him against the United States. So soon as he understands that they will not, he will cease to do the things which justify and oblige the United States to seek redress, and so relieve Mexico and the Mexican people of all danger of suffering directly or indirectly for General Huerta's offenses.[44]

The Constitutionalists had no intention of joining Huerta, but neither would they, in effect, authorize the American invasion of Mexico. If the United States pressed its invasion, the Constitutionalists would fight both Huerta and the Americans.[45] Wilson's demand of Carranza amounted to a request that the Constitutionalists recognize United States predominance in Mexican affairs. By his proposal for the appointment of high commissioners, Carranza had said to Wilson: If you truly oppose Huerta and support us let us join in a high commission and act in concert. But Wilson desired a much larger role in Mexican affairs than that of friend of revolutionaries. He desired control over Mexico's destiny, and it was this that the group around Carranza were determined to deny him.

To meet the criticisms leveled at the occupation of Veracruz and to guide and inform the American public and the world of his true intentions in Mexico, Wilson granted an interview on April 27 to Samuel G. Blythe of the *Saturday Evening Post*. The interview highlights Wilson's paradoxical position as it had evolved by 1914, on the one hand his understanding of and sympathy for the Mexican Revolution and, on the other, his determination to control it and shape it according to American experience. The conflict between these two motives appeared clearly in one of the president's eloquent formulations: "My ideal is an orderly and righteous government in Mexico; but my passion is for the submerged 85 percent of the people of that republic who are now struggling toward liberty."[46]

Profoundly moved by the struggle of the Mexican people to

[44] Bryan to Letcher, April 24, 1914, 812.00/11651 and Wilson Papers, Ser. 2. Drafted by Bryan and revised by the president.
[45] Louis Hostetter to Secretary of State, n.d. (received April 24, 1914), Wilson Papers, Ser. 2. Hostetter quoted General Obregón's refusal of an offer from the federal commander at Guaymas to join forces against the United States.
[46] Samuel G. Blythe, "A Conversation with President Wilson," *The Saturday Evening Post*, May 23, 1914, in *Public Papers: The New Democracy*, 1: 111.

change and improve their society, Wilson still felt it his "duty" to intervene and to attempt to shape the development of the revolution.[47] His comments in late April 1914 show unmistakably that he understood the forces at work in Mexico and approved. They deserve to be quoted at some length to establish clearly Wilson's attitude toward the revolution:

I challenge you to cite me an instance in all the history of the world where liberty was handed down from above. Liberty always is attained by the forces working below, underneath, by the great movement of the people. That, leavened by the sense of wrong and oppression and injustice, by the ferment of human rights to be attained, brings freedom.

It is a curious thing that every demand for the establishment of order in Mexico takes into consideration, not order for the benefit of the people of Mexico, the great mass of the population, but order for the benefit of the old-time regime, for the aristocrats, for the vested interests, for the men who are responsible for this very condition of disorder. No one asks for the order because order will help the masses of the people to get a portion of their rights and their land; but all demand it so that the great owners of property, the overlords, the hidalgos, the men who have exploited that rich country for their own selfish purposes, shall be able to continue their process undisturbed by the protests of the people from whom their wealth and power have been obtained.

The dangers that beset the Republic are held to be the individual and corporate troubles of these men, not the aggregated injustices that have been heaped on this vastly greater section of the population that is now struggling to recover by force what has always been theirs by right.

They want order—the old order; but I say to you that the old order is dead.[48]

---

[47] Wilson knew what a difficult task this would be. In November 1913, for example, James Bryce warned him that "from what I saw of that country when I travelled there and from what I have seen since of other Spanish-American countries, I should fear that nothing can be done from outside to better their conditions except at a dangerous cost to the benevolent neighbor." Bryce to W.W., November 7, 1913, Wilson Papers, Ser. 2. Wilson replied: "I am a bit daunted by your opinion of Latin-America and the possibilities of development within it, and I must admit that there is much to be said for your thesis. We are laboring through rather blind ways in Mexico but I have considerable hope that a solution may come which is not altogether inconsistent with the ideals of constitutional development." W.W. to Bryce, November 21, 1913, Wilson Papers, Ser. 2.

[48] *Public Papers: The New Democracy*, 1: 111–112. Some of Blythe's transitions have been omitted to make the quote conversational.

Wilson told Blythe he based American policy on three points: (1) no territorial aggrandizement for the United States; (2) no personal aggrandizement by American investors or capitalists; (3) settlement of the agrarian question by constitutional means. Wilson emphasized that the desire for land was the main cause of unrest in Mexico, and outlined the history of the rural enslavement of Mexico's peasantry.[49] Wilson concluded, "To some extent the situation in Mexico is similar to that in France at the time of the revolution. There are wide differences in many ways, but the basic situation has many resemblances."[50]

The president then turned to his concept of the part the United States should play in the Mexican Revolution:

It is my part, as I see it, to aid in composing those differences [between rich and poor in Mexico] so far as I may be able, that the new order, which will have its foundation on human liberty and human rights, shall prevail. . . .

I hold this to be a wonderful opportunity to prove to the world that the United States of America is not only human but humane; that we are actuated by no other motives than the betterment of the conditions of our unfortunate neighbor, and by the sincere desire to advance the cause of human liberty.

The situation [in Mexico] is intolerable, and requires the strong guiding hand of the great Nation on this continent that, by every appeal of right and justice, and the love for order, and the hope for peace and prosperity, must assist these warring people back into the paths of quiet and prosperity. We have an object lesson to give to the rest of the world; an object lesson that will prove to the skeptical outsider that this nation rises superior to considerations of added power and scorns an opportunity for territorial aggrandizement; an object lesson that will show to the people of this, our own hemisphere that we are sincerely and unselfishly the friends of all of them, and particularly the friends of the Mexican people, with no other idea than the idea and the ideal of helping them compose their differences, starting them on the road to continued peace and prosperity, and leaving them to work out their own destiny, *but watching them narrowly and insisting that they shall take help when help is needed.* . . .

They say the Mexicans are not fitted for self-government; and

---

[49] Wilson's understanding of the land question echoed the memoranda supplied to him by Constitutionalist agent Luis Cabrera, supra, pp. 128–129.

[50] *Public Papers: The New Democracy,* 1: 116–117.

to this I reply that, *when properly directed,* there is no people
not fitted for self-government.[51] (Italics added.)

The Constitutionalists now began to move steadily toward Mexico City, and once again the welfare of the diplomats and foreigners became a prime concern in Washington. On May 7,
Bryan sent instructions to George C. Carothers, special American representative with the Constitutionalists, to impress upon
Villa and Carranza the need to exercise great care in capturing
Mexico City.[52] The next day Wilson discussed with his cabinet
the need to be prepared to march on Mexico City. The secretary
of war, Lindley Garrison, informed Wilson that 25,000 army
troops were available for such an expedition.[53] And on May
12 the secretary of the navy, Josephus Daniels, informed the
president that a total of 17,000 men from all services were in
or near Veracruz and some 4,000 sailors and marines were
available for immediate service on the west coast of Mexico.
Daniels reassured the president that this force was adequate to
handle any emergency and that no additional troop movements
were necessary.[54] The president reassured the British that the
United States was prepared to act should the necessity arise,
but he regarded further military intervention as unnecessary and
refused to accept formal responsibility for the welfare of foreigners in Mexico.[55]

Constitutionalist troops under General Pablo González occupied
Tampico on May 14 and Huerta's downfall became certain.
The Constitutionalists advanced steadily toward Mexico City,
despite a deepening split between Villa and Carranza.[56] The
American diplomats with the Constitutionalists worked anxiously
to preserve unity among the revolutionaries and, following
Huerta's resignation on July 15, to facilitate the negotiations
for the surrender of the federal forces. Carranza ignored Ameri-

---

[51] *Ibid.,* pp. 112, 118, 119. See also Wilson's address at Independence
Hall, Philadelphia, July 4, 1914, *Public Papers: The New Democracy,*
1: 144.
[52] Bryan to Carothers, May 7, 1914, Wilson Papers, Ser. 2.
[53] Lindley Garrison to W.W., May 8, 1914, Wilson Papers, Ser. 2.
[54] Daniels to W.W., May 12, 1914, Wilson Papers, Ser. 2.
[55] Bryan to American Embassy, London, May 9, 1914, Wilson Papers,
Ser. 2. Bryan to Brazilian Minister, Mexico City (in charge of American
interests), May 16, 1914, Wilson Papers, Ser. 2. W.W. to Bryan, May
22, 1914, Wilson Papers, Ser. 3, 8: 359.
[56] Letcher to Secretary of State, June 4, 1914, Wilson Papers, Ser. 2.

can pressure and refused to accept anything but unconditional surrender, which was signed on August 13. One week later he rode in triumph into Mexico City.

A.B.C. MEDIATION

As a result of the landing at Veracruz, O'Shaughnessy was handed his passports, and what diplomatic relations existed between the United States and Mexico were terminated. On April 25 the representatives in Washington of Brazil, Argentina, and Chile (A.B.C.) offered their good offices for the "peaceful and friendly settlement of the conflicts" between the United States and Mexico. Wilson accepted the same day, and three days later Huerta accepted. On April 29, Carranza accepted mediation in principle, but he rejected the request of the mediators for a cease-fire between Mexican factions. The Constitutionalists insisted that Huerta had caused the conflict between the United States and Mexico which was "independent of our struggle for liberty and right."[57] The civil war would continue; there would be no armistice.

The mediators took a far more comprehensive view of their intervention and withdrew their invitation to Carranza to participate. They informed him: "All difficulties which have contributed to bring about the present situation of Mexico, directly or indirectly affect the solution of the conflict pending between Mexico and the United States, and consequently we understand that they must be made the subject-matter of consideration in the settlement of negotiations for the full success of which we have deemed the suspension of hostilities to be indispensable."[58]

President Wilson took yet a third position toward the mediation effort. He desired to use it to further his plans to eliminate Huerta and to control the development of the Mexican Revolution, and he informed the mediators:

No settlement could have any prospect of permanence or of proving acceptable to public opinion in the United States or to the practical judgment of the Government of the United States which did not include these features:

First, the entire elimination of General Huerta;

Second, the immediate setting up in Mexico of a single provisional

[57] Carranza to the mediators, April 29, 1914, *Foreign Relations, 1914,* p. 518.
[58] Mediators to Carranza, May 3, 1914, *Foreign Relations, 1914,* pp. 518–519.

government acceptable to all parties and pledged to proceed at
once to the establishment of a permanent government constituted
in strict accordance with the Constitution of Mexico and committed
to the prosecution of such reforms as will reasonably assure the
ultimate removal of the present causes of discontent.

This government ventures to suggest that the essence of any hopeful settlement would of necessity be a concert of the contending
elements of the republic and that such a concert can be obtained
only upon the basis of such reforms as will satisfy the just claims
of the people of Mexico to life, liberty and independent self-
support.[59]

The United States entered the mediation not to settle its quarrel
with any Mexican faction but, in Robert Lansing's words, "to
restore peace between Mexican factions and to obtain guarantees
from them which will insure the reestablishment of constitutional
government in Mexico. The real quarrel of the United States
is with the intolerable conditions which exist and not with the
factions except so far as they are the causes of these conditions.
In reality, therefore, the mediation is between the factions and
not between the United States and either one of the factions."[60]

As if Lansing's description were not sufficiently unreal, to this
mediation between Mexican factions the mediators invited and
then disinvited one of the major factions and that faction, even
if reinvited, would not have attended. Turning the unreality
into surreality, or slapstick, Niagara Falls was chosen as the site
for negotiations. The president selected J. R. Lamar and
F. W. Lehman as American commissioners to the mediation
conference.

The Constitutionalists sought to maintain friendly relations with
the United States, but they refused to change their attitude toward the mediation.[61] When the proceedings opened at Niagara

---

[59] "Confidential Memorandum" to the mediators, n.d. [c. April 30, 1914],
Wilson Papers, Ser. 2.
[60] Robert Lansing, "Memorandum on Place of Conferences of Mediators
and Representatives to attend on behalf of the United States," May
1, 1914, Wilson Papers, Ser. 2. Lansing understandably observed that
"the situation of the United States in the present attempted mediation
is, therefore, so novel as to take the case out of any rule which may
be adduced from precedents." Lansing also had acquired a good understanding of the causes of the Mexican Revolution. See Robert Lansing,
"The Mexican Situation," Private Memorandum, May 4, 1914,
812.00/13976.
[61] R. Zubaran Capmany (Constitutionalist agent at Washington), Memorandum, May 4, 1914, 812.00/23426.

Falls on May 20 only the mediators and representatives of Huerta and the United States were present. The conference was dominated by events in Mexico and by the absent Constitutionalists. The extent of their control of the conference and of Mexican-American relations was reflected in the changing nature of American proposals for a settlement.

At the opening session the mediators proposed that Huerta appoint as foreign minister a man acceptable to the Constitutionalists, to the Mexican neutrals, and to the United States. Huerta would then resign and the new provisional president would make provision for elections and the necessary reforms. The mediators suggested Pedro Lascuráin, foreign minister under Madero, as a possible candidate.[62] To avoid incorporating Huerta in any way into the new Mexican government, President Wilson suggested a provisional triumvirate composed of someone like Lascuráin, one Constitutionalist, and one chosen by these two.[63] Meanwhile the president tried but failed to persuade the mediators to reinvite the Constitutionalists.[64]

On May 23, Huerta's representatives announced the general's willingness to retire, provided his resignation would bring about peace and a compromise settlement. To this end, the mediators urged the United States to enforce an armistice between the factions in Mexico which meant, of course, compelling the Constitutionalists to cease hostilities. This evoked a lengthy statement from the president. He informed the American commissioners:

It is clear to us that the representatives from Mexico are keenly aware that General Huerta no longer has the force or standing to insist on anything; and they of course cannot expect us to supply him with the force or influence he lacks. We get the impression that the Mexican representatives are chiefly anxious that we should by some means intervene to prevent the complete success of the revolution now in progress. We on our part cannot afford in right or conscience to do that and can only act in the spirit and for the purposes expressed in the propositions I shall presently state . . .

---

[62] Special Commissioners to Secretary of State, May 20, 1914, Wilson Papers, Ser. 2, and 812.00/23435. All communications from the commissioners were received and deciphered at the White House, showing Wilson's close interest and supervision.

[63] Secretary of State to Special Commissioners, May 21, 1914, Wilson Papers, Ser. 2.

[64] Secretary of State to Special Commissioners, May 21, 1914, Wilson Papers, Ser. 4, casefile 471, and 812.00/23452C, drafted on Wilson's personal typewriter; and Special Commissioners to Secretary of State, May 22, 1914, Wilson Papers, Ser. 2.

Please present to the mediators as you have occasion and in the
way you think best the following considerations and conclusions
by which we feel we must be guided:
First, we can deal only with the facts in Mexico as they now
stand. Concerning them it is too late to exercise any choice or
effect any change.
Second, we must deal with those facts, if possible, and get our
solution out of them without the use of the armed force of the
United States.
Third, the elimination of Huerta by one process or another is
now clearly inevitable, the only question remaining being the
method, the occasion and the circumstances of his elimination.
Fourth, the object of our conferences, now is to find a method
by which the inevitable can be accomplished without further bloodshed. By inevitable we mean not only the elimination of Huerta but
the completion of the revolution by the transfer of political power
from Huerta to those who represent the interests and aspirations
of the people whose forces are now in the ascendancy.
Fifth, to attempt to put a stop to the present processes of revolution before we have a peaceful method to suggest would be impracticable and futile because based upon no definite program. It
would, moreover, in all probability, very soon force active intervention upon us and delay and confuse all we have hoped for.
Sixth, we can at the present stage of things do little more than
set the stage for a settlement and demand guarantees that a settlement will be effected. Before we can insist on the acceptance of
anything by the Constitutionalists, even the cessation of arms, we
must know what it is that we are to insist that they accept. The
whole settlement obviously depends, if there is to be no force used
by the United States, on the acceptance of the program by the
Carranzistas. The use of force by the United States against them
could be justified only by their rejection of terms of such a character
that refusal on their part to accept them would be clearly indefensi-
ble, terms which meant the full attainment of the just objects
of revolution without further bloodshed.
Seventh, we are inclined to believe that it would be unwise to
attempt to work out the details of the reforms involved anywhere but at Mexico City and through the proposed provisional
government.
We suggest that a prompt agreement upon a clear program which
the Constitutionalists can accept is the best and only way to stop
the process of arms.[65]

---

[65] Secretary of State to Special Commissioners, May 24, 1914, Wilson
Papers, Ser. 2, and 812.00/23452d, drafted on Wilson's personal
typewriter.

Out of a desire to avoid offending the mediators, Commissioners Lamar and Lehman did not read any part of the president's telegram to them, but said only that the president desired that a specific plan be formulated, one so just that the Constitutionalists would accept its terms.[66] Their decision to spare the mediators introduced yet another falsity into the conference, for in their ignorance of Wilson's preferences the mediators continued to propose plans unacceptable to the United States.

President Wilson remained committed to the creation of a provisional Mexican government, but the victories of the Constitutionalists were leaving the conferees behind. On May 26 the president indicated that a single provisional president might be preferable to a triumvirate or other collective interim regime. In that case the provisional president would have to be a Constitutionalist:

What influences our thought and our preferences in this matter is entirely the state of the facts and the method of dealing with them in such a way as to carry out a program of peace and accommodation. Events have moved very fast and very far since mediation was agreed upon and we are endeavoring to interpret those events[;] and to adjust each step to a program which necessitated intervention and coercion would involve the interests, the welfare, and the pride of the Mexican people much more deeply than an accommodation with the Constitutionalists carried out upon equitable terms. Even the occupation of Veracruz seemed for a little while to bring the danger of war with a whole people.[67]

The president's instructions virtually eliminated further American military intervention and sought to push the conferees to formulate a settlement that took account of the growing predominance of the Constitutionalists in Mexico, a settlement that the United States could then reasonably pressure the Constitutionalists to accept. But the mediators continued to present ideas that would have denied the Constitutionalists the victory they were winning on the battlefield. On May 26 they suggested that Huerta appoint a foreign minister and then resign. The

[66] Special Commissioners to Secretary of State, May 25, 1914, Wilson Papers, Ser. 2, and 812.00/23444.
[67] Secretary of State to Special Commissioners, May 26, 1914, Wilson Papers, Ser. 2, accompanied by Wilson's notes in hand and on his personal typewriter indicating he composed this dispatch, and 812.00/23444. The United States had been sufficiently uncertain how the Constitutionalists would react to the seizure of Veracruz to suspend arms shipments into Constitutionalist areas.

foreign minister would appoint a cabinet of four—one Huertista, one Constitutionalist, and two neutrals—to constitute a board of provisional government. The board would call elections and "devote special attention" to the agrarian question and other reforms. The provisional government would be recognized immediately by the United States and the A.B.C. powers. American forces would begin withdrawal within fifteen days and complete evacuation within thirty days, unless requested to remain. The mediators took the position that to adopt a plan envisioning the transfer of power to a Constitutionalist was inconsistent with the spirit of the original proposal for mediation.[68]

The arrival of this proposal disappointed the president. In reply he stated that "the most serious and pressing question with regard to any plan, the question by which it must, whatever our preference, be tested is this, who would put it into operation if the victorious party refused to accept it?"[69] To establish a provisional government by force, especially the force of the United States, would only invite other revolutions:

Certain things are clearly inevitable in Mexico as things now stand, whether we act or not. One of these is the elimination of Huerta. Another is resistance, and successful resistance, to any arrangement which can be made to seem to be a continuation of the Huerta regime.

It would in our judgment be futile to set up a provisional authority which would be neutral. It must, to be successful, be actually, avowedly, and sincerely in favor of the necessary agrarian and political reforms, and it must be pledged to their immediate formulation, not merely "requested to devote special attention" to them.

And it will be impossible for the United States to withdraw her hand until this government is finally and fully satisfied that the program contemplated will be carried out in all respects. . . .

The case lies in our mind thus: the success of the Constitutionalists is now inevitable. The only question we can now answer without armed intervention on the part of the United States is this, Can the result be moderated, how can it be brought about without further bloodshed, what provisional arrangement can be made which will temper the whole process and lead to elections in a way that will be hopeful of peace and permanent accommodation? If we do not successfully answer these questions, then the settlement must come by arms, either ours or those of the Constitutionalists.

[68] Special Commissioners to Secretary of State, May 26, 1914, Wilson Papers, Ser. 2, and 812.00/23445.
[69] Secretary of State to Special Commissioners, May 27, 1914, Wilson Papers, Ser. 2, and 812.00/23445.

Every plan suggested must, therefore, of necessity be subjected to the test of these questions. We will not make war on the Mexican people to force upon them a plan of our own based upon a futile effort to give a defeated party equality with a victorious party.[70]

The president saw that the Constitutionalists were winning on the battlefield.[71] He understood and sympathized with the Mexican Revolution, but he declined to identify American policy with the Constitutionalists, to recognize their belligerency, or to make available the military supplies they needed to gain their victory. He clung to the idea of establishing a provisional government even to the point of insisting on the installation of a Constitutionalist as provisional president. Until and after the mediatory commission adjourned in failure and irrelevance, he persistently cast the problem in the following terms:

The problem is how peace is to be secured for Mexico, and that means simply this, How is the triumph of the Constitutionalist Party, which is now clearly triumphant, to be accepted and established without further bloodshed; or, to put it differently, How are representatives of that party to be placed in control of the government under conditions which can be approved and assented to and earnestly pressed for acceptance [by the Constitutionalists] by the government of the United States. We are not seeking a plan which we would be willing to enforce by arms but a plan which will promptly bring peace and a government which we can recognize and deal with. Recognition or nonrecognition is the only means of compulsion we have in mind. A plan which would require the backing of force would if acted on do Mexico more harm than good and would postpone peace indefinitely, not secure it.[72]

The president feared that the pursuit of full military victory by the Constitutionalists might not end but prolong the civil war indefinitely.[73] A memo of a conversation between an American and Huertista representative at Niagara Falls suggested that

[70] Secretary of State to Special Commissioners, May 27, 1914, Wilson Papers, Ser. 2, drafted on Wilson's personal typewriter and carrying revisions in his handwriting; and 812.00/23445.
[71] "It ought to be conclusive even with the Mexican representatives that unless the United States is to intervene with arms and practically conquer Mexico, which nobody desires, the only alternative to such a plan as we propose is the armed entrance of Carranza into Mexico City and the assumption of the provisional presidency by Carranza himself." Secretary of State to Special Commissioners, Wilson Papers, Ser. 2, drafted on Wilson's personal typewriter; and 812.00/23445a.
[72] Ibid.
[73] H. P. Dodge (Secretary to the Commissioners) to Secretary of State, June 16, 1914, 812.00/12288.

three motives lay behind the president's policy, in addition to
his desire to promote the spread of constitutional government.
They were (1) to restore peace in Mexico "in order to avoid
the complications which continued disorder might create with
the possibility of even leading up to a conflict with Mexico";
(2) to protect the interests of Americans and other foreigners
in Mexico; and (3) to prevent any other nation interfering in
political matters pertaining to America.[74]
   Regardless of the motives behind the president's policy, the
Constitutionalists firmly but without serious hostility denied
Wilson the control he desired over Mexico's destiny. On May
29, Constitutionalist Agent Rafael Zubaran Capmany delivered
a letter from Carranza to the American commissioners. Carranza
objected to the continuation of the conference without Constitutionalist representatives, but he omitted any reference to accepting an armistice, the chief conditions imposed by the A.B.C.
mediators. At the same time an article inspired by the Constitutionalists appeared in *The New York Times* indicating that the
Constitutionalists would accept mediation only of the Tampico
and other incidents, the occupation of Veracruz, and the elimination of Huerta. They refused to agree to mediate anything touching Mexico's internal affairs, neither the creation of a provisional
government, the settlement of the land question, nor the recognition through mediation of any of the acts of Huerta's government.[75] Wilson and Bryan saw a possible change for the better
in Carranza's mention of participation in the conference, and
they renewed their pressure on the mediators to admit the Constitutionalists to the talks.[76] The mediators yielded to the extent
of inquiring of Carranza whether his letter signified that he
had accepted the terms of mediation. Carranza replied ignoring
the mediators' terms but appointing three commissioners: Iglesias
Calderón, Luis Cabrera, and José Vasconcelos.[77] The mediators
answered immediately saying that in their view Carranza had
not accepted the terms of the mediation.
   Carranza's initiative had brought accredited Constitutionalist

---

[74] Memorandum of a conversation between Frederick W. Lehmann and
Don Luis Elguero, June 9, 1914, *Foreign Relations, 1914*, pp. 530–532.
[75] Special Commissioners to the Secretary of State, May 31, 1914,
812.00/12130.
[76] Bryan to Special Commissioners, May 31, 1914, 812.00/23451.
[77] Correspondence in Secretary Dodge to Secretary of State, June 15,
1914, 812.00/12270.

representatives near the conference, and on June 16 they met in Buffalo with the American commissioners. The results of their four-hour conference doomed to failure another phase of the president's policy. The Constitutionalists argued that Mexico was entitled to "fight out their own fight in their own way" just as the United States had been during the American civil war. They argued that permanent peace would follow only a Constitutionalist victory. A compromise or a solution imposed from the outside could not be enforced unless the United States was prepared to intervene militarily to enforce it. The Americans presented the president's plan: no recognition of Huerta in any way, the appointment of a Constitutionalist provisional government, and the implementation of reforms by the provisional president. But the Constitutionalists adamantly opposed any sort of outside interference:

They declined to discuss names or to propose names for Provisional President, saying that no one would be satisfactory that was appointed by the mediators, even if it was Carranza himself, because anything that came from the mediators would not be accepted by their party or by the Mexican people. Their manner was courteous [,] expressing regret that they should decline what was [done] in mistaken kindness; but their statement was so explicit, their objection so prositive, their spirit so defiant that we asked them if we were to understand if they were expressing their own views or the views of Carranza. To this they emphatically replied that they were absolutely instructed by Carranza to deliver this as his final answer. We inquired again if they meant this to be accepted as final and to be reported to Washington; they said they did and that under no consideration would Carranza accept the result of mediation no matter how far it might be in his favor.[78]

The American commissioners advised the president that since Consitutionalist participation in any plan was now out of the question the United States should present its own plan to the conference with the reservation that all plans must be referred to the Constitutionalists and that the United States would accept only that plan acceptable to the Constitutionalists. Accordingly, on June 17 the mediators and the United States presented for discussion their proposed settlements.[79] Since the Constitutionalists refused to have anything to do with any proposals touching Mexico's internal affairs, the mediators subsequently presented

[78] Special Commissioners to Secretary of State, June 16, 1914, Wilson Papers, Ser. 2, and 812.00/23477.
[79] *Foreign Relations, 1914,* pp. 539–541.

yet another plan calling on the factions to meet to discuss internal
affairs and the formation of a provisional government. This for-
lorn proposal was incorporated into a protocol and signed by
the conferees on June 24 with the proviso that Brazil, Argentina,
Chile, and the United States would recognize a provisional government formed in this way.[80]

CONSTITUTIONALIST VICTORY AND AMERICAN DISENGAGEMENT
The United States urged Carranza to send a representative to
treat with Huerta. Carranza replied that to accept the plan
formulated at Niagara Falls "would be tantamount to com-
pounding felony."[81] Repeated overtures to Carranza produced
expressions of appreciation for the attitude of the United States,
but the Constitutionalists would treat with Huerta only on the
basis of "unconditional surrender."[82] At this time Carranza indicated that there would be no provisional government but a
period of "revolutionary military rule." During this period the
revolutionary government would inaugurate immediate reforms
and restore order to the country.[83]

Disturbed by the prospect of a revolutionary dictatorship and
by the uncertainties connected with the imminent occupation
of Mexico City, Wilson warned the Constitutionalists to protect
foreign lives and property, to grant a generous amnesty to military and political opponents, and to eschew punitive measures
against the Roman Catholic church.[84] Carranza replied that
those who were entitled to protection would not be molested.
"Property rights will be respected and the property and rights
of foreigners will be accorded the most ample guarantees."[85]
Wilson reemphasized this point several days later, warning:
Excesses of any kind, even towards their own people, and especially
extreme measures against political opponents or representatives of
the Church, if such things should occur in connection with their

---

[80] For copies of the conference protocols see Secretary Dodge to Secretary
of State, July 3, 1914, 812.00/12421.
[81] Leon J. Canova to Secretary of State, July 6, 1914, 812.00/12429,
and Wilson Papers, Ser. 2.
[82] Silliman to Secretary of State, July 10, 1914, 812.00/12469, and Wilson
Papers, Ser. 2.
[83] *Ibid.*
[84] Bryan to John R. Silliman, July 23, 1914, *Foreign Relations, 1914,*
pp. 568–569; original draft in Wilson's shorthand, n.d. [July 23, 1914?],
Wilson Papers, Ser. 2.
[85] Silliman to Bryan, July 27, 1914, *Foreign Relations, 1914,* p. 573.

assumption of power at Mexico City, might make it morally impossible for the United States to recognize a new government. If we did not recognize it could obtain no loans and must speedily break down. The existence of war in Europe would clearly make it impossible to obtain assistance anywhere on the other side of the water even if such excesses as we have alluded to did not themselves make it impossible.[86]

The changeover at Mexico City took place peacefully, and on August 22, Carranza assumed executive authority in accord with the Plan of Guadaloupe. As unity among the revolutionaries broke down altogether,[87] Wilson hastened to withdraw American forces from Veracruz. On November 10 the convention of Aguascalientes declared Carranza in rebellion and appointed Villa commander in chief of the Conventionist forces. Carranza withdrew his forces to the state of Veracruz and retained the Constitutionalist title for the movement. On November 13 the United States informed the Mexican factions and the powers that the United States would evacuate Veracruz in ten days. Wilson had delayed evacuation until the Constitutionalists agreed not to persecute those in Veracruz who had cooperated with the American forces during the occupation.[88] The Constitutionalists, who were in de facto control of the area, gained control of Veracruz after the departure of the American troops.

Villa quickly forced the Carranzistas on the defensive, and as winter approached the Conventionists appeared to be close to victory. Early in December, Secretary Bryan wrote to the president, "The situation seems to be clearing up in Mexico. Villa and Zapata are working in harmony and Gutiérrez seems to be about to assume control over most of the country. The occupation of Carranza is not likely to last long."[89] Bryan proposed sending a stern warning to Gutiérrez similar to the one sent the previous July to Carranza and Villa. The president

---

[86] Bryan to Silliman, July 31, 1914, *Foreign Relations, 1914*, p. 577; original draft in Wilson's shorthand and on his typewriter, July 29, 1914, Wilson Papers, Ser. 2.

[87] Silliman to Secretary of State, September 23, 1914, *Foreign Relations, 1914*, p. 605.

[88] Bryan to Brazilian Ambassador (for Carranza), to Carothers (for Villa), and to Canova (for Gutiérrez, Conventionist provisional president), November 13, 1914, *Foreign Relations, 1914*, pp. 621–622. Copies also went to the American missions in London, Rome, Paris, Berlin, and Madrid and to the ambassadors of these countries in Washington.

[89] Bryan to W.W., December 2, 1914, Wilson Papers, Ser. 2.

approved the idea but suggested that the representations be made unofficially. "I am heartily glad," the president replied, "to see things clearing up, as they seem to be in Mexico. I pray most earnestly it may be indeed the beginning of the end."[90] The two men had mistakenly applauded at the pause between movements, not at the climax of the revolutionary symphony. As the new year began, the Constitutionalists fought back hard, and Mexico entered its bloodiest period of civil war. The overthrow of the Huerta government and the withdrawal of United States troops from Veracruz, however, ended the first phase of the Wilson administration's involvement in the Mexican Revolution. The president did not again significantly engage the United States in Mexican affairs until June 1915.

---

[90] Wilson to Bryan, December 3, 1914, Wilson Papers, Ser. 2.

Before the victorious Constitutionalists could enter Mexico City, the European powers had plunged the world into war. From its beginning the world war exerted a great influence on the response of the United States to the Mexican Revolution. That influence is difficult to pin down in the diplomatic documents and the papers of American statesmen, but the effects of the war on the President's Mexican policy were immediate and far-reaching. Two points deserve mention in this regard. They are, first, the coincidence of crises in European-American and particularly German-American relations with efforts of the United States to promote a settlement in Mexico and, second, the preoccupation across the United States with the war in Europe and not with the Mexican Revolution.

Two examples stand out in regard to the coincidence of crises in German-American relations with American efforts to settle the Mexican civil war. First, the president's speech of June 2, 1915, calling on the Mexican factions to unite and threatening American action if they refused, came in the midst of the *Lusitania* crisis and a national war scare. And second, the American chief of staff, General Hugh L. Scott, was sent to the border on April 22, 1916, to decide what should be done with Pershing's forces inside Mexico. His trip began less than four days after the president's note of April 18, 1916, threatening to sever diplomatic relations with Germany unless she changed her methods of submarine warfare against passenger- and freight-carrying ships. Scott's unsuccessful discussions with General Obregón about border protection and withdrawal of American forces from Mexico began some ten days after the president's note.

Sporadically, certain events born of the Mexican Revolution sparked controversy and Congressional inquiries and on one occasion raised the threat of war. The murder of seventeen Americans at Santa Isabel, the Villista raids into the United States, and the clashes between Constitutionalist and American forces at Parral and Carrizal were such events. Before the spectacle of the nightmarish slaughter in Europe, however, the temper of the American people remained pacific. The president exercised his relative freedom of action, and the crises in Mexican-American relations found relief at the negotiating table. Through it all the country stood hypnotized by the Great War. Describing

the year 1915, Arthur S. Link observed: "The one central
reality of American life between the sinking of the *Lusitania*
and the final settlement of the *Arabic* controversy in October
1915 was the ever-present possibility of war with Germany.
Every decision that the president and his colleagues made during
this period was affected if not controlled by this fact."[1] During
the final two years of the first Wilson administration, the nation
responded to the Mexican Revolution in an atmosphere of preoccupation, uncertainty, and dread fostered by World War I.

TWO UNSUCCESSFUL INITIATIVES
The divisions that had appeared among the Mexican revolutionaries in the wake of the victory over Huerta worsened in
the first days of 1915. New splits occurred among those who
had broken with Carranza and Obregón. On January 16, the
Convention deposed the provisional president, Eulalio Gutiérrez,
and itself assumed the government. Gutiérrez took the field with
a small force and issued an impotent proclamation stripping
Villa and Zapata of their commands. On January 28, General
Obregón's forces occupied Mexico City, though the Zapatistas
continued to occupy the outlying suburbs and control the city's
water supply. Carranza then decreed Mexico's capital would be
Veracruz but could not force the foreign diplomats to move there.
   The Constitutionalists regarded Mexico City as a "white ele-
phant." They could not and did not intend to take and hold
the city by a static defense but sought instead to use their forces
against Villa's main force. Accordingly, they made little provision for the welfare of the citizens, foreign and Mexican, within
the city. They extorted money from the local merchants by
threatening to allow the hungry masses to sack the city. This
was good politics—playing on economic grievances and animosity
toward foreigners—as well as profitable. Obregón, understandably, imprisoned merchants who refused to pay taxes or
to accept Constitutionalist fiat currency. The Brazilian ambassador, Cardoso de Oliveira, in charge of American interests,
reported on March 9 that "starvation [is] worse than ever on
account of impossibility to obtain any means of transportation
of food."[2] Bryan protested to Carranza and Villa about the

---

[1] Arthur S. Link, *Wilson: The Struggle for Neutrality, 1914–1915* (Princeton, N.J.: Princeton University Press, 1960), p. 588.
[2] Oliveira to Secretary of State, March 9, 1915, *Foreign Relations, 1915*,
p. 665.

6. First Chief Venustiano Carranza, ca. March 1915 (Prints and Photographs Division, Library of Congress)

154 Controlling Revolution

treatment of Americans in Mexico City and warned that the American government would "hold personally accountable those responsible for suffering caused American lives or property."[3] Carranza denied that Obregón had in any way prevented the entry of food, and insisted that the suffering resulted from the civil war and from the obstructive actions of the merchants in Mexico City. Carranza asserted that all available transportation was required for military purposes. This assertion carried weight, for on March 11 Obregón was forced to evacuate the city, and it was to change hands a number of times before finally falling to the Constitutionalists.

Address to Mexico and the World

In addition to the apparent chaos in Mexico, rumors continued to reach Washington describing vague intentions of the European belligerents to restore order in Mexico after their war ended. On March 15, House wrote to Wilson from Paris:

Since I have been over here every now and then Mexico raises its head.

It could be of enormous advantage to your prestige if you could place that problem well on the road to settlement before this war ends. I have heard it time and again, not directly but through others, that the belligerent governments will become insistent that order be restored there.

Winslow tells me that he hears it constantly in Berlin.

I have wondered whether you have taken the matter up with the A.B.C. Powers as you contemplated when I left. This seems to me to be the wisest solution. I think you have now given them every chance to work it out themselves, and help should be offered them and insisted upon.[4]

In mid-April the American ambassador in Rome, T. N. Page, reported on French financial maneuvers with regard to Mexico and warned the president against the possibility of European intervention in Mexico after the war:

I am wondering now if, when the war closes, France may not think it will be an opportunity for her to prove that she is stronger than she was at the close of the American civil war, and may not wish to undertake some work of reorganization in Mexico, especially if she can secure the cooperation of European powers.

Unquestionably, there was considerable exasperation in some quarters in Europe over the situation last spring and summer, and

---

[3] Bryan to Oliveira, March 6, 1915, *ibid.*, p. 660.
[4] House to W.W., March 15, 1915, Wilson Papers, Ser. 2.

7. President Woodrow Wilson, ca. September 1919 (Prints and Photographs Division, Library of Congress)

I cannot help thinking that when this present war closes there
will be more than one country in Europe ready to utilize the great
forces which will be released from service here, for the purpose
of recouping in some measure on the other side of the Atlantic
the losses they have suffered.[5]

That Page was mistaken was not, of course, evident in early
1915, and the president took his warning seriously. He forwarded
the ambassador's letter to Bryan with the following comment:
Here is some extremely interesting matter from our Ambassador
at Rome.

The part which will especially arrest your attention, I dare say,
as it did mine, is the information given by the representative of
the Morgans as to the plans (not to say designs) of the French
bankers. And if these plans were indeed entertained and given
countenance by the French Government, I think Mr. Page is right
in forecasting that France will be more troublesome after the
war (provided, of course, the Allies are in any measure victorious)
than she could have been before.[6]

From April 6 to April 15 a crucial battle raged at Celaya
between the forces of Villa and Obregón. The result was a crush-
ing defeat for Villa. Carothers reported on April 20 that Villa's
infantry had been completely routed and that Villa himself admitted having suffered 2,500 killed, wounded, and captured.[7]
Immediately after Obregón's victory John Lind submitted a
memorandum to Secretary Bryan urging the prompt recognition
of Carranza. Lind argued persuasively that Villa was finished
militarily and that recognition of Carranza would hasten the
restoration of peace and orderly government. The United States,
Lind observed, had recognized Juárez though he, like the Constitutionalists, had not occupied Mexico City. Prophetically Lind
warned that "if the Angeles and Huertas are encouraged by our
nonaction, a condition of affairs may again arise where our
government will be called upon to express a choice or preference."[8]

Bryan forwarded Lind's memorandum to the president along
with a draft of a proclamation Carranza intended to issue out-

[5] T. N. Page to W.W., April 19, 1915, Wilson Papers, Ser. 2.
[6] Wilson to Bryan, May 14, 1915, Wilson Papers, Ser. 2, written on
Wilson's personal typewriter and initialed "W.W."
[7] Carothers to Secretary of State, April 20, 1915, 812.00/14897.
[8] Lind to Secretary of State, April 21, 1915, Wilson Papers, Ser. 2. Lind
was apparently referring to Felipe Angeles, a professional soldier who
had deserted Carranza and had become one of Villa's chief lieutenants.

lining the future political conduct of the Constitutionalist revolutionary government. It guaranteed to foreigners their legal property rights, promised compensation for just damages resulting from the revolution, gave priority to the reestablishment of law and order, proclaimed freedom of religion, pledged a solution to the agrarian problem through compensation and due process, and described the procedures for resumption of constitutional government. In short, the proclamation pledged the Constitutionalists to meet every condition desired by the Wilson administration. Despite these assurances the president felt the right moment had not arrived for recognition of any faction. Many things could happen in the next few days, he told Bryan, and he wanted in particular to await the "first hand impressions" of yet another special agent to Mexico, Duval West.[9]

In his evaluations of Carranza, Villa, and Zapata, West described accurately what he had seen, but through ignorance, oversight, or calculation he failed to report that the Carranzistas were on the verge of military victory in Mexico. West's reports conveyed the profoundly mistaken impression that none of the Mexican factions could pacify and rebuild their country.[10] According to West, most Mexicans would thus favor action by the United States along three lines. The United States could lend its moral and financial support to some of the existing parties in the field, the United States could select some person, party, or faction as "best representative" of the desires of the Mexican people, and the United States could look to the Mexican constitution to see which officer retained a legitimate right to succession. The course ultimately followed by Wilson and Lansing during the summer and fall of 1915 closely resembled the options presented by West.

The president thus received little evidence during the spring of 1915 that Mexico faced anything but indefinite chaos and anarchy. Lacking reliable information about the considerable military capacities of the Constitutionalists, he discounted their

---

[9] Wilson to Bryan, April 21, 1915, 812.00/17536. The president directed West to go to Mexico in early February. West arrived in Veracruz on March 24. For an account of West's instructions and mission see Clendenen, *The United States and Pancho Villa*, pp. 155–159.
[10] For West's reports see West to Secretary of State, April 5, 1915. 812.00/20721; and Bryan to W.W., forwarding West's report, May 18, 1915, 812.00/24272a.

8. General Álvaro Obregón (seated), ca. 1920 (Prints and Photographs Division, Library of Congress)

victories at Celaya and, later, at León.[11] Rather than reports of Constitutionalist progress, the President received countless despatches describing widespread starvation and suffering in Mexico. A few among his closest advisers emphasized the chaos and anarchy and urged the president to act. On May 24, for example, Secretary Bryan forwarded to the president for his use in the preparation of a policy statement a memorandum from Leon J. Canova, assistant chief of the Latin American division:

The reports which the Department has been receiving from all parts of Mexico convey only a small impression of the misery which must prevail in that country today. I hereto attach an abstract from sundry reports recently received from Mexico in relation to the widespread starvation.

I feel that this country has a great work before it, and, that the Administration is on the threshold of its opportunity.

July and August are approaching. The first signalizing the anniversary of Huerta's departure from Mexico; the second the anniversary of the triumphal entry of the Revolutionists into Mexico City. Since then they have done nothing but sink their country deeper, and still deeper, in the throes of anarchy, until the country is prostrate in misery, famine is increasing and absolutely no hope seems to be left . . . .

Should relief measures be decided upon, it would be effort wasted, unless, when we went in it would be on a big enough scale to master the situation. In the meantime an absolute embargo should be put on arms and ammunition going into Mexico.[12]

---

[11] The Constitutionalists gained another major victory at León on May 23. Initially, both sides claimed a victory. Firm reports that Obregón had won reached Washington on June 7, five days after the president's statement. See Silliman to Secretary of State, June 7, 1915, 812.00/15159.

[12] Bryan to W.W., May 27, 1915, Wilson Papers, Ser. 2. The secretary of the interior, Franklin K. Lane, lobbied for recognition and support of Eduardo Iturbide, former governor of the federal district of Mexico. In a dramatic episode, Canova had helped Iturbide escape from Mexico and death before a Villista firing squad, perhaps explaining Canova's inability to believe Mexico could ever be pacified without full-scale American military intervention. For a somewhat melodramatic account of Lane's and Canova's efforts on behalf of Iturbide, see Link, *Wilson: The Struggle for Neutrality,* pp. 471–476. The president was searching for a policy, and it was natural for these men to press their views and candidates, wildly inappropriate though they were. Nothing in the documents indicates that the president gave serious thought to supporting an émigré coalition, like Iturbide's, without roots in Mexico or an effective military force. See also Lane to W.W., May 26, 1915, June 5, 1915, July 1, 1915, and House to W.W., July 1, 1915, n.d. [July

The president shared an inclination with some of his advisers to attribute the prolongation of the Mexican civil war to the personal ambition, pride, and greed of the major leaders. Carranza was singled out for particularly heavy criticism because of his unyielding prosecution of the war and his abrupt rejections of American ideas for a settlement. David Lawrence, a journalist close to the president, sent Wilson a memorandum in late May that accurately reflected the prevailing myths, half-truths, and prejudices governing American policy during this period. Lawrence assumed that Mexico had collapsed economically and politically: "From the United States Government must come the real impetus which will make a settlement possible." He also believed that the United States could bring peace and stable government to Mexico "without the use of physical force."[13] In addition to the two military movements in Mexico, Lawrence said, there were at least three separate émigré "intrigues" going on, all claiming to possess the support of the American government and one claiming the personal approval of the president. The way out of this tangle, Lawrence recommended, was for the United States to begin negotiations in Washington with representatives of the various factions. "When I realize that the leaders of the intrigues which are now going on are appealing to those very military subordinates [willing to accept a compromise settlement] and are telling them that an amalgamation of the liberal elements will be given the support of the United States Government, it occurs to me that the most direct way to accomplish results would be for the American Government to undertake frankly to bring into harmony such elements as are willing to harmonize."[14]

Lawrence hoped in this way to split the reasonable subordinates from their unreasonable chiefs, to overcome the great obstacle, as it was perceived in Washington, of the ambition and cupidity of the major leaders:

I am confident that as soon as it becomes generally known that the United States Government intends to recognize soon an amalgamation of the best elements in Mexico, there will be a flocking

---

5, 1915?], and July 19, 1915, all in Wilson Papers, Ser. 2. The president, as he often did, may have borrowed some procedural ideas, in this case from Lane, without committing himself to any particular outcome or individual.

[13] Lawrence to W.W., May 27, 1915, Wilson Papers, Ser. 2.

[14] *Ibid.*

of individual chiefs to the support of such a combination. I should expect Carranza to be stubbornly opposed to this and with him the circle of politicians who have constantly advised him against all manner of compromises. I have every reason to believe, however, that General Obregon, who has lately had personal differences with Carranza, would not stand by Carranza. General Villa has shown himself amenable to compromises and one of his representatives here assured me recently that he would again be willing to fall in with any plan of amalgamation to the Constitutionalist cause.[15]

Out of this welter of intrigue, prejudice, and misinformation and in the midst of crisis with Germany, the president formulated his policy.[16] With the help of Secretary Bryan, the president drafted a statement on Mexico and released it to the press on June 2. "Mexico is apparently no nearer a solution of her tragical troubles than she was when the revolution was first kindled," the president's statement read, only a few days after the decisive battle of the civil war:

And she has been swept by civil war as if by fire. Her crops are destroyed, her fields lie unseeded, her work cattle are confiscated for the use of the armed factions, her people flee to the mountains to escape being drawn into unavailing bloodshed, and no man seems to see or lead the way to peace and settled order. There is no proper protection either for her own citizens or for the citizens of other nations resident and at work within her territory. Mexico is starving and without a government.

In words that suggested Duval West's recommendations, as well as those of his other advisers, the president declared:

It is time, therefore, that the Government of the United States should frankly state the policy which in these extraordinary circumstances it becomes its duty to adopt. It must presently do what it has not hitherto done or felt at liberty to do, lend its active moral support to some man or group of men, if such may be found, who can rally the suffering people of Mexico to their support in an effort to ignore, if they cannot unite, the warring factions of the country, return to the constitution of the Republic so long

---

[15] Ibid.

[16] A letter from the chief of staff, General H. L. Scott, to Z. L. Cobb, collector of the port of El Paso, indicated the preoccupation in Washington with Europe: "The papers seem to be full of the intentions of the Administration to do something in Mexico; just what, we do not know. It would seem better, however, to finish our troubles one at a time, and the European trouble seems more insistent." Scott to Cobb, June 1, 1915, The Papers of Hugh Lennox Scott, Library of Congress, General Correspondence, Box 18 (hereinafter cited as Scott Papers).

in abeyance, and set up a government at Mexico City which the
great powers of the world can recognize and deal with, a government with whom the program of the revolution will be a business
and not merely a platform. I, therefore, publicly and very solemnly,
call upon the leaders of faction in Mexico to act, to act together,
and to act promptly for the relief and redemption of their prostrate
country. I feel it my duty to tell them that, if they cannot accommodate their differences and unite . . . this Government will be con-
strained to decide what means should be employed by the United
States in order to help Mexico save herself and serve her people.[17]

Though misinformed, the president realized that the situation
in Mexico could change rapidly. In helping the president prepare
the statement, Secretary Bryan had been anxious to leave the
administration the widest possible latitude. An early draft had
stated that if the factions did not unite the United States would
"look for other means" to bring about unity. Bryan warned:
"What I fear is that the papers will attempt to put a construction
upon it which will exclude the possibility of recognizing either
one of the factions if, upon investigation, you should find it
better to recognize one of those factions than to invite the organization of a new faction. It is possible that by the time you are
ready to act Carranza might exert an influence that would
justify his recognition. It is possible that it might be wise to encourage Angeles if he should show sufficient support."[18] The president agreed: "I am entirely open to anything that events may
open to us, even the recognition of Carranza if he should develop
the necessary influence and begin to bring real order out of
chaos. But I think our statement ought to precipitate things
(in the chemical sense) and open up either this or some
other channel of action."[19]

The president's statement produced a varied reaction among
the Mexican revolutionaries. González Garza, the president of
the Convention, seized on the statement as a pretext for seeking
a *rapprochement* with the Constitutionalists. His eagerness cost
him his position. On June 9 Villa replied, denying the absence
of government and minimizing the suffering in Mexico, but accepting the proposal for a conference of revolutionaries. Villa
also sent a note to Carranza urging that the factions unite. The
note to Carranza identified the risks both for Mexico and for

---

[17] Statement by the President, June 2, 1915, *Foreign Relations, 1915,*
pp. 694, 695.
[18] Bryan to W.W., June 2, 1915, 812.00/15122a.
[19] W.W. to Bryan, June 2, 1915, 812.00/15133½.

the United States in the president's declaration: that the United States would back a reactionary grouping and, if it did not succeed, that the United States would intervene.[20] Carranza's reply came indirectly in the form of a manifesto to the Mexican nation urging all factions to submit to the Constitutionalists. The manifesto also proclaimed the substance of the ideas on the future political conduct of the Constitutionalists that had been communicated to President Wilson in late April.[21]

No option had been eliminated, including American military intervention, and on June 16, Lansing, who had now succeeded Bryan as secretary of state, sent the president a copy of a memorandum he had prepared some months before suggesting that if the United States government decided to use force in Mexico it should attempt to obtain the approval and at least token participation of the A.B.C. powers.[22] Next day, acting perhaps on information from David Lawrence,[23] Wilson wrote to Lansing, "I have been feeling the past twenty-four hours or so, that it is possible we were not using all the influences we might use in Mexico to guide what is taking place there." He suggested telling Carranza

that it was within the possibilities that we might recognize him, as things are now apparently shaping themselves—at any rate that that possibility was not excluded by anything we had yet determined upon—but that he need not expect us to consider that course seriously unless he went the full length of conciliation and conference with all factions with a view to the accommodation upon which the opinion of the world now insists. He cannot in our view afford to insist upon establishing his own dominion unless he first makes a genuine effort to unite all parties and groups.[24]

---

[20] For Villa's notes see Bonilla to Secretary of State, June 11, 1915, 812.00/15389. Lansing forwarded Villa's reply to Wilson; see Lansing to W.W., June 15, 1915, 812.00/15389.

[21] Lansing sent the president a letter from Constitutionalist representative in Washington Eliseo Arredondo that included a copy of Carranza's message. Lansing to W.W., June 17, 1915, Wilson Papers, Ser. 4, casefile 471.

[22] Lansing to Secretary of State, March 8, 1915, copy sent to the president, June 16, 1915, 812.00/15283$\frac{1}{2}$. On June 11, Canova had suggested that the Central American republics could be persuaded to request joint action with regard to Mexico, *ibid.*

[23] Lawrence to W.W., June 16, 1915, Wilson Papers, Ser. 2.

[24] W.W. to Lansing, June 17, 1915, The Papers of Ray Stannard Baker, Library of Congress, State Department Folder, Ser. 1, Box 11, written on Wilson's personal typewriter (hereinafter cited as R. S. Baker Papers); and Lansing to W.W., June 17, 1915, 812.00/15285$\frac{1}{2}$.

Lansing drafted a note on this basis and, with Wilson's approval, sent it to J. R. Silliman, a vice-consul and special representative of the president, for communication to Carranza.[25] The Constitutionalist leader rebuffed the president's idea. Appealing to logic and history, Carranza replied, "History furnishes no example in any age or any country of a civil war terminating by the union of the contending parties. One or the other must triumph." Carranza, reported Silliman, had declared that under no circumstances would he treat with Villa; that there was no expediency that could induce him to make any offer whatever. Villa and his associates must submit to military trial or leave the country. He appeared somewhat perplexed that the Government of the United States should be concerned for adjustment [and] conciliation [upon a] common basis since any revolutionary Government established upon such theories would inevitably and necessarily soon be found to be disappointing ineffective and fruitless. The intimation of possible recognition did not in the least affect his impassive face. He did not want recognition conditioned on conciliation. The determination of the United States to adopt any other measures than the recognition and support of the Constitutionalist cause would be a regrettable injustice and great calamity for two friendly nations. If the Government of the United States will maintain [a] neutral attitude the Constitutionalist cause will subdue the opposition.[26]

The president disregarded the Constitutionalist's words and victories. He continued to believe such chaos existed in Mexico that Mexicans alone could not save their country. He cherished hopes of establishing constitutional government in Mexico and felt compelled by the possibility of war with Germany to achieve a solution that would end the disorders in Mexico in order to free the United States to deal with the war in Europe.

Conference on Mexico

On June 22 the president instructed Lansing to work out the plans for a Pan-American conference on Mexico and seemed to eliminate military intervention: "Do you not think it would be well to see the A.B.C. men now to ascertain whether they would be willing (that is, whether their governments would be willing) to cooperate with us in advice and political action (rec-

---

[25] Lansing to Silliman, June 18, 1915, 812.00/15261a.
[26] Silliman to Secretary of State, June 22, 1915, 812.00/15288. Silliman interviewed Carranza on June 21.

ognition and the like)—in bringing order out of chaos there?"[27]
He remained set against allowing "private interests" to gain
any sort of control over the Mexican government.[28]

The reports from Mexico, meanwhile, continued to emphasize
disorder and suffering without providing any assessment of Constitutionalist progress or prospects.[29] The president wanted action
and on July 2 pressed Lansing to get on with the conference.[30]
Lansing submitted a tentative plan to the president on July 5.
Lansing based his plan on three assumptions. First, the "old
aristocratic party" could not be included in any settlement. The
problem was "the harmonizing of the factions representing the
Revolution." The intrigues of reactionary Mexican groups along
the border would increase the desire of the revolutionaries to
unite of their own accord, though Carranza's military successes
in southern Mexico decreased the chances for spontaneous reuni-
fication. Third, there was little hope that Carranza would agree
to an armistice or a conference of revolutionaries. His military
successes and his own stubbornness argued against it. Though
Lansing now recognized that the Carranzistas were winning militarily, he could not overcome the long-standing prejudice that
Carranza and his followers could not pacify Mexico. Only with
this in mind does his recommendation to the president seem
remotely in touch with reality. Lansing proposed that American
policy be based on six propositions:

1. It is manifest that, in view of the personal animosities, jealousies
and ambitions of the factional leaders nothing can be accomplished
through them to restore peace and stable government.

2. Carranza, Villa, and other factional leaders must retire and
not seek dominant leadership.

3. This Government will not recognize as legal any government
headed or controlled by any one of these leaders and will exert
its moral influence to prevent the establishment of such a government in any part of Mexico.

4. The determination of this Government to eliminate the present

---

[27] W.W. to Lansing, June 22, 1915, 812.00/15338½.
[28] W.W. to W. G. McAdoo, June 22, 1915, The Papers of William Gibbs
McAdoo, Woodrow Wilson Correspondence, Library of Congress.
[29] For example, this report from the American consul at Veracruz:
"Crisis is considered here to have arrived at a point that it is time
a remedy, come from where it may, is needed to stop the present unbear-
able situation in which even our own lives are at stake." Tumulty to
W.W., July 2, 1915, Wilson Papers, Ser. 2.
[30] W.W. to Lansing, July 2, 1915, 812.00/15408½, written on Wilson's
personal typewriter.

factional leaders by withdrawal of moral support should be notified in plain terms to the various factions.

5. An invitation should be issued to the factions by the American Government, agreeing to identical action, to meet in conference through their leader chiefs for the purpose of organizing a coalition provisional government with the understanding that, provided such government is unquestionably representative of the bulk of the revolutionary element, this Government and the other governments cooperating with it, will recognize it and renew diplomatic relations with Mexico.

6. This Government will aid so far as possible such coalition government by preventing arms and ammunition from reaching parties hostile to it and by employing such means as it may properly employ to insure the stability and permanency of such government until constitutional government can be restored.[31]

The president replied enigmatically. On the one hand, he seemed to accept Lansing's scheme without reservations: "The suggestions contained in your letter of the fifth furnish an excellent foundation, it seems to me, for planning something definite and final in the Mexican matter, and run very nearly along the lines of my own thought." On the other hand, Wilson raised the one objection that, when taken seriously, as Wilson would one month later, vitiated Lansing's whole approach: "Is there not reason to fear that without the present factional leaders, who seem to represent the strongest that has been thrown to the surface, we would be in a wallow of weaknesses and jealousies down there, unless some man (perhaps Angeles) could be commended to the trust of the rest?"[32] The president asked several questions about the leading émigrés and, acting on a suggestion from Colonel House, proposed that Paul Fuller, another of his confidential agents to Mexico, be commissioned to keep in touch with the émigré factions.[33] Lansing approved the idea, and Fuller took up the task immediately.[34]

---

[31] Lansing to W.W., July 5, 1915, 812.00/15410½A.

[32] W.W. to Lansing, July 8, 1915, 812.00/15412½.

[33] House to W.W., n.d. [July 5, 1915?], Wilson Papers, Ser. 2. House had been making contacts himself and apparently suggested Fuller yet another of the President's former confidential agents to Mexico, in order to relieve himself of the responsibility and to make the process of contacting the factions more efficient. See W.W. to Lansing, July 7, 1915, 812.00/15411½

[34] See Fuller to Lansing, July 19, 1915, Correspondence, 11: 1823, The Papers of Robert Lansing, Library of Congress (hereinafter cited as Lansing Papers); Fuller to Lansing, July 20, 1915, ibid., p. 1861; and Lansing to Fuller, July 13, 22, 1915, ibid., pp. 1827, 1869.

On July 17, Canova informed Lansing that he had been in touch with representatives of Villa, Zapata, and Gutiérrez and with men representing the émigrés Iturbide, Aurelio Blanguet, Manuel Mondragón, and Félix Díaz. Canova's premise was that neither Carranza's army nor his civilian advisers, "who, though educated, are of anarchistic and criminal proclivities," could restore order in Mexico: "I am, therefore, convinced," he told Lansing, "that the hour has arrived to take action." Canova offered a fantasy as a solution, one that recalls the Bay of Pigs operation during the Eisenhower and Kennedy administrations:

If you will authorize me, I feel quite confident that within ten days, and without interrupting regular duties, I can submit to you the names of a group of men who will be worthy of confidence, and who will, by that time, have the endorsement of all the Mexican elements except Carranza himself and some of his immediate advisers. I am assured that 5,000 officers and men can be assembled by this group just across the Rio Grande, as soon as the encouraging word is spoken; that 20,000 men, mostly the trained soldiers of the old Federal Army, coming largely from Villa's ranks, will rally to it; that in all probability, Villa's entire army will join the movement. . . . The Carrancista element will, in a large part, come over to this new movement. . . .

9. Francisco (Pancho) Villa and his men on the march, ca. January 1914 (Prints and Photographs Division, Library of Congress)

All of the various groups feel that with the tacit approval of President Wilson they can accomplish the salvation of their country. . . .

The opinion prevails among these groups that if the Administration can close its eyes to the operation of the new movement, and at the same time restrict, or place an embargo on, the shipment of arms and ammunition to Carranza, the problem will not be a serious one, and that Carranza will not be able to offer any real opposition for more than two months. The new movement will have the advantage of being a disciplined force, and will undertake the restoration of peace and order under conditions which will be laid down by President Wilson.[35]

Various other plans surfaced during July in anticipation of the Pan-American Conference. The president listened and committed himself to none of them.[36] Meanwhile, planning for the conference proceeded according to the proposal Lansing had submitted to the president.

Conditions in Mexico City grew worse in late July, and the president feared that a crisis there might defeat his hopes to avoid American intervention.[37] Little could be done except to send stern protests to Carranza, Villa, and Zapata and hurry into the Pan-American Conference. Villa's defeats had made him desperate, adding another problem to the already tangled situation. "Villa is now dedicating to extortion," Carothers reported on August 5, "the cupidity he formerly used for military purposes."[38]

Lansing met with the ambassadors of Brazil, Chile, and Argentina and the ministers of Bolivia, Uruguay, and Guatemala at the initial sessions of the conference on Mexico on August 5 and 6. Lansing prepared a detailed summary of the meetings and sent it to the president, who was still at his summer home in Cornish, New Hampshire. The conferees decided on two steps: "*First,* to send a communication to the factions inviting them to an immediate conference, the communication to be signed by all the conferees. . . . *Second,* to work out at once

---

[35] Canova to Lansing, July 17, 1915, 812.00/15531½.

[36] See H. L. Scott to Captain James H. Reeves, July 9, 1915, Scott Papers, General Correspondence, Box 19; and House to W.W., July 19, 1915, Wilson Papers, Ser. 2.

[37] W.W. to Lansing, July 29, 1915, 812.00/15629½; Lansing to W.W., August 2, 1915, Wilson Papers, Ser. 2.

[38] Carothers to Secretary of State, August 5, 1915, 812.00/15658. See also Carothers to Secretary of State, August 3, 1915, 812.00/15626.

a plan of selecting a government to be recognized by the countries represented in case the first step failed."[39] Lansing had
no doubts that the first step would fail. "In the second step,"
he wrote the president, "lies our hope." Lansing added: "In
the discussions, I found that there was unanimous agreement
that Carranza was impossible, that even if he triumphed it would
mean continued disorder. The disposition was to eliminate from
consideration as the head of a government to be recognized
all the previous heads of factions and to seek a man who would
withdraw the secondary chiefs to him."[40]

The Chilean ambassador, Eduardo Suárez Mújica, originated
the idea of a communication to the factions and submitted a
draft to the conferees. Lansing included the note in his letter
to the president. The note appealed to the factions—apparently
all factions, inside and outside Mexico—to come together in
a conference and to agree on a provisional government that
would adopt the first steps toward a "constitutional reconstruc-
tion" of the country and "issue the first and most essential of
them all, the immediate call to general elections."[41] The signatories of the note offered their good offices in bringing about
such a conference of factions.

Wilson approved the appeal to the factions and the plan to
consider what to do if it failed. The president added: "Would
suggest, however, that this point be dwelt upon: the first and
most essential step in settling affairs of Mexico is not to call
general elections. It seems to me necessary that a provisional
government essentially revolutionary in character should take
action to institute reforms by decree before the full forms of
the constitution are resumed. This was the original program
of the revolution and seems to me probably an essential part
of it."[42]

Though he could not know it, Carranza had won a crucial
point with the president. For over a year Carranza had been
arguing the necessity of a temporary revolutionary dictatorship,
and Wilson had at last agreed. To be sure, the president apparently still supported Lansing's plan to create a provisional

[39] Lansing to W.W., August 6, 1915, Wilson Papers, Ser. 2, and 812.00/
15715½A. The stenographic records of the meetings on August 5 and 6
are at 812.00/15714½ and 812.00/15715½, respectively.
[40] Lansing to W.W., August 6, 1915, Wilson Papers, Ser. 2.
[41] Ibid.
[42] W.W. to Lansing, August 8, 1915, 812.00/15752½.

10. Secretary of State Robert Lansing, ca. December 1917 (Prints and Photographs Division, Library of Congress)

government by drawing together elements from all the factions. Other changes would have to follow soon, for the mistaken view that an unending stalemate existed in Mexico, the view largely responsible for the plan to harmonize the factions, was rapidly becoming untenable. On August 3, Constitutionalist forces under Major General Pablo González took Mexico City for the last time, putting an end to the uncertainty and suffering in the city. Moreover, to keep Villa solvent and to prevent his depredations against foreigners from disqualifying him as an alternative to Carranza, Lansing found it necessary to allow him to acquire funds by exporting stolen cattle into the United States.[43] When the president challenged this, Lansing replied:

The reason for furnishing Villa with an opportunity to obtain funds is this: We do not wish the Carranza faction to be the only one to deal with in Mexico. Carranza seems so impossible that an appearance, at least, of opposition to him will give us an opportunity to invite a compromise of factions. I think, therefore, it is politic, for the time, to allow his faction to remain in arms until a compromise can be effected. . . . I believe he is desperate on account of lack of money.[44]

The conference had appointed a committee to consider what to do if the appeal to the factions was unsuccessful. On August 7, Paul Fuller, who was assisting Lansing at the conference, informed Lansing of the strangely anticlimactic recommendation of the committee. If the factions inside Mexico accepted the suggestion, then the conferees would recognize the government established by common agreement. Failing this, the conferees would recognize the government formed by "any group" that accepted the suggestion and granted participation to any other faction, parts of any other faction, or elements outside any faction.[45]

On August 10, Lansing sent the president a stenographic record of the first two conference meetings. Early in the meeting on August 5, Lansing had set out his basic premises.

The problem is the restoration of a stable government in Mexico, for the people, as a result of the chaotic condition there, are suffering untold woes, the last, of course, being famine. War is bad enough but now they have famine added to it.

---

[43] Lansing to W.W., August 6, 1915, 812.00/15751A.
[44] Lansing to W.W., August 9, 1915, Wilson Papers, Ser. 2. For the correspondence about the arrangement to sell Villa's cattle, see 812.00/15751½.
[45] Fuller to Lansing, August 7, 1915, 812.00/15717½.

I think we should start with the proposition—at least that is my view—that the right of revolution is inherent in man. Men have a right to revolt against those whom they consider unjust rulers. . . . They have done that in Mexico and have succeeded in their revolutionary movement. Then immediately after their victory the revolutionists split into factions not based on any great principle, but along personal lines. The result is that the revolution itself, while it is represented by all these factions combined is unable to accomplish its purpose, unable to restore a stable and responsible government in Mexico. Now this has been going on for a year, not only the people of Mexico have endured much, but we who have had representatives in Mexico, have still no government to which we can go for the protection of our rights.[46]

The problem for the conference, Lansing said, was to answer several questions:

What government can we recognize that will be stable; that can respond to its international obligations; and that will instantly, from a humanitarian standpoint, bring peace to the people of Mexico who have suffered so much. . . . Where can we find a government that it is right and expedient for us to recognize? Can we recognize any one of the existing factions? Is it possible to restore government in that way? If we can not

and here Lansing proposed the course he favored,

is it possible for us to recognize a group of men who would establish a provisional government—for it is bound to be a provisional government—until they can restore constitutional government?[47]

Lansing was convinced that recognizing Carranza would not help answer these questions. "I doubt very much as to his personality being strong enough or one that would be able to restore peace in Mexico," he declared on August 5. "I am afraid he has not the idea of surrendering his will to constitutional government." Lansing hoped to split the Constitutionalists and specifically mentioned Obregón as one who might be able to unite all the revolutionaries and treat the situation with common sense instead of arrogance.[48]

During the meeting on August 6, Paul Fuller asked the question that enabled Lansing to reveal his concept of what would happen if Carranza rebuffed the appeal for unity. "Suppose [Villa's] army of the north rallies to that invitation," Fuller suggested,

---

[46] Minutes of the First Latin American–United States Conference, August 5, 1915, 812.00/15714½, copy sent to the president; Lansing to W.W., August 10, 1915, 812.00/15864A.
[47] Ibid.
[48] Ibid.

"or the army of the south—Zapata—answers to that invitation, and Mr. Carranza refuses?" Lansing's reply indicated that he had adopted the reasoning and at least some of the specifics of Canova's proposal. Though Lansing realized the need to deal only with the major revolutionary factions inside Mexico, his plan was hardly more workable than Canova's:

I think we must bear in mind that we must be prepared to go ahead immediately upon a manifest rejection of the first plan, because the people of Mexico are starving and if we have any friendship for Mexico and her people it is our duty to do what we can to relieve it, and the only way we can relieve it is by exerting our influence for the re-establishment of stable government. So far as the suggestion made by one of the gentlemen in regard to Carranza, I think I can say that Carranza probably has ammunition long enough to last him two months and no more. If there should be an embargo placed on arms and ammunition he could not continue for a long period. Furthermore, I believe that as soon as a government is recognized in Mexico you will find that there are men in this country, not only Americans, but Mexicans, who will furnish the finances to carry on that government and will pay the soldiers in gold instead of paper money, you will see immediately desertions from all the factions . . . so that the act of recognition will have a tremendous strengthening of those whom we decide to recognize. I think we should bear in mind the men that will win the people, . . . In other words, if there are any of the underchieftains of Carranza who can be approached so that they would withdraw their adherence from Carranza . . . if we could select a man who would draw materially from the Carranzistas as well as to obtain the adherence of the other faction, we have the very elements of a stable government in itself, and recognition of that government would give it such prestige that I believe it would restore stable government in Mexico. If we could find the right man, his personality would be the guaranty of good government, the guaranty of the protection of property, and the guaranty of justice in dealing with those who are opposing him.[49]

At a time when the president desired above all else to promote peace and stability in Mexico, and when it appeared to be arriving through a Constitutionalist victory, the secretary of state was embarked on a course that promised to prolong the civil war, mix in the reactionary émigré groups, and thus threaten the accomplishments of the revolution. Alarmed by these prospects and aware of the growing dominance of the Constitu-

---

[49] Lansing to W.W., August 6, 1915, 812.00/15715½.

tionalists in Mexico, the president withdrew his approval from Lansing's plan and imposed a different meaning and direction on the conference. "I think it would be unwise for the conference to take for granted or insist upon the elimination of Carranza," he wired to Lansing. "It would be to ignore some very big facts. It seems to me very important that the plan now formed should leave the way of action open in any direction and not assume a beginning over again with a clean sheet of paper to write on. Carranza will somehow have to be digested into the scheme and above all the object of the revolution will have to be in any event conserved."[50]

Lansing had obviously been moving toward the achievement of a very specific program that envisioned the elimination of Carranza and the formation of a provisional government based on a coalition of revolutionaries. The president's telegram demolished this plan and ordered Lansing to protect the goals of the revolution and to avoid committing the United States to any specific outcome. The president had, in effect, returned to the original purpose of his speech of June 2; to bring pressure on the Mexican revolutionaries, but to await events and to avoid American military intervention. It seems likely that the president and secretary of state never thoroughly understood one another's intentions until after the conference had begun. Communication was awkward and slow between Washington and the president's summer home in New Hampshire. The president's view of the Mexican Revolution had not changed. He remained, as always, profoundly sympathetic but paternalistic, approving the revolution and desiring to supervise it. What his telegram demonstrated was his ability to recognize, to accept, and to adjust to changes in the situation in Mexico and in his own understanding of that situation. By mid-August, Villa had been crushed and had to be held up and controlled by American subsidy. The Constitutionalist victory had become so complete that it could be ignored or overridden only at the price of massive American intervention. Wilson saw this, saw that however much he disliked him, Carranza had won, and saw that Carranza's victory really meant a victory for his own hopes as well. The outcome was not exactly as he wanted it, but it came close. To change it would involve the United States in a war against the Mexican people and the Mexican Revolution.

---

[50] W.W. to Lansing, August 11, 1915, 10 A.M., 812.00/15753½.

The last-minute influences that might have caused the president to turn the conference around remain clouded. Two days before Wilson sent Lansing the new instructions, Colonel House forwarded to him part of a letter from Lincoln Steffens. House told the president: "John Lind thinks as Steffens does." Steffens had written House that it was all too plain what was going on in Washington:

Carranza has practically conquered Mexico in the military sense. . . . In other words the revolution is coming to an end with Carranza and the Carranzistas on the top. I believe the dominating parties of that group are sincere, earnest radical. . . . I trust they are like some of the best reformers we have ever known in this country.

And the opposition is perfectly comprehensible to me, for the same reason that I have seen the same opposition arise to reform movements in this country. The Church and other privileged interests here and abroad in Mexico are desperately bent upon robbing Carranza and the revolution of the fruits of their victory, and it must not be done.

And this conference, it seemed to me, was organized for that very purpose. . . .

I cannot understand why our Administration does not recognize the Carranza Government. I heard that you [House] felt that one could not deal with Carranza. Well, some men can't; Mr. Fuller can't when he wants him to make concessions to the Catholic Church—the Harvester Trust can't when it wants concessions; nobody can move Carrenza backward. But when I was talking with him and he discovered that I was friendly to the purpose of the revolution, he showed himself to be a most suggestible mind. He is a slow-minded, honest, quick-tempered and determined revolutionist; a gentleman, but a radical.[51]

Perhaps this plea, together with the mounting evidence of Villa's unsuitability and the reports of Constitutionalist successes, persuaded the president. In any event, when the conference reassembled on August 11 at the Biltmore Hotel in New York City, Lansing dutifully reversed himself and carried out the president's instructions which must have arrived, at the earliest, a few hours before the meeting began. The conferees soon turned to a consideration of what to do if the appeal to the factions were unsuccessful. Lansing dominated the discussion. He had two points to make. First, according to the instructions from

---

[51] Steffens to House in House to W.W., August 9, 1915, Wilson Papers, Ser. 2.

the president, he indicated that Carranza could not be eliminated from consideration if the Carranzistas remained united and rejected the appeal to join with the other factions.

My opinion is just this, we must not take a very small body of men that do not represent in a general way the body of the revolution, and attempt to establish them in the face of general opposition because if we do we are not supporting the body of the revolutionists and it seems to me that is essential to success. For that reason we cannot eliminate consideration of the Carranzista element which is apparently a great body of the revolution at the present time. If they should stand firmly together we have a new problem to face and we cannot decide it at this conference. If a portion of the Carranzistas should adhere to those who consent to enter into the Conference, or should share in the conference, then there would be a body of revolutionists that would be able to maintain a stable government, and unless there is something of that sort we have got to take up the question again.[52]

Ambassador Dionicio da Gama of Brazil objected and indicated that his government was doubtful about any government which excluded Carranza, because Carranza now held Mexico City and most of the country. Lansing's reply indicated that the United States intended at least to try to bring all the factions together, and if Carranza were eliminated and replaced by, say, Obregón, so be it.

Lansing made his second point over the objections of Paul Fuller. The conferees, Lansing argued successfully, could deal only with the revolutionary factions inside Mexico. "I do not believe we can ever reach a solution of this," he declared, "if we attempt to harmonize what might be called the reactionaries and the revolutionists; they will never come together without another revolution." Fuller objected that exclusion of this element would only bring another decade of revolution. Lansing replied: "I am afraid I cannot agree with Mr. Fuller. I am convinced that you must have a provisional government founded on the revolution."[53] Later, in remarks prepared before the arrival of the president's telegram, Lansing elaborated this point:

The participants in the revolution and the advocates of the reforms, for which the revolution was carried on by Madero originally and later by the Constitutionalist armies in suppressing the re-

---

[52] Lansing sent the president a stenographic record of the second session of the conference, Lansing to W.W., August 14, 1915, Wilson Papers, Ser. 2, and 812.00/15754½.
[53] *Ibid.*

actionary movement under Huerta, are entitled to exercise the rights of sovereignty in the establishment of a government for Mexico and in putting into force the reforms which the Mexican people have willed through the success of [the] revolution. . . . The Mexicans who resisted the revolution led by Madero, the Mexicans who supported the Huerta revolt against the constitutional government, and the Mexicans who oppose the principle of reform of the revolution, are not entitled to participate in the initial reestablishment of government in Mexico.[54]

The appeal would be sent, in short, only to military and civilian leaders who were Villistas, Zapatistas, and Carranzistas. Copies of the appeal were sent out on August 11 to all prominent military and civilian authorities who, with one or two exceptions, were members of one of these factions. Aware of the crucial importance of Carranza's response, Lansing tried hard to win the Mexican leader's agreement to the peace plan. To this end David Lawrence acted as an envoy between Lansing and Eliseo Arredondo, Constitutionalist agent in Washington.[55] Zapata, Villa, and their generals replied as individuals and agreed to the conference.[56] To a man, the Carranzista leaders demonstrated their unity and loyalty to their chief by referring the appeal to Carranza for reply. For his part, Carranza kept silent, though on August 24 the Constitutionalist foreign minister sent a curious, almost insulting query asking if the signatories of the appeal had acted in a private or official capacity.[57]

Lansing himself had recognized during the session in New York City that if the appeal failed to split the Constitutionalists a new situation would be created. Determined to exhaust the possibilities of persuasion, the president and Lansing dispatched David Lawrence to Veracruz to meet personally with Carranza. Lawrence left in great secrecy and took the fictitious name "Laguirre" during his mission. Lawrence's reports of his meet-

---

[54] *Ibid.*

[55] See Lawrence to Lansing, August 15, 1915, 812.00/15866½, August 15, 1915, 812.00/15867½, August 18, 1915, 812.00/15868½; and Lansing to Lawrence, August 16, 1915, 812.00/15867¼, August 17, 1915, 812.00/15866½.

[56] Villa replied on August 16, Llorente to Secretary of State, August 19, 1915, 812.00/15826. All of the replies are summarized in Canova to Secretary of State, August 30, 1915, 812.00/16472.

[57] Silliman to Lansing, August 24, 1915, 812.00/15898. The signatories replied simply that they had acted officially. See Lansing to Ambassador Domicio da Garza, September 1, 1915, 812.00/16251a.

ings with Carranza could have been written a year before when the president had been trying to persuade Carranza to negotiate with Huerta. "He rejected [the] idea of even accepting in principle [a] conference as proposed, because it implies acceptance of foreign mediation in internal affairs."[58] Next day, Lawrence reported that Carranza was impossible to deal with because he doubted the United States would intervene and recommended that the United States recognize Carranza and require him to protect foreign interests.[59] The president thought this bad advice and, surprisingly, revealed to Lansing some doubts about the usefulness of confidential agents: "The usual thing has happened: A man is sent down to explain our exact position and purpose and within a day or two sends up a comprehensive plan of his own entirely inconsistent with what he was sent to say." Ruefully, Wilson observed: "It is a great pity, but it is clear that nothing can be done either with or through Carranza."[60]

The Constitutionalists won a series of decisive victories against Villa in early September, routing his troops, forcing Villa to flee to the mountains, and occupying Torreón on September 9. Carranza thus spoke from a position of strength on September 10 when he formally rejected the proposal of the Pan-American Conference.[61] The Mexican leader offered instead to meet on the border with the United States and Latin American conferees to discuss international questions and to determine if his government were entitled to recognition.

RECOGNITION ON CARRANZA'S TERMS

Lansing's view of the Carranzistas changed remarkably in just one month. Forwarding Carranza's rejection of the Pan-American appeal, Lansing declared to the president: "The Carranzistas are undoubtedly stronger and more cohesive than they have ever been. In fact, I have almost reached the conclusion that they are so dominant that they are entitled to recognition. If they are not recognized, I cannot see what will be gained

---

[58] Canada to Secretary of State (for "Laguirre"), August 29, 1915, 812.00/16014½, sent to the president on August 31.
[59] Canada to Secretary of State (for "Laguirre"), August 30, 1915, 812.00/16016½. For Wilson's reservation of recognition, see W.W. to Lansing, August 31, 1915, 812.00/16015½.
[60] W.W. to Lansing, August 31, 1915, 812.00/16017½.
[61] Silliman to Secretary of State, September 10, 1915, 812.00/16988.

by recognizing any other government, since the present war would continue and be prolonged by strengthening the opposition to Carranza, who, I feel certain, would win in the end."[62] The conference had acted, Lansing added, when it seemed that the surest way to pacify Mexico was to harmonize the factions. Now it seemed that the quickest way to restore peace was to recognize Carranza. One problem remained. The conferees had invited all of the factions to unite in a conference, and all but the Carranzistas had accepted. An obligation rested on the United States and the other signatories of the appeal to deal honorably with those who had accepted the plan.

Lansing got around this difficulty by proposing to the president that the conference proceed on the basis that the replies to the appeal indicated that there were really only two factions in Mexico: Villista and Carranzista. Accordingly, the conferees would receive statements from these two and then decide which would be recognized.[63] The president and Lansing also intended to keep faith with the other groups in Mexico by inviting them to a conference and inquiring of them the terms upon which they would submit to Carranza. This second procedure was necessary because, in the president's words, "of the probable necessity we shall be under, because of the utter alteration of conditions since our suggestion of a conference was conveyed to them, of recognizing [Carranza] as the head of the Republic."[64]

This approach bore no relation to that of a month earlier and was chiefly designed to save face for the Wilson administration and impart a veil of consistency to an erratic policy. When the conference met on September 18, Lansing blandly asserted that to recognize either Carranza or Villa was consistent with the original plan of the conferees.[65] He was unable, however, to persuade the Latin Americans to agree to two conferences of Mexicans as he and the president had hoped. After considerable garbled and inconsequential discussion, the conferees accepted Lansing's lead and commissioned him to receive statements from representatives of Villa and Carranza. Lansing was

---

[62] Lansing to W.W., September 12, 1915, 812.00/16988.
[63] Lansing to W.W., September 15, 1915, 812.00/16989¼A. See also W.W. to Lansing, September 13, 1915, 812.00/16989½.
[64] W.W. to Lansing, September 18, 1915, 812.00/16989½.
[65] For the stenographic record of this conference, see 812.00/24281.

to report back to the conferees, who would then make a recommendation about recognition to their governments.

During the following days Lansing accepted résumés—actually summaries of previously expressed positions—from the Villista and Carranzista representatives. On October 9 the conference reconvened. Lansing recommended that Carranza be recognized and, after discussion, the Latin American diplomats agreed to recommend recognition to their governments. The home governments responded favorably and, after a final meeting on October 18, the United States extended de facto recognition to Carranza on October 19. The Latin American nations followed suit within the next few days. On the same day he granted recognition, Wilson prohibited the export of arms and munitions to Mexico, but instructed the secretary of the treasury to allow arms to be exported for the use of the de facto government.

Though the United States had extended de facto recognition to Carranza's government, Wilson and Lansing still retained their desire to supervise and control developments in Mexico. Lansing provided a striking example of this on October 19 by handing Arredondo a lengthy list of points on which the United States government desired to receive assurances. The list included restoration of constitutional guarantees, reestablishment of the judicial system, protection of foreign property, settlement of all just claims of foreigners, just compensation for lands redistributed during agrarian reform, and an early resumption of negotiations on the Chamizal dispute.[66] Almost every point involved Mexico's internal affairs in the most intimate way.

On October 10, the day after the way was finally cleared to recognize Carranza, Lansing wrote for his diary an account of

---

[66] The memorandum is marked in Lansing's handwriting: "Handed a copy to Arrendondo to use on seeing Carranza. October 19/15 RL." 812.00/16548½. Lansing's memo to Arredondo was based in part on a similar list formulated by Canova, see Canova to Lansing, October 13, 1915, 812.00/20667. From this time on Canova turned out a steady flow of memoranda on Mexico, every one of which breathed hostility to Carranza and the aims of the Mexican Revolution, and conveyed a willingness to go to war against Mexico to achieve satisfaction on the sort of points Lansing had communicated to Arredondo. Canova provided Henry P. Fletcher, the ambassador-designate, with a 79-page memo containing the most important of these on February 10, just before Fletcher left for Mexico. The Papers of Henry P. Fletcher, Library of Congress, General Correspondence, Box 4 (hereinafter cited as Fletcher Papers).

the efforts of the Wilson administration to promote peace in
Mexico. If Lansing wrote sincerely and introspectively, the entry
convicts him of profound self-deception and casts serious doubt
on the reliability of his other private observations on foreign
policy. He failed to mention, for example, his conversion through
Wilson's telegram of August 11 from an opponent to an advocate
of Carranza. Instead, Lansing cast himself as the prime agent
in the move to recognize Carranza. Of his conduct during the
negotiations, he wrote:
At the outset the dislike for Carranza by the members of the Conference was so strong that I doubted very much whether they
could be brought to accept him, and yet as a matter of expendiency
I felt that he must be recognized. . . .
    The plan of carrying on the negotiations which I determined
to follow as the only one to bring the desired result, the recognition
of Carranza, was to lay a foundation in philosophy which would
appeal strongly to the Latin mind. . . .
    . . . After much discussion it was unanimously agreed that the
logic of the situation was that the revolution was triumphant and
so was an exercise of the real sovereignty of the Mexican people,
that the revolutionary authorities were the de facto agents of the
sovereign, and that the Carranzista faction was the dominant element among the revolutionaries and therefore should be considered
the true agents of the people. The logical conclusion was that
that faction should be recognized as the de facto government. Re-
luctantly and after many hours of debates the Latin American
conferees were won over by the very logic of the case, and finally
agreed without a dissenting voice to the recognition of Carranza.[67]
    Lansing then turned to the relationships one to another of Ger-
many, Mexico, and the United States. Despite the reservations
engendered by his misleading description of his personal role
in the Pan-American negotiations, Lansing's remarks on Germany, eighteen months before the United States entered the
war, are striking:
I am not sanguine as to the future and my doubt has increased
as it is reported that Obregon and the other military leaders of
Carranza's factions are strongly anti-American and very friendly
with the Germans.
    There is no doubt, however, in my own mind as to the policy
which [we] should pursue for a time at least and that is not to
intervene to restore order in Mexico. We must try to keep on
good terms with Carranza and give him financial aid. We must

---

[67] Diary, October 10, 1915, Lansing Papers.

send an ambassador to Mexico as soon as improved conditions give a shadow of an excuse. We must keep a close watch on German agents in Mexico and along the border and prevent them if possible from causing further revolution and unrest. . . .

Looking at the general situation I have come to the following conclusions:

Germany desires to keep up the turmoil in Mexico until the United States is forced to intervene; *therefore, we must not intervene.*

Germany does not wish to have any one faction dominant in Mexico; *therefore we must recognize one faction as dominant in Mexico.*

When we recognize a faction as the government, Germany will undoubtedly seek to cause a quarrel between that government and ours; *therefore we must avoid a quarrel regardless of criticism and complaint in Congress and the press.*

It comes down to this: Our possible relations with Germany must be our first consideration; and all our intercourse with Mexico must be regulated accordingly. It is the only rational and safe policy under present conditions, but we might as well understand that the American people will not approve it, though the future may and I have no doubt, will justify the wisdom of the course adopted.[68]

Judging from his summary of the negotiations that preceded recognition, Lansing's views on Germany and Mexico represented a retrospective, self-aggrandizing synthesis of the views of a number of people, particularly the president. Whatever their origin, Lansing's diplomatic syllogisms testify to the great influence of the war in Europe on the administration's response to the Mexican Revolution.

During his annual message to Congress in early December, the president summarized developments in Mexican-American relations. Wilson noted a basic similarity between the Mexican and the American revolutionary experiences, and he emphasized the right of every people to revolt against despotic government. It was a theme he had struck frequently during the difficult months past to justify his policy of support for and attempted supervision of the Mexican Revolution. It was one to which he returned in 1916 when the two nations came close to war:

We have been put to the test in the case of Mexico and we have stood the test. Whether we have benefited Mexico by the course we have pursued remains to be seen. Her fortunes are in

---

[68] *Ibid.*

her own hands. But we have at least proved that we will not
take advantage of her in her distress or undertake to impose upon
her an order and government not of her own choosing. Liberty
is often a fierce and intractable thing, to which no bounds can
be set, and to which no bounds of a few men's choosing ought
ever to be set. Every American who has drunk at the true foun-
tains of principle and tradition must subscribe without reservation
to the high doctrine of the Virginia Bill of Rights, which in the
great days in which our government was set up was everywhere
amongst us accepted as the creed of free men. That doctrine is,
"That government is, or ought to be, instituted for the common
benefit, protection, and security of the people, nation, or community"; that "of all the various modes and forms of government
that is the best which is capable of producing the greatest degree
of happiness and safety, and is most effectually secured against
the danger of maladministration; and that, when any government
shall be found inadequate or contrary to these purposes, a majority
of the community hath an indubitable, inalienable, and indefeasible
right to reform, alter, or abolish it in such manner as shall be
judged most conducive to the public weal." We have unhesitat-
ingly applied that heroic principle to the case of Mexico, and
now hopefully await the rebirth of the troubled Republic, which
had so much of which to purge itself and so little sympathy from
any outside quarter in the radical but necessary process. We will
aid and befriend Mexico, but we will not coerce her; and our
course with regard to her ought to be sufficient proof to all America
that we seek no political suzerainty or selfish control.[69]

Wilson made the same point in unadorned terms to a meeting
of the Democratic National Committee on December 8:

Why, I have been in companies where it seemed as if I were
the only man who really believed down in his heart that a people
had the right to do anything with their government that they
damned pleased to do, and that it was nobody else's business what
they did with it. That is what I believe. If the Mexicans want
to raise hell, let them raise hell. We have got nothing to do with
it. It is their government, it is their hell. And after they have
raised enough of it, it will sit so badly on their stomachs that they
will want something else. They will get down to hard pan and
make a government that will stay put, but unless you let them
have it out, they won't have a government that will stay put.[70]

Wilson had never willingly allowed the Mexican people to

[69] Annual Address to Congress, December 7, 1915, *Public Papers: The
New Democracy*, 1: 408–409.
[70] Cited in Arthur S. Link, *Wilson: Confusions and Crises, 1915–1916*
(Princeton, N.J.: Princeton University Press, 1964), p. 200.

"have it out." Carranza and the Constitutionalist leaders had succeeded in having it out, but only by defying an insistent United States government that constantly sought to prevent the culmination of the revolution, to force a compromise in the midst of revolutionary strife, and to forestall revolutionary destruction and violence. Only in relative terms had Wilson allowed the Mexican Revolution to go its own way, only in the European and American context, where to intervene in Latin America was considered a natural and even exalted duty, a belief to which Wilson contributed by his frequent interventions in the Caribbean.

This should not be allowed to prejudice an understanding of where Wilson stood and to what ends he attempted to use the power of the United States. He used American military power directly against the military tyrant Huerta, and Wilson's opposition was a necessary if not sufficient condition of Huerta's overthrow. Thereafter, Wilson remained firmly committed to the objectives of the revolution in Mexico. His errors derived from fruitless attempts to impose without the use of military force compromise solutions on revolutionaries engaged in a civil war. His errors toward the revolutionaries in Mexico were those of a misinformed but well-intentioned maiden aunt, not those of a Metternich. Only by a play on the term could Wilson be considered a counterrevolutionary. He made no attempt to "counter" the Mexican Revolution or to turn back the clock in the sense one normally understands as counterrevolutionary. Rather, he attempted prematurely to "sublimate" the revolutionary struggle into constitutional channels.

Wilson identified with the objectives of the Mexican Revolution and desired to be free to deal with the belligerents in Europe. He refrained from using force to implement his inappropriate compromises and gracefully accepted the triumph of the Mexican Revolution and the defeat of his policies when to have used military force would have involved the United States in a war against a people and their revolution.

In the final months of 1915 the Carranzista government worked to consolidate its victory and to return peace to Mexico. The destruction of Villa remained a paramount concern. Villa, unable to survive without fighting, destroyed his own army by attacking fixed positions, first at Agua Prieta, then at Hermosillo. "By the end of November, Villa was finished as a major factor in Mexican politics."[1] He retained, however, sufficient strength and freedom of action to conduct savage raids, and his defeats had turned him bitterly anti-American. In mid-December the Mexican government negotiated the surrender of many of Villa's men and pressed its efforts to capture Villa or to drive him out of the country.[2]

Senator Albert Fall of New Mexico had long opposed the Wilson administration's Mexican policy. Fall owned extensive interests in Mexico and spoke for all those who wished to turn back the clock and perpetuate foreign economic domination of Mexico. To embarrass the Wilson administration, Fall introduced a resolution, adopted by the Senate on January 6 at a time when peace seemed to be returning to Mexico, whose tenor can be judged from its first article: "Is there a government now existing in the Republic of Mexico?" The president was requested to give answers to this and a number of questions concerning protection of foreign lives and property in Mexico and to make available to the Senate, in effect, all of the diplomatic correspondence sent and received since the Tampico incident.[3] On January 10, before the president could reply, a band of Villistas stopped a train near the cattle station of Santa Isabel and murdered seventeen American mining employees. Only one American in the party, Thomas B. Holmes, escaped.[4] The murders supplied ammunition to the enemies of the administration's policies, but Wilson was determined to ride out the crisis. He was aided in this by the energetic attempts of the Carranza government to capture and punish those responsible. Pablo López,

---

[1] Clendenen, *The United States and Pancho Villa*, p. 214. The United States allowed Carranza to reinforce Agua Prieta by shipping men and supplies across American territory.

[2] *Foreign Relations, 1915*, pp. 779–780.

[3] *Foreign Relations, 1916*, pp. 463–464.

[4] See Clendenen, *The United States and Pancho Villa*, pp. 225–227.

the leader of the ambush, was captured in April and shot.[5]

In his reply to the Fall resolution on February 17, Secretary Lansing gave the administration's answer to the calls of Theodore Roosevelt, Fall, and others to use military force against Mexico. The Mexican government, Lansing reported, was not constitutional but military, "like the majority of revolutionary governments." It had promised to hold elections and had pledged to protect foreigners and their property and to honor just claims. Incidents, like that at Santa Isabel, had declined in number but would continue, Lansing stated. The years of revolutionary disturbance made it difficult to end banditry and outrages in a short time.[6]

Villa himself made it impossible to hold to this tolerant approach. Early in the morning of March 9, Villa struck the town of Columbus, New Mexico, with a force of about five hundred men, killing fifteen American soldiers and civilians and wounding seven. A small American cavalry detachment pursued the raiders into Mexico and inflicted heavy losses on Villa's rear guard before returning to the United States.

THE DECISION TO ENTER MEXICO

Prior to the attack on Columbus the Wilson administration had learned that Villa was operating near the town without serious opposition from the Mexican government.[7] The first response from Washington after the attack occurred was to emphasize the seriousness of the situation and to ask the Mexican government to pursue and destroy the raiders.[8] By four o'clock on the day of the raid, the president had decided to send American troops into Mexico after Villa. Lansing met with Arredondo and informed him of the intentions of the American government. I told him that I thought the attack was made in accordance with a definite plan on the part of Villa to compel this Government to invade Mexico, and that I sincerely hoped he would advise

---

[5] *Ibid.*, p. 226.

[6] *Foreign Relations, 1916*, pp. 470–471.

[7] Customs Collector Z. L. Cobb to Secretary of State, March 8, 1916, 2 P.M., received March 8, 5 P.M., 812.00/17368: "Villa forces south of Columbus have not been attacked and are not being pursued according to private admissions in Juarez because of insufficient troops under Juarez command and failure of detachments from Chihuahua." See also Cobb to Secretary of State, March 8, 1916, 3 P.M., received March 8, 7 P.M., 812.00/17369.

[8] Secretary of State to Silliman, March 9, 1916, 812.00/17377; and Wilson Papers, Ser. 2.

his Government to raise no objection to the pursuit by American troops into Mexico of the attacking forces; . . . that I thought the case of "hot pursuit" by a punitive expedition was a very different thing from the deliberate invasion by an expeditionary force with intent to occupy Mexican territory. . . .

I said to him that if there should be objection raised and serious trouble should result, his Government would be playing directly into the hands of Villa and would do the very thing that Villa wished them to do. He replied—"I know that is so and I will do what I can to avoid any trouble of this sort."

I told Arredondo that we had already telegraphed to Mr. Silliman as to the facts but that I was not sure yet whether troops had actually crossed the border, although I believe they had done so; that we did not seek the consent or cooperation of the Mexican Government as we felt it would cause resentment against Carranza and make the political situation most difficult.[9]

Ironically, Henry P. Fletcher, Wilson's choice for ambassador to Mexico, took his oath of office on March 9, the day of the attack that postponed his arrival in Mexico for almost a year. Fletcher was sworn on the day he left Chile, where he had been ambassador, to return to Washington.[10]

On the afternoon of March 10, after discussing with the cabinet whether he should wait for Carranza's permission to pursue Villa, the president announced: "An adequate force will be sent at once in pursuit of Villa with the single object of capturing him and putting a stop to his forays. This can and will be done in entirely friendly aid of the constituted authorities in Mexico and with scrupulous respect for the sovereignty of that Republic."[11] The president had emphasized the capture of Villa. The orders that went to the commanding general of the southern department, Frederick Funston, emphasized a more practicable objective. Funston was ordered to organize an adequate force under command of Brigadier General John Pershing and to send the force into Mexico in pursuit of Villa. "These troops will be withdrawn to American territory," the orders read, "as soon as the de facto Government of Mexico is able to relieve them of this work. In any event the work of these troops will

---

[9] "Memorandum of Conversation with Mr. Arredondo," March 9, 1916, 4 P.M., 812.00/17510½, signed "Robert Lansing."
[10] Fletcher took the oath on instructions received from the Department of State on February 26. See Fletcher to Secretary of State, April 13, 1916, Fletcher Papers, General Correspondence.
[11] Secretary of State to all Consular Officers in Mexico, March 10, 1916, 812.00/17426a; and Wilson Papers, Ser. 2, March 9, 1916.

be regarded as finished as soon as Villa's band or bands are known to be broken up."[12]

The president had ordered troops into Mexico without the permission of the Mexican government. At least three considerations dictated immediate action. First, he knew that unless he acted as he did Congress might pass a forceful resolution and in the process take control of foreign policy out of his hands. Second, his military advisors informed him that pursuit of Villa to be effective had to begin at the earliest possible moment. Last, the November election was only seven months away, and the president could not again disregard outrages against Americans without handing the Republicans an issue with which to discredit and defeat him.

The Mexican government's reply to Lansing's original note was received in Washington at 8:15 A.M. on March 11. The note expressed regret over the raid and cited a precedent for joint action, an arrangement for reciprocal crossings of the border concluded in the 1880s between Mexico and the United States to control marauding Indians. The Mexican government proposed a similar reciprocal arrangement, to come into effect "if the raid effected at Columbus should unfortunately be repeated at any other point of the border."[13]

On March 12, General Funston requested that the militia of Arizona and New Mexico be called out to protect the towns along the border. The president and Secretary of War Baker turned down the request in an attempt to prevent speculation in the United States and Mexico that war was imminent.[14]

From this time the debate between the Mexican and American governments about the pursuit of Villa became curiously vague. Words were chosen to imply far more than was meant and, at times, neither American nor Mexican diplomats seemed able to read. On March 12, Arredondo informed Lansing: "If the Government of the United States does not take into consideration the mutual permission for American and Mexican forces to cross into the territory of one another in pursuit of bandits and insists in sending an operating army into Mexican soil, my

[12] Baker to W.W., March 10, 1916, Wilson Papers, Ser. 2. Baker's letter included a copy of a proposed statement for the press, a memorandum for the chief of staff, and the orders to General Funston.

[13] Silliman to Secretary of State, March 10, 1916, 12 midnight, 812.00/17415.

[14] Baker to W.W., March 12, 1916, Wilson Papers, Ser. 2.

Government shall consider this act as an invasion of national territory."[15] Now, if the Mexican government meant to treat as invaders any American force sent after Villa, why had it not said so? Instead, it had raised the question of reciprocal crossing rights without, as before, stressing that the arrangement would come into force only if raids occurred in the future. In a similar lapse of precision Wilson accepted the arrangement for reciprocal crossings but, strangely, failed even to mention Pershing's expedition. Lansing instructed Silliman to say: "The Government of the United States understands that in view of its agreement to this reciprocal arrangement proposed by the de facto Government, the arrangement is now complete and in force and the reciprocal privileges thereunder may accordingly be exercised by either Government without further interchange of views."[16]

Now, if the United States government intended to send Pershing into Mexico in defiance of the original Mexican proposal and in face of a threat of war—or was it actually a threat?—why had it not said so? Officially, the two governments resembled young men with acute hearing holding speaking trumpets to their ears and pretending not to hear one another. Before receiving Lansing's reply, Carranza increased the tension by publishing an appeal to the Mexican people to "be prepared for any emergency that may arise." The Constitutionalist government, the appeal continued, "will not admit, under any circumstances and whatever may be the reasons advanced and the explanation offered by the Government of the United States about the act it proposes to carry out, that the territory of Mexico be invaded for an instant and the dignity of the Republic outraged."[17]

The chief of staff, Major General Hugh Scott, fearing that the Mexican government would resist Pershing's force and even strike at American territory, ordered the War College to advise him whether the militia should be called.[18] The president remained convinced that the force should be sent and had Lansing

---

[15] Note dated March 11, 1916, read to Lansing by Arredondo, March 12, 1916, 4 P.M., 812.00/17501.
[16] Lansing to Silliman, March 13, 1916, 3 P.M., 812.00/17415, marked "Seen and approved by the President March 13th."
[17] John W. Belt to Secretary of State, March 12, 1916, midnight, received March 13, 11 P.M., 812.00/17458.
[18] Scott to Secretary of War, March 13, 1916, Scott Papers, General Correspondence, Box 2.

give a reassuring statement to Arredondo and the press. The pursuit of Villa on Mexican soil by American troops in no way infringed Mexican sovereignty, the president argued, and was undertaken in order to avoid intervention.[19] A similar instruction was sent to General Funston ordering him to limit the actions of the force to the pursuit of Villa and stressing that "neither in size nor otherwise should the expedition afford the slightest ground of suspicion of any other or larger object."[20]

At five-thirty on the afternoon of March 13, John W. Belt, a special American representative in Querétaro (the interim Mexican capital), handed Lansing's note accepting the reciprocal arrangement to the Mexican foreign minister, Jesús Acuña. Finding in the note only an acceptance of the Mexican proposal and, perhaps, assuming that this meant no American troops would cross the border, Acuña responded warmly. "It was plainly evident," Belt reported, "that the reply created a favorable impression and an already delicate situation has thus been remedied."[21]

Belt's encouraging report arrived early March 14, and at eight o'clock that evening Lansing informed all American consular officers in Mexico that American troops would "shortly" cross the border in pursuit of Villa. Lansing's message informed the consuls of Belt's encouraging interview.[22] Still later in the evening a message arrived from General Pershing saying that Carranza's troops would probably oppose his entry into Mexico. Pershing added that he would send a small force across the border the following morning unless he received other instructions.[23] When the president saw the message, he stated that if Pershing were correct he would not allow the American force to cross the border for to force entry in such circumstances would bring war

---

[19] Cited in Link, *Wilson: Confusions and Crises,* p. 212.

[20] Adjutant General to Commanding General, Southern Department, March 13, 1916, 812.00/17457.

[21] Belt to Secretary of State, March 13, 1916, 6 P.M., received March 14, 12:20 A.M., 812.00/17455.

[22] Secretary of State to All American Consular Officers in Mexico, March 14, 1916, 8 P.M., 812.00/17455. Sent to all American diplomatic missions in Latin America on March 16, 1916, *ibid.*

[23] General Funston to the Adjutant General, March 14, 1916, The Papers of Frank Polk, Yale University Library, cited in Link, *Wilson: Confusions and Crises,* p. 212.

with Mexico.[24] Wilson decided, however, to go as far as he
could to test Carranza's determination. The next day, March
15, the following orders were sent to General Funston: "The
President understands that the de facto Government of Mexico
will tolerate the entry of our expedition into Mexico in accordance with the statement of the first chief and the reply
of Secretary Lansing, which we telegraphed to you. If the military representative of the de facto Government of Mexico refuses
to tolerate your crossing the border, wire fully what he says
about his instructions before crossing and await further orders."[25]

Acting Secretary of State Frank L. Polk wired Belt in
Querétaro that the local Mexican commanders along the border
had apparently received no orders and intended to resist the
American troops. Polk instructed Belt to find out whether any
instructions had been issued to the local commanders and how
the Mexican government would react if the American force
crossed in face of a protest.[26]

At the White House, Joseph Tumulty, the president's secretary,
argued in favor of crossing the border whatever Carranza's response, stressing that the cabinet was unanimously in favor and
warning the president he would lose the election unless he acted.
Wilson answered magnanimously:

There won't be any war with Mexico if I can prevent it, no matter
how loud the gentlemen on the hill yell for it and demand it.

It is not a difficult thing for a president to declare war, especially
against a weak and defenceless nation like Mexico. . . . The thing
that daunts me and holds me back is the aftermath of war, with
all its tears and tragedies. I came from the South and I know
what war is, for I have seen its wreckage and terrible ruin. It
is easy for me as President to declare war. I do not have to fight
it, and neither do the gentlemen on the Hill who now clamor
for it. It is some poor farmer's boy, or the son of some poor widow
away off in some modest community, or perhaps the scion of a
great family, who will have to do the fighting and dying. I will
not resort to war against Mexico until I have exhausted every
means to keep out of this mess. . . . Men forget what is back

---

[24] House Diary, March 17, 1916, The Papers of Edward M. House, Yale
University Library, cited in Link, *Wilson: Confusions and Crises,* p. 213.
[25] Copy in Baker to W.W., March 15, 1916, Wilson Papers, Ser. 2.
[26] Polk to Belt, March 15, 1916, 812.00/17524a. This telegram was delayed
and reached its destination on March 18, after the crisis had passed.
See Rodgers to Secretary of State, March 18, 1916, 812.00/17525.

of this struggle in Mexico. It is the age-long struggle of a people to come into their own, and while we look upon the incidents in the foreground, let us not forget the tragic reality in the background which towers above this whole sad picture. The gentlemen who criticize me speak as if America were afraid to fight Mexico. Poor Mexico, with its pitiful men, women, and children, fighting to gain a foothold in their own land![27]

Tumulty was moved, but he remained unconvinced. The acquiescence of the Mexican government removed the grounds of crisis and tragedy. Later the same day, March 15, General Funston wired that American troops had crossed the border without opposition, and that local military representatives appeared to be cooperating.[28] A report from Silliman, describing a meeting with Obregón, Acuña, and the new secretary of foreign relations, Cándido Aguilar, confirmed Funston's report: "Upon being asked whether it could be said in advance what would be the attitude of the Mexican Government [toward] the announced plan of sending American troops into Mexico for the immediate pursuit and capture of Villa, all the Secretaries said the attitude would be one of approval and acquiescence. Secretary of War [Obregón] added that his commanders would be instructed to cooperate with American commanders in the campaign."[29]

The next day, Secretary of War Baker sent Funston the strictest orders to avoid friction with the forces of the Mexican government: "Upon no account or pretext, and neither by act, word, or attitude of any American commander, shall this expedition become or be given the appearance of being hostile to the integrity or dignity of the Republic of Mexico, by the courtesy of

[27] J. P. Tumulty, *Woodrow Wilson as I Know Him* (Garden City, N.Y.: Doubleday, Page, 1921), pp. 157–160, cited in Link, *Wilson: Confusions and Crises,* pp. 213–214. Tumulty acquired a reputation for fictionalizing his conversations with Wilson, but this account of Wilson's aversion to war with Mexico corresponds with that of House and with the order to Funston to wait for instructions if his troops met opposition at the border.
[28] Copy in Baker to W.W., March 16, 1916, Wilson Papers, Ser. 2. The Pershing expedition crossed the border in two columns, one from Columbus and one from Culberson's ranch in southwestern New Mexico. The Culberson column reached the rendezvous, Colonia Dublán, on March 17 and was joined by the column from Columbus on March 20.
[29] Silliman to Secretary of State, March 15, 1916, *Foreign Relations, 1916,* p. 491.

which this expedition is permitted to pursue an aggressor upon the peace of these neighboring Republics."[30] On March 17 Congress passed a concurrent resolution approving the president's actions and reiterating the president's pledge not to interfere in any way in Mexico's domestic affairs.[31]

Though both governments had acted as if they were ready for war, both were willing to compromise to avoid it. Wilson had used his prerogatives very cleverly to discover whether the Mexican government would allow Pershing to cross over and pursue Villa. Faced with Wilson's apparent willingness to go to war if Pershing were denied entry, the Mexican government had yielded before superior force, knowing that only war with the United States could imperil the success of the revolution. President Wilson, on the other hand, had himself been prepared to yield in order to avoid war against the revolutionaries, though the Mexican government had no way of knowing this. In the days and weeks that followed, Carranza sought to limit the dangers involved in future "punitive expeditions" and to persuade and, later, to compel the American government to withdraw Pershing's force from Mexico. Time and the vast open spaces of north-central Mexico favored Carranza's efforts, and he used his allies well.

MEXICO OPPOSES INTERVENTION

Carranza first tried through diplomacy to accomplish both his objectives. The Mexican government maintained that the original proposal for reciprocal crossing rights was intended only to open the whole subject and that detailed negotiations should have followed. Instead the United States had "without notice" sent an expedition into Mexico. The Mexican government, declared Arredondo, could not authorize the crossing of the border by expeditionary forces until the terms of the reciprocal

---

[30] Copy in Baker to W.W., March 16, 1916, Wilson Papers, Ser. 2. On the advice of General Scott and General Tasker H. Bliss, assistant chief of staff, American troops were authorized to take up defensive positions if menaced by forces of the Mexican government, "and if actually attacked they will of course defend themselves by all means at their command, but in no event must they attack or become the aggressor with any such body of troops."

[31] U.S., Congress, Senate, Concurrent Resolution No. 17, 64th Cong., 1st sess., March 17, 1916, text in *Foreign Relations, 1916,* pp. 491–492.

agreement had been precisely fixed.[32] On March 19, Arredondo submitted a draft agreement that set limits on the number of troops that could be sent, 1,000, the distance they might travel, 60 kilometers from the border, and the length of their stay, no more than five days.[33] Though the numbers would change during the negotiations, the Mexican government held firm to these principles of limiting size and later type of force, time, and distance.[34]

On March 20, Arredondo revealed that the Mexican government desired an agreement embodying these limitations, with the understanding that Pershing's force would then conform to them. Polk summarized Arredondo's remarks for the president:

I told him I assumed that this proposed agreement would cover future movements of troops and as to the present expedition, we would do everything we could to conform in general to the terms suggested by him. His reply was that the proposed terms were meant to cover this particular expedition and his suggestion was that the agreement should be made at once and that we could then slowly withdraw our troops so as to meet all the terms—that is to say, that there should not be more than one thousand troops over the border and that they should not go more than sixty kilometers from the border into Mexico. I told him that this would be difficult, if not impossible, for obvious reasons. His point is that the chances of catching Villa are slight; that our troops may have to venture a great distance into Mexico; that Villa will hide in the mountains, and it will mean a campaign of months in the heart of Mexico. All this will be very dangerous to existing relations. He thought that our troops could now be secretly withdrawn and the statement then made that Villa had fled into the interior of Mexico. I told him he could tell General Carranza that this Government was most anxious to meet his views in every way possible; that the arrangement proposed would probably be satisfactory to cover all future campaigns, but as to this particular campaign I felt sure that you would wish to have reports showing the progress of this campaign and the chances of success before

---

[32] F. L. Polk, Memorandum of Conversation with Arredondo, March 18, 1916, 812.00/18494. See also Arredondo to Secretary of State, March 18, 1916, 812.00/17920; and Polk, Acting Secretary of State, to Arredondo, March 19, 1916, 812.00/17920.

[33] Arredondo to Secretary of State, March 19, 1916, 812.00/18481.

[34] At this point, no one in Washington knew exactly how many American troops had gone into Mexico. See Scott, Acting Secretary of War, to Secretary of State, March 20, 1916, 812.00/18957.

you could consider reducing the forces in Mexico and withdrawing
it to the limits suggested.[35] The next day the president and Generals Scott and Bliss agreed
to a draft for reciprocal rights of pursuit that envisioned a limit
on distance traveled (to be negotiated), but set neither a limit
on time nor a limit on the number of troops that could be
sent.[36] The negotiations thus remained as Polk and Arredondo
left them on March 20, though additional efforts were made
to reach agreement. The American government would accept
some limitations on its freedom to pursue border raiders and
desired to exclude Pershing's expedition from the agreement.
The Mexican government desired more stringent limitations and
insisted that they apply to the American troops already in Mexico in order to speed their departure.[37]

Diplomacy had failed, and the Mexican government turned
to sterner measures. On March 31, Special Representative James
Rodgers reported that Carranza and Obregón believed they
would soon have to request the withdrawal of American troops.
And on April 6 the Mexican government rescinded the secret
agreement by which it had allowed supplies for Pershing to
be shipped on the Chihuahua railroad to "civilian" consignees.

At this time United States forces in Mexico totaled 6,675 officers and men. A total of 19,468 were deployed along the border
in varying numbers, ranging from thirty-four men and one
officer at Crooks Tunnel, Arizona, to 2,799 men and 117 officers
at Douglas, Arizona.[38] Considering the factors working against
them, Pershing's troops performed well. By pushing themselves
relentlessly during their first weeks in Mexico they managed
to locate and to fight and even to surprise bands of Villistas.
Time and even the small victories worked against overall success,
as the Villistas became more and more dispersed and less and
less vulnerable. Late in March Pershing himself warned the chief

---

[35] Polk to W.W., March 20, 1916, 812.00/17743.
[36] See enclosures in Polk to Lansing, March 21, 1916, 812.00/24290. Eventually the United States accepted limitations on time and distance of
pursuit but would not limit size or composition of the pursuing force.
See Lansing to Arredondo, April 4, 1916, National Archives, Personal
and Confidential Letters of Secretary of State Lansing to President Wilson, 1915–1918, pp. 306–309.
[37] See also Arredondo to Lansing, March 27, 1916, 812.00/17650½;
Lansing to Arredondo, April 4, 1916, 812.00/17650½; and W.W. to
Lansing, March 30, 1916, 812.00/17713½.
[38] Baker to W.W., April 5, 1916, Wilson Papers, Ser. 2.

of staff not to become optimistic over the capture of Villa. Scott replied that the whole country was very optimistic.[39]

The Mexican government continued to stiffen its resistance to the presence of American troops. Early in April, General Funston reported threatening movements of Mexican troops and growing hostility from Carranza's generals, including those most friendly to the United States. Unless Villa were captured quickly and Pershing's force could be withdrawn "gracefully and victoriously," he warned that the United States would have to fight and fight hard.[40] Funston, like Lansing and others in the administration, appeared to have forgotten that Pershing's mission was to disperse the Villistas, an attainable objective, not to capture Villa, probably unattainable. But the confusion over mission did not prolong Pershing's presence in Mexico. The Wilson administration would not withdraw Pershing until satisfied that raids like that against Columbus would not be repeated and, if repeated, could be dealt with on the basis of a mutually satisfactory treaty arrangement. While these conditions remained unfulfilled, Pershing stayed in Mexico. The longer Pershing stayed, the more far-reaching became Wilson's conditions for withdrawal. Before Pershing's force was withdrawn in early 1917, Wilson would attempt without success to use the promise of evacuation of American troops from Mexico to persuade the Mexican government to accept American supervision of the outcome of the revolution.

Less than two weeks away from his threatening note to Germany, Wilson commissioned House to sound out "opinion" on withdrawing the Pershing expedition. House reported that the "consensus of opinion" was almost entirely against withdrawing the troops. House added that he had not "given any indication of why it should be done further than to say that the foreign situation seemed to justify extreme caution in this direction."[41]

On April 12 bloodshed occurred between American troops and the townspeople of Parral, Chihuahua. Having received an invitation from a Carranzista officer to visit Parral, Major Frank Tompkins led a detachment from the 13th Cavalry into the town. No one would admit having extended an invitation. A crowd gathered. Tompkins attempted to withdraw. Someone

---

[39] Pershing to Scott, n.d. [March 31, 1916?], Scott Papers, General Correspondence, Box 22. Scott to Pershing, April 14, 1916, *ibid.*
[40] Funston to Scott, April 5, 1916, *ibid.*
[41] House to W.W., April 7, 1916, Wilson Papers, Ser. 2.

fired. The troopers returned the fire, and death and injury resulted on both sides. Carranza lamented the incident, and insisted that American troops be withdrawn from Mexico. Carranza told Arredondo to "make it clear to the Secretary of State that the American forces cannot stay any longer on our territory for other incidents more serious than this and which we must avoid at any risk may develop."[42] Lansing replied through Rodgers that American troops had entered Mexico in an attempt to capture Villa and would be withdrawn "as soon as the object of the mission is accomplished."[43] Rodgers reported next day that Luis Cabrera had informed him that "every high official of de facto government insisted upon immediate withdrawal [of] American troops. . . . Generals Carranza and Obregón are determined to secure withdrawal at once."[44] A report from General Pershing two days later underlined the seriousness of the situation. Pershing reported that the attitude of the populace and the government was so hostile and threatening that in order to continue the pursuit it would be necessary for his command to occupy the territory through which it operated and to control the railroad.[45]

Granting Pershing's requests would have altered fundamentally the character of the punitive expedition and increased the likelihood of war with Mexico, a possibility made more likely by the Mexican government's determination to force the withdrawal of American troops. These two factors combined with a third—the threat of war with Germany resulting from the president's note of April 18—to produce, first, a review of the future of the punitive expedition, second, a basic change in the disposition of Pershing's force, and third, a fresh American initiative to reach agreement on border protection and withdrawal of the expedition from Mexico.

General Scott arrived in El Paso on April 21. His orders, dated April 19, instructed him to secure from Funston his best information on Villa's whereabouts and on the public and official sentiment in the areas of Mexico through which Pershing had passed. Scott was to emphasize to Funston the limited purposes of the

[42] Arredondo to Lansing, April 12, 1916, 812.00/17866. See also Arredondo to Lansing, April 13, 1916, 812.00/17865; Arredondo to Lansing, April 13, 1916, 812.00/17867.
[43] Lansing to Rodgers, April 14, 1916, 812.00/17866.
[44] Rodgers to Lansing, April 15, 1916, 812.00/17872.
[45] Pershing to Funston, April 17, 1916, *Foreign Relations, 1916*, p. 522.

expedition and to stress the importance of respecting Mexican sovereignty. Scott was also to discuss with Funston a plan for concentrating Pershing's forces, "and maintaining an establishment in Mexico as a means of compelling the *de facto* Government to take up and pursue to an end the chase of Villa and the dispersing of whatever bands remain organized. Discuss with him the extent to which this concentration ought to take place, the number of troops that would be used, and the extent to which the border could adequately be protected with the remaining troops in his Department; also, what, if any, additional troops would be needed for a more or less prolonged continuation of a deadlock of this kind."[46] In short, the president sent General Scott on this mission to dispose Pershing's troops in such a way as to free the administration to deal with Germany. Scott was to accomplish this by concentrating Pershing's command, thus minimizing the occasions for conflict, and by guaranteeing the protection of the border.[47]

The report of Scott and Funston reads, in retrospect, as a brief for withdrawal, though this was not their recommendation: Whereabouts Villa unknown. Variously reported in different directions. He is no longer being trailed. Pershing has been obliged to withdraw Colonel Brown's force to Satevo [*sic*] account lack food and forage. Animals much run down by little food and long swift marching. It is evident Carranza troops concentrating to oppose our southward advance. There are three courses open, one to drive our way through by force after recuperation and seizure of railroad to supply large reinforcements that would be necessary for this purpose. It is believed that this will not result in capture of Villa who can go clear to Yucatan. Second course open is for Pershing to concentrate forces somewhere near Colonia Dublan [approximately 100 miles south of Columbus, New Mexico] where water rations to include May fifteenth and considerable forage are now on hand. At this point road from Columbus strikes Mexican Northwestern Railroad and protection can be given Mormon colonists. These troops can be maintained here indefinitely as an incentive to Carranza forces to kill or capture Villa if we have use of Mexican Northwestern Railroad. One other course open to remove our troops from Mexico as it is felt that longer they stay south Casas Grandes more acute will be present situation.

[46] Memorandum for General Scott from the Secretary of State, April 19, 1916, Scott Papers, General Correspondence, Box 23.
[47] See Baker to W.W., April 20, 1916, Wilson Papers, Ser. 2, for an indication that the president originated the idea of concentrating Pershing's command.

With Villa hiding very small chance exists of finding him in a population friendly to him and daily becoming more hostile to us. Realizing that first course cannot be considered General Funston and I recommend second course. Approach of rainy season which will make Columbus road impassable will make it necessary for us to have use of Mexican Northwestern Railroad from Juarez to Casas Grandes.[48] The generals' plan for concentration on Colonia Dublán was approved the next day and soon put into operation.[49]

THE SCOTT-OBREGÓN CONFERENCE

General Scott was a highly effective negotiator, and before he could return from the border the president decided to use the general's diplomatic skills. On April 22, perhaps with some prompting from Mexico City,[50] Lansing proposed to Carranza that General Scott meet with General Obregón or some other high military official to discuss Mexican-American military cooperation.[51] General Scott opposed the idea because he believed Carranza was jealous of Obregón,[52] and because he knew that he had no way of compelling his Mexican counterparts to agree to his terms. "Do you think anyone," he wrote his wife, "would be likely [to] come out of a conference with you with credit on the subject of selling one of the children—with no way of compelling you—he would not only be refused but likely to be abused in addition—that would be my condition & I don't want to subject myself or the U.S. to it. . . ."[53] Despite Scott's misgivings, the two governments quickly settled arrangements for the conference which began on the evening of April 28 with an official call on Obregón in Juárez by Scott and Funston. Scott's instructions to discuss the "future military operations"

---

[48] Scott to Secretary of War, April 22, 1916, Scott Papers, General Correspondence, Box 22.
[49] Adjutant General to Scott, April 23, 1916, ibid.
[50] Bliss to Scott, April 27, 1916, ibid.: "Secretary of War says that original suggestion for conference was made in Mexico City and probably originated with General Obregon. First formal suggestion, however, was made by our State Department." See Lansing to Secretary of War, April 22, 1916, Personal and Confidential Letters from Secretary of State Lansing to President Wilson, 1915–1918.
[51] Lansing to Rodgers, April 22, 1916, 812.00/17966a.
[52] Scott to Secretary of War, April 22, 1916, Scott Papers, General Correspondence, Box 22.
[53] Scott to Mrs. Mary M. Scott, April 24, 1916, Scott Papers, Family Correspondence, Box 5.

of American forces in Mexico reiterated the position already taken by the American government. Scott was instructed to point out that depredations on American soil could not be tolerated, and that even one additional occurrence might make it impossible to control public opinion in the United States. The dispatch of American troops into Mexico was not intended as a hostile act, and, if the Mexican authorities would only cooperate, the affair would appear simply as two governments cooperating to suppress a cause of irritation to their friendly relations. Scott was empowered to propose that American forces be regrouped in northern Mexico while the Mexican government's troops drove northward, thus catching Villa between them. This hardly constituted a concession, for the administration had already approved a plan to concentrate Pershing's forces in the north. If Obregón presented a peremptory demand for withdrawal, Scott would say that that question was a diplomatic one to be handled by those responsible for foreign affairs.[54]

After two days of official calls, the substantive meetings began on April 30. At the first meeting Obregón politely but firmly declined to discuss anything but withdrawal. He turned aside all requests for cooperation and use of Mexican railroads and maintained that Villa was dead or innocuous. There was now no cause for American troops to remain in Mexico. "We evidently came to discuss one question, Obregón another," Scott and Funston reported. The American generals recommended that the administration adhere to its plan to concentrate Pershing's command and to keep it in Mexico. Scott broke off the conference amicably when a deadlock seemed imminent. He feared that the Mexican military leaders would foolishly provoke a war with the United States.[55]

After conferring with Obregón, Scott received two telegrams from Washington. In the first, Secretary of War Baker indicated that the administration was prepared to concede the elimination of Villa, but would insist that complete withdrawal from Mexico could take place only "as soon as we are assured of the safety of our border from further aggression." Baker repeated the

---

[54] Adjutant General to Chief of Staff, April 26, 1916, Scott Papers, General Correspondence, Box 22.
[55] Scott, Funston to Secretary of War, Wilson Papers, Ser. 2, and 812.00/18020. See also Scott to Mrs. Mary M. Scott, April 30, 1916, Scott Papers, Family Correspondence, Box 5.

earlier instructions to Scott to propose the removal of American forces to a location nearer the border from which it would be possible to act independently or in cooperation with the forces of the Mexican government.[56] In the second telegram Scott was instructed to stall if a deadlock seemed imminent in order to gain time to pull together Pershing's scattered troops.[57]

In his first reaction to Obregón's refusal to cooperate, Scott had expressed his misgivings more clearly in a letter to his wife than he had to his superiors in Washington.[58] Now, in response to these two telegrams from Washington, Scott made himself understood. "Every source of information leads us to believe," he wired the secretary of war, "that Mexican Generals are certain of our entire lack of preparedness, feeling that they can cope successfully with the United States and propose to attempt it unless we retire at once." He added:

An American correspondent reported to us that he showed to Obregón afternoon April 30th press forecast from Washington, D.C. of our instructions. Obregon turned at once to Trevino and said in substance that one mile or five hundred across the border was the same thing so far as it affected the sovereignty of Mexico. We feel that last conference covered so much of latest instructions which have been rejected that in present temper of Mexicans no good will result from proposing them again and we expect flat ultimatum to get out of Mexico at once or take the consequences. If acceded to this will be a complete victory for Mexican [over] the United States in the eyes of the Mexican people already arrogant and encourage further aggressions. We feel that the border should be greatly strengthened at once to allow concentration of regular troops to meet expected eventualities in Mexico, repel invasion at many border points and cause Mexicans to feel that the United States is able and willing to repel attacks and we believe that if attacks can be prevented at all this prevention will be best accomplished by show of strength.[59]

In his nightly letter to his wife, General Scott wrote that he and Funston had put it squarely to the president either to with-

---

[56] Adjutant General to Scott, April 30, 1916, Scott Papers, General Correspondence, Box 22, and 812.00/18030. All of Baker's replies were undoubtedly approved, and perhaps drafted, by Wilson.
[57] Adjutant General to Scott, April 30, 1916, 812.00/18031.
[58] Scott to Mrs. Mary M. Scott, April 30, 1916, Scott Papers, Family Correspondence, Box 5.
[59] Scott to Secretary of War, May 1, 1916, Scott Papers, General Correspondence, Box 23, and 812.00/18033.

draw from Mexico or get ready to fight. Scott recalled that
two weeks earlier he had urged the withdrawal of Pershing,
on the ground that over 100 Columbus raiders had been killed—the
remainder driven 400 miles south of the border and dispersed which
constituted a sufficient punishment and the psychological moment
had arrived to withdraw of our own motion—especially as we were
not on Villa's trail had no correct idea of his whereabouts & had
no right under those circumstances to go slashing around Mexico
at random which we would not permit in our country—a clash
with Mexicans was considered most imminent such as actually occurred afterward at Parral and was liable to spread over a large
section if not the whole of Mexico—and a peremptory demand
for our withdrawal would surely soon be received—the original
order to Funston was drawn with the object of not committing
us to too much—this has all come about and the time has passed
to withdraw without loss of prestige in our estimation—now get
ready with large force to resist attack not only on Pershing but
on the whole border for the Mexicans are foolish and ignorant
enough to believe they can cope with us successfully and mean
to make the attempt and the only way to prevent attack on us
if it can now be prevented at all is by a show of competent force
to convince them that we are able and willing to punish aggression—this [is] a very serious moment while peace and war are
hanging in the balance. . . .[60]

President Wilson understood the gravity of the situation and
chose to stand and fight, if necessary, to protect the borders
of the United States. Scott was instructed to call another meeting
and to tell Obregón that the United States would not withdraw
from Mexico until satisfied that the danger to its border had
been removed. If Obregón refused to consider any other course
than the one he had already taken, Scott was to declare to
him that the United States would concentrate its troops in
northern Mexico. If they were attacked or if their defensive
operations were obstructed, "the consequences, however grave,
will rest upon General Obregón."[61] The administration backed
up this tough stand on the same day by alerting the militia
of Arizona, New Mexico, and Texas.[62] Late in the evening of

[60] Scott to Mrs. Mary M. Scott, May 1, 1916, Scott Papers, Family
Correspondence, Box 5.
[61] Secretary of War (?) to Scott, Funston, n.d. [May 1, 1916?], Wilson
Papers, Ser. 2.
[62] For copies of the letters to the governors of these states, see Secretary
of War to Governors of Arizona, Texas, and New Mexico, May 1, 1916,
812.00/18144½.

May 1, when war seemed close, the secretary of war arranged
with Scott a phrase "Send them at once" to signal the breakdown of the conference and the moment to dispatch the militia.[63]
In addition, Funston was ordered to halt all shipments of arms
across the border into Mexico.

General Scott had correctly estimated the depth of the desire
of the Mexican leaders to force the withdrawal of American
troops. But he had miscalculated their attitude and intentions.
Though they were revolutionaries, Carranza, Obregón, and the
others desired to avoid war with the United States, as they had
demonstrated by allowing the Pershing expedition to cross into
Mexico in the first place. Accordingly, Obregón approached
one of Scott's informal agents, A. J. McQuatters, on the evening
of May 1, and requested a private meeting with Scott. The
two generals met about midnight May 2 at the Paso del Norte
Hotel. The only others present were McQuatters, an interpreter, and a stenographer.

Obregón's objective was to secure a time limit for withdrawal,
and he failed to achieve this during twelve hours of continuous
negotiations. Nonetheless, the agreement finally drawn and submitted for approval declared: "The Government of the United
States has decided to gradually withdraw the forces of the punitive expedition." The agreement pledged the Mexican government to strengthen its forces along the border and to pursue
or destroy any lawless bands still abroad in northern Mexico.
The intention of the Wilson administration to regroup in northern Mexico was written into the agreement as though it represented a partial withdrawal. "The decision of the American
government to continue the gradual withdrawal of the troops
of the punitive expedition from Mexico was inspired by the
belief that the Mexican government is now in a position and
will omit no effort to permit the recurrence of invasion of American territory and the completion of the withdrawal of American
troops will only be prevented by occurrences arising in Mexico
tending to prove that such belief was wrongly founded."[64]

Obregón had, in fact, won only a highly qualified pledge from
Scott that American troops would be withdrawn. There was,

---

[63] Secretary of War to Scott, May 1, 1916, 10:25 P.M., Scott Papers,
General Correspondence, Box 23.
[64] Scott to Secretary of War, May 2, 1916, Scott Papers, General Correspondence, Box 23, and 812.00/18097.

as mentioned, no time limit, and the concentration on Colonia Dublán would shorten lines of communication and make it possible for Pershing to remain in Mexico as long as necessary to protect the border. Scott revealed this as his intention in his report on the twelve-hour negotiations and the agreement with Obregón.[65] He wrote his wife: "I don't know whether my arrangement is worded to suit the administration or not but the practical results are there—the President has all along stated his policy not to remain indefinitely in Mexico [B]y this he can gradually withdraw keeping rate of withdrawal in his own hands to stop if conditions [fail to] improve."[66]

On May 3, the day Obregón and Scott agreed on withdrawal, Secretary Baker sent the president a report from General Pershing that underlined the general's earlier reports of the difficulties facing his expedition and of the need to expand and alter its character in order to capture or kill Villa and his men. Pershing declared:

It is very probable that the real object of our mission to Mexico can only be attained after an arduous campaign of considerable length. . . . Our various forces have had to rely for their guidance upon the inaccurate knowledge of untried American employees, or else upon the uncertain information of frightened or unwilling natives. Thus have well laid plans often miscarried and the goal has moved further and further into the future. While this is all true as to ourselves, almost the exact contrary is true as to Villa and his men. Villa is entirely familiar with every foot of Chihuahua, and the Mexican people, through friendship or fear, have always kept him advised of our every movement. He carries little food, lives off the country, rides his mounts hard and replaces them with fresh stock taken wherever found. *Thus he has had the advantage since the end of the first twenty-four hours after the Columbus raid occurred.* [Italics added.]

Success then will depend (a) Upon our continuing occupation of as many distinct localities as possible in the territory to be covered; (b) the establishment of intimate relations with a sufficient number of reliable inhabitants in each locality to insure their assistance in obtaining trustworthy information; (c) a very full and accurate knowledge of the country through which we may operate, to be obtained by careful study and reconnaissance; (d) the maintenance of ample and regular lines of supply, especially through

---

[65] *Ibid.*
[66] Scott to Mrs. Mary M. Scott, May 4, 1916, Scott Papers, Family Correspondence, Box 5.

the large extent of unproductive or mountainous territory; and
a sufficient number of men and animals to occupy localities and
keep fresh columns constantly at work.[67]

This was a formula for military occupation and almost certainly
for war with Mexico. Small wonder, then, that Wilson found
so much to his liking the agreement negotiated by General Scott.
On May 4 he announced to the press his approval, and on
May 5 Baker submitted to the president the draft of a statement
to be released when Carranza accepted the agreement. The proposed statement described the arrangement for gradual withdrawal and announced the president's intention to receive Arredondo as Mexico's ambassador and to direct Fletcher to proceed to Mexico City.[68] Everything seemed arranged, and General
Scott prepared to leave El Paso. Scott remained dissatisfied with
the agreement but realized that it would enable the president
to concentrate on relations with Germany. "I am not satisfied
with that agreement even tho' it has been approved," he wrote
his wife, "yet it will free the President's hands for the German
situation."[69]

On May 7 word came from Mexico City that Carranza was
generally satisfied with the agreement but desired to omit the
reasons cited for American withdrawal, which included the dis-
persion of the Villistas and the assumption by the Mexican government of the obligation to protect the border.[70] On the same
day, news reached Washington that a force of Mexicans had
attacked near Glen Springs, Texas, killing three soldiers and
a nine-year-old boy. An attack had also occurred at Boquillas,
Texas, and, though the raiders were driven off by mining employees, two Americans were abducted. Obregón immediately
asked Scott if this would affect their agreement, and Scott replied
that the United States would carry it out without catching at

[67] Baker to W.W., May 3, 1916, Wilson Papers, Ser. 2, forwarding Pershing's report dated April 14, 1916.
[68] Baker to W.W., May 5, 1916, Wilson Papers, Ser. 2. Lansing had
also endorsed the Scott-Obregón agreement and had recommended that
Fletcher be sent to Mexico City. Following the comments in his diary
of the previous October, Lansing advised the president that Carranza's
problems were primarily financial and that Fletcher would be able to
help in the solution of the financial problems, which were, in Lansing's
mind, the chief obstacles to the pacification of the country. See Lansing
to W.W., May 4, 1916, Wilson Papers, Ser. 2, and 812.00/24290c.
[69] Scott to Mrs. Mary M. Scott, May 5, 1916, Scott Papers, Family
Correspondence, Box 5.
[70] Rodgers to Secretary of State, May 7, 1916, 812.00/18081.

pretexts to declare it void.[71] American troops had, nonetheless, pursued the raiders into Mexico.

Next day the generals met, and Obregón declared that the Mexican government could not accept the agreement, "on the ground that no date was set for complete withdrawal and the agreement was therefore too indefinite and a danger to Mexico."[72] Obregón offered instead a verbal agreement not to be ratified or reduced to writing for the protection by each nation of its own side of the border. The Mexican general also proposed that Pershing begin his withdrawal and that troops of Generals Treviño and Gómez follow the American force to the border. Once again Scott and Funston allowed their fears to speak and informed the secretary of war:

We feel that the whole proposition is redolent with bad faith, that Mexicans are convinced that they are not able to carry out agreement even if ratified and they desire to keep the United States troops quiet until Mexican troops are in position to drive them out of Mexico by force. . . . We expect many attacks along whole border similar to latest attack in Big Bend [of the] Rio Grande. Our line is thin and weak everywhere and inadequate to protect border anywhere if attacked in force. There is no adequate reserve. There are now many calls for help on border which cannot be given, and we think the border should at once be supported by at least one hundred fifty thousand additional troops. We have struggled for a different result with all our intelligence, patience, and courtesy, hoping against hope for a peaceful solution but are now convinced that such solution can no longer be hoped for. In order to give some added protection to border points exposed to raids it is recommended militia of Texas, New Mexico, and Arizona be called out at once, final action as to that of other states to be deferred until receipt by us of Obregon's proposal [in writing].[73]

The next day, the president mobilized the militia of the border states. Scott had not altogether closed the door in rejecting Obregón's proposal. By asking for the proposal in writing he allowed the Mexican leaders to alter their approach if, as he hoped, they were impressed by the decision to mobilize.[74] His hopes were in vain.

---

[71] Scott to Mrs. Mary M. Scott, May 8, 1916, Scott Papers, Family Correspondence, Box 5. The Mexicans had no connection with Villa.
[72] Scott, Funston to Secretary of War, May 8, 1916, Scott Papers, General Correspondence, Box 23.
[73] *Ibid.*
[74] Scott to Mrs. Mary M. Scott, May 9, 1916, Scott Papers, Family Correspondence, Box 5.

On May 9, Obregón's colleague on the Mexican delegation, Juan Amador, brought a letter to General Scott confirming the rejection of the proposed agreement.[75] Scott seized the occasion to warn Amador that an attack on Pershing's forces would result in the destruction of the Mexican government. Amador replied in a conciliatory way.[76] Later in the same day at a formal meeting of the conference, Obregón offered two propositions. One provided for the establishment along the border of zones to be occupied and protected by the forces of each nation on its own territory. The other proposed that General Scott declare that the mission of the punitive expedition had been accomplished. Withdrawal would begin immediately and continue until complete. Scott replied that the border zones could best be arranged after withdrawal. Instead of immediate withdrawal, he proposed that the United States begin a gradual withdrawal, stopping first at Namiquipa and then moving north gradually until the president was convinced that the Mexican government could protect the border. Withdrawal would be made complete when this became clear. Neither side had yielded an inch. Despite the impasse, Scott was willing to continue the conference and thought he detected some signs of softening in the Mexican attitude.[77]

The final session of the conference occurred on May 11. It ended amicably and raised false hopes within the Wilson administration that the Mexican government had accepted the substance of the American position. Obregón declared that General Treviño would take ten thousand troops into the Parral and eastern Rio Grande districts and conduct a vigorous campaign against all bandits in order to convince the United States that it was safe to withdraw its forces from Mexico.[78] Scott believed in Obregón's protestations and he and other high officials pub-

---

[75] Obregón to Scott, May 9, 1916, 812.00/18126.

[76] *Foreign Relations, 1916,* p. 546.

[77] Scott, Funston to Secretary of War, May 9, 1916, Wilson Papers, Ser. 2; and Scott to Mrs. Mary M. Scott, May 11, 1916, Scott Papers, Family Correspondence, Box 5. Carranza also desired to continue the conferences. See Robert Lansing, Memorandum of Interview with Mr. Arredondo, May 11, 1916, 812.00/17714½, and 812.00/24286.

[78] Scott, Funston to Secretary of War, May 11, 1916, 812.00/18998. See also Funston to Adjutant General, May 12, 1916, No. 1357-A, Wilson Papers, Ser. 2; and Scott to Secretary of War, May 12, 1916, Wilson Papers, Ser. 2.

licly implied that an end was near to the border troubles and to the disagreements with the Mexican government. On this hopeful note, the Scott-Obregón conference ended.

THE THREAT OF WAR

Reports began arriving from Mexico immediately after the Scott-Obregón conference that dissipated hopes for Mexican-American cooperation. On May 15, Silliman reported that the governor of Coahuila had received instructions to attack the American troops who had crossed the border in pursuit of Mexicans who had raided at Glen Springs and Boquillas. During the next few days a number of reports mentioned large Mexican troop concentrations along the border. American officials understandably believed that the Mexican government had begun preparations to force Pershing's withdrawal and to repel any further attempts to pursue raiders into Mexico. Obregón insisted that the movements were made to comply with the pledges given to protect the border. Silliman reported on May 20 that the governor of Coahuila had requested the withdrawal of the force pursuing the Glen Springs raiders; if they were not withdrawn, the governor would attack.

These reports disturbed the Wilson administration, and it prepared for the worst. But the president was unwilling to retreat from his decision to assure the protection of American borders. In a letter detailing his plans to strike into Mexico in case of war, General Funston told General Scott, "In my opinion we are in more imminent danger of a rupture within the next few days than we have been since the turmoil began in Mexico."[79] General Scott shared his concern over the threatening developments.[80] The administration had no choice but to wait for Carranza's next move.

That move came in the form of a rambling and abusive note from the Mexican government delivered on May 31.[81] The military preparations of the previous days had obviously been intended to put force behind this diplomatic initiative. On the day the note was delivered in Washington, it was published in the newspapers in Mexico City. The note began with a review

---

[79] Funston to Scott, May 29, 1916, Scott Papers, General Correspondence, Box 23.
[80] Scott to Colonel H. T. Allen, May 31, 1916, *ibid.*
[81] *Foreign Relations, 1916,* pp. 552–563. The note was dated May 22.

of events since the raid on Columbus. At that time, the note read, the United States acting either precipitately or in error had dispatched American troops into Mexico. Though the Mexican government had responded with friendship it had not authorized this crossing, and it immediately attempted to negotiate a reciprocal agreement to cover the protection of the border. The United States insisted on excepting the punitive expedition and, when the Mexican government rejected this and asked for the withdrawal of Pershing's force, the American government proposed a military conference. The Mexican government had not approved the agreement reached by the military conferees because of the conditions attached to American withdrawal. During the conference, more American troops crossed into Mexico in pursuit of the Glen Springs raiders. This second crossing without the permission of the Mexican government could only be considered an invasion of Mexican territory, and these troops must be withdrawn immediately.

The note asserted that responsibility for the protection of the frontier was not exclusively Mexican. Moreover, when a raid occurred, it was a matter for "pecuniary reparation and a reason to provide for a combined defense, but never the cause for the American forces to invade Mexican soil."[82] Ominously, the note requested a clarification of the intentions of the United States toward Mexico. Much had been said, it continued, about the friendship of the United States for Latin American peoples; much had been said about the absence of any desire to intervene in the domestic affairs of Mexico. But the military acts of the United States government contradicted these declarations. The objective of the Columbus expedition—the destruction of Villa's forces—had been accomplished, yet the expedition remained in Mexico. Some acts of the United States seemed intended to make it difficult for the consolidation of the Mexican government to occur. In particular, the United States had delayed and detained shipments of arms and munitions to the Mexican government. Withdrawal of all American troops from Mexico would be the surest proof of the intentions of the United States government.

Opinion in Mexico was dangerously inflamed and, as the American government prepared its reply, events seemed to lead toward war. On June 7, General Funston reported that Luis

---

[82] *Ibid.*, p. 556.

de la Rosa and Aniceto Pizaña, leading spirits of the Plan of San Diego, were preparing to conduct raids along the border.[83] Three days later the raids began, and Lansing promptly warned the Mexican government that further raids by de la Rosa's band would threaten peaceable relations with the United States. Fortunately, on June 12, de la Rosa and forty of his men were captured. Raids across the border continued, nonetheless, and captured documents indicated that members of the Mexican army were taking part.

Still holding the initiative, the Mexican government chose to risk war in order to compel Pershing to withdraw. General J. B. Treviño informed General Pershing on June 16 that he would attack if American troops were moved to the south, east, or west of their present location. Pershing replied that he had received no orders from the United States government to this effect and that he would continue to use his own judgment as to when and in what direction to move his forces. Pershing informed General Funston: "Shall continue reconnaissance necessary to keep in touch movement of Carranza forces."[84] President Wilson had elected to stand and fight, if necessary, to protect American borders, which seemed to require the presence of American troops in Mexico. Now, Carranza had decided to stand on the inviolability of Mexican sovereignty. War came close. With the proper incident as midwife, it would arrive.

The American army prepared for war.[85] President Wilson remained committed to the defense of the country's borders against raids from Mexico. The crisis with the Mexican government

---

[83] The conspirators of the plan of San Diego plotted a revolution in the states of Texas, Oklahoma, New Mexico, Arizona, Colorado, Nevada, and California to establish an independent republic controlled by Mexicans, Negroes, and Indians. The new republic would remain independent or become a part of Mexico. The originators of the movement were then to assist the Negroes to take six more American states and to form a Negro republic.

[84] Funston to Adjutant General, forwarding copy of telegram from General Pershing, June 16, 1916, 812.00/18544, received at War Department on June 17.

[85] Memorandum for Chief, War College Division from General Scott, June 16, 1916, Scott Papers, General Correspondence, Box 23. Scott requested plans for "the invasion of Mexico on the lines of the various railways from the north." He added that the American reply to the Mexican note would be sent the following week. The Army's plans should be ready to be implemented at once.

coincided with the Democratic National Convention held in St.
Louis, June 14–16. Wilson composed much of the party platform, and the section on Mexico accurately summarized his
intentions:
    The want of a stable responsible government in Mexico, capable
of repressing and punishing marauders and bandit bands, who have
not only taken the lives and seized and destroyed the property of
American citizens in that country, but have insolently invaded our
soil, made war upon and murdered our people thereon has rendered
it necessary temporarily to occupy by our armed forces, a portion
of the territory of that friendly state. Until, by the restoration
of law and order therein, a repetition of such incursions is [made]
improbable, the necessity for their remaining will continue. Intervention, implying, as it does, military subjugation, is revolting to
the people of the United States, notwithstanding the provocation
to that course has been great, and should be resorted to, if at
all, only as a last recourse. The stubborn resistance of the President
and his advisers to every demand and suggestion to enter upon
it, is creditable alike to them and to the people in whose name
he speaks.[86]
    Secretary Lansing composed the reply to the Mexican note
of May 31. With revisions by the president and Secretary of
War Baker, the note was ready on June 18.[87] Before sending
the note, the president authorized the mobilization of the militia
of all the states of the union, some 125,000 men, for duty on
the border. On June 19, acting under orders similar to those
of General Treviño, Mexican authorities at the port of Mazatlán
fired on a boat from the U.S.S. *Annapolis* and seized members
of the crew who were ashore on a diplomatic mission. An American sailor and a Mexican were killed, and a number of Mexicans
wounded. The American consul at Mazatlán obtained the release
of the arrested Americans by blustering a bit and reminding
the authorities of the seriousness of precipitating an international
incident.
    The American reply went to Mexico the next day. It restated

---

[86] Copy of the platform of the Democratic party in Wilson Papers, Ser.
2, for June 16, 1916. Only one of the drafts in the Wilson Papers refers
to Mexico, praising the president for avoiding intervention. The section
of the platform on international affairs is almost entirely in Wilson's
words. Apparently Mexico was left out until the convention met.
[87] See W.W. to Lansing, June 18, 1916, 812.00/18516½; and Baker to
W.W., June 18, 1916, *ibid.* The draft of the note bearing the president's
handwritten revisions is at Lansing to W.W., June 15, 1916, 812.00/18450.

the American position in forceful terms. American troops had entered Mexican territory, the note asserted, in face of the inability or unwillingness of the Carranza government to suppress the vicious lawlessness and violence that had prevailed in Mexico for three years. "Can the *de facto* Government doubt," the note asked, "that if the United States had turned covetous eyes on Mexican territory, it could have found many pretexts in the past for the gratification of its desire? Can that Government doubt that months ago, when the war between the revolutionary factions was in progress, a much better opportunity than the present was afforded for American intervention, if such has been the purpose of the United States as the *de facto* Government now insinuates?"[88] The United States government could not allow outlaws to invade and plunder American territory and then to retreat with impunity into Mexico. The inability of the Mexican government to suppress the raiders only made stronger the duty of the United States to deal with them. If the Mexican government should attack American troops pursuing outlaws, the United States government would regret the grave consequences that would follow, but it would not recede from its determination to prevent invasions of American territory and to remove the dangers that threatened Americans living along the border.

General Scott was convinced that there would be war: "It seems to me we are verging rapidly towards war. I told the President to look out for an attack upon Pershing by the national forces of the Mexican government; that there will be no way to stave off war, and that we should at once seize all the border towns—Cananea, El Tigre, Nacozari, etc.—and shove the Mexicans into the desert."[89] The day before the note was sent, Colonel House wrote the president, "I have been praying that we could get out of the Mexican difficulty without war, but it looks now as if it were inevitable. If it comes to that, I hope you will prosecute it with all the vigor and power we possess, for to do less, will entail unnecessary loss of life and an infinite amount of criticism."[90] Rodgers reported from Mexico that Carranza and his civilian associates hoped to avoid war but that

[88] *Foreign Relations, 1916,* p. 589.
[89] Scott to Colonel H. J. Slocum (with Pershing's forces), June 20, 1916, Scott Papers, General Correspondence, Box 23.
[90] House to W.W., June 19, 1916, Wilson Papers, Ser. 2.

the military, which Rogers regarded as in control of the government, were eager for war.[91]

Lansing proposed on June 21 that the United States avoid using the word "intervention" if it went into Mexico because the term was so distasteful to Latin Americans. Lansing also suggested that copies of the American reply be sent to the Latin American countries represented in Washington to make sure that these nations would understand the American viewpoint should war with Mexico occur.[92] Wilson approved the suggestion immediately, fearing from stories in the newspapers that hostilities had already begun.[93]

What Wilson mistook for the beginnings of war was another serious incident between Mexico and the United States. Earlier that day, June 21, two American cavalry troops conducting a reconnaissance mission to maintain contact with the Mexican government's troops had blundered into a fight with a well-prepared Mexican force just outside the town of Carrizal in northeastern Mexico. The patrols had been sent out to gather information not to fight. On the evening of June 20, Troop C, 10th Cavalry, commanded by Captain Charles T. Boyd, had encountered Troop K, also of the 10th Cavalry, commanded by Captain of Captain Boyd as senior officer present. Together the American Lewis Morey. The patrols joined forces under the command force totaled eighty-four men including two civilian guides. General Felix U. Gómez, the Mexican commander at Carrizal, knew of the presence of the American force and the night before had requested orders. He had been instructed to remain at Carrizal and to prevent the American troops from passing through the town.[94] Early the next morning the troopers approached Carrizal. Boyd requested permission to pass through the town on a peaceful mission, and Gómez refused, saying that the troops must go north. The Mexican general suggested a conference. Afraid of an ambush, Boyd rode forward with an interpreter

[91] Rodgers to Secretary of State, June 20, 1916, 812.00/18517.
[92] Lansing to W.W., June 21, 1916, 812.00/18533A. For the note to the Latin American countries, see Lansing to Argentine ambassador, June 21, 1916, 812.00/18534b, and Wilson Papers, Ser. 2; same to diplomatic representatives in Washington of Brazil, Chile, Bolivia, Columbia, Costa Rica, Cuba, Dominican Republic, Ecuador, Guatemala, Haiti, Honduras, Nicaragua, Panama, Peru, Paraguay, Salvador, Uruguay, and Venezuela.
[93] W.W. to Lansing, June 21, 1916, 812.00/18533½.
[94] Clendenen, *The United States and Pancho Villa,* p. 280.

to parley. Gómez suggested that he might be able to obtain permission from General Treviño for the Americans to pass through the town, but Boyd insisted on passing through the town immediately. Overconfident and spoiling for a fight, he led his men forward. The Americans dismounted about 300 yards from the Mexican position and advanced on foot into strong rifle and machine gun fire. The fight continued for an hour with the American troops advancing slowly. A Mexican detachment flanked Morey's troop and another attacked the men holding the horses and scattered the animals. Under this pressure, with its officers dead or wounded, the American force disintegrated. Fourteen Americans and thirty Mexicans died, forty-three Mexicans were wounded, and twenty-five Americans were captured. The remainder of the men made their way back to camp as best they could. Boyd had been killed and Morey, who was wounded, wrote his first report of the fight hidden in a hole 2,000 yards from the battlefield.[95]

News of the battle and its possible meaning for Mexico and the United States saddened Wilson. On June 22 he wrote House:

The break seems to have come in Mexico; and all my patience seems to have gone for nothing. I am infinitely sad about it. I fear I should have drawn Pershing and his command northward just after it became evident that Villa had slipped through his fingers; but except for that error of judgment (if it was an error) I cannot, in looking back, see where I could have done differently, holding sacred the convictions I hold in this matter.

Right or wrong, however, the extremist consequences seem upon us. But INTERVENTION (that is the rearrangement and control of Mexico's domestic affairs by the U.S.) there shall not be either now or at any time if I can prevent it.

We as yet know nothing from our officers about the affair at Carrizal. We shall no doubt have heard from them before this reaches you.[96]

With Boyd dead and the American cavalrymen scattered over the countryside, a precise account of the fight took some time to piece together. The president would not act until he was

---

[95] This account draws on the official report of the inspector general of the United States army, see W. M. Ingraham, Acting Secretary of War to W.W., October 9, 1916, Wilson Papers, Ser. 2; and on Clendenen, *The United States and Pancho Villa,* pp. 279–282, and Link, *Wilson: Confusions and Crises,* pp. 303–306.
[96] W.W. to House, June 22, 1916, copy in R. S. Baker Papers, Ser. 1, folder on E. M. House's correspondence with W.W., Box 1.

certain. There was no automatic assumption that the Americans had been right and the Mexicans wrong. Funston revealed this on June 22 in an urgent request for information from Pershing that bordered on a reprimand:

Why in the name of God do I hear nothing from you. The whole country has known for ten hours through Mexican sources that a considerable force of your command was apparently defeated yesterday with heavy losses at Carrizal. Under existing orders why were they there so far from your line. Being at such a distance I assume that now nearly twenty-four hours after affair news has not reached you who was responsible for what on its face seems to have been a terrible blunder.[97]

Pershing immediately recommended that he attack and seize the state of Chihuahua and the railroad he would need for reinforcements and supplies. His notice of these intentions apparently crossed in transit orders from Washington directing him to take no actions until a report of the battle had reached Washington and orders had been issued from there.[98]

On June 24, Arredondo delivered a note from the Mexican government that attributed the encounter at Carrizal to the violation of General Treviño's orders to Pershing not to advance east, south, or west. Again Wilson chose not to yield his right to protect American territory, and he personally composed the reply that went to Rodgers in Mexico City next day.

You are hereby instructed to hand to the Minister of Foreign Relations of the defacto Government the following:

"The Government of the United States can put no other construction upon the communication handed to the Secretary of State of the United States on the twenty fourth of June by Mr. Arredondo, under instruction of your Government, than that it is intended as a formal avowal of deliberately hostile action against the forces of the United States now in Mexico, and of the purpose to attack them without provocation whenever they move from their present position in pursuance of the objects for which they were sent there, notwithstanding the fact that those objects not only involved no unfriendly intention towards the Government and people of Mexico, but are on the contrary, intended only to assist that Government in protecting itself and the territory and

---

[97] Funston to Pershing, June 22, 1916, Punitive Expedition Records, Box 70, National Archives, cited in Clendenen, *The United States and Pancho Villa,* p. 281.
[98] Baker to Chief of Staff, June 22, 1916, Wilson Papers, Ser. 2, and Funston to Adjutant General, June 23, 1916, *ibid.*

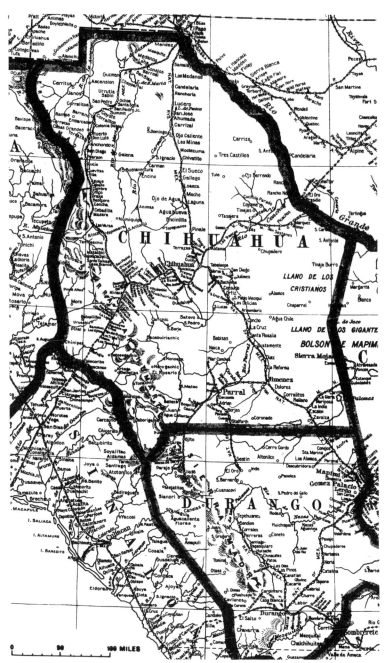

State of Chihuahua, from a Pan American Union Enlarged Map of Mexico ca. 1915 (Geography and Map Division, Library of Congress)

people of the United States against irresponsible and insurgent bands of rebel marauders.

"I am instructed, therefore, by my Government to demand the immediate release of the prisoners taken in the encounter at Carrizal, together with any property of the United States taken with them, and to inform you that the Government of the United States expects an early statement from your Government as to the course of action it wishes the Government of the United States to understand it has determined upon, and that it also expects that his statement be made through the usual diplomatic channels and not through subordinate military commanders."

CONFIDENTIAL. If you are asked, or opportunity offers, you may state that the expectation of an early statement means that the Government of the United States will not wait many hours for a reply.[99]

Apparently convinced that Carranza would reject his ultimatum, the president began to compose a message to Congress asking authority to employ the armed forces.[100] As he had done after the Tampico incident, Wilson took liberties with the facts. Though he had seen Captain Morey's account of the battle at Carrizal,[101] he intended to tell Congress that the Mexican troops had attacked the American cavalry. The Mexican government could not or would not protect the frontier. Wilson, therefore, intended to ask Congress for authority to employ the armed forces as needed. It might become necessary to clear northern Mexico of armed forces of every kind and to require a suspension of all Mexican military operations until constitutional government was reestablished in Mexico.

RETREAT FROM WAR

The president's mail ran easily ten to one against war.[102] Moved,

---

[99] Lansing and Rodgers, June 25, 1916, 812.00/18574. The original text dictated by the president is in Wilson Papers, Ser. 2, June 24–25, 1916.
[100] This account of the president's proposed message to Congress is based on Link, *Wilson: Confusions and Crises,* pp. 312–313. See also Baker to W.W., June 26, 1916, Wilson Papers, Ser. 2, proposing that the president ask Congress for authority to employ the armed forces along the border and to enter Mexico, if necessary, in order to protect against raiders. Baker also proposed that the United States forestall British occupation of Tampico by intervening there as well as in northern Mexico. See Baker to W.W., June 26, 1916, 812.00/18791$\frac{1}{2}$, forwarded to Lansing by the president on July 20.
[101] Funston to Secretary of War, June 25, 1916, *Foreign Relations, 1916,* p. 596.
[102] See Wilson Papers, Ser. 2, June 16–30, 1916.

but not persuaded, Wilson waited for the Mexican government's response. His patience and his skillful use of the means of coercion short of war were rewarded on June 28 when Rodgers reported that the Mexican government intended to release the prisoners. Now Wilson could give himself over to public opinion with good conscience. Two days later, before the Press Club in New York City, he responded in kind to the Mexican government's conciliatory gesture with a stirring speech:

Of course, it is the duty of the Government, which it will never overlook, to defend the territory and people of this country. It goes without saying that it is the duty of the administration to have constantly in mind with the utmost sensitiveness every point of national honor.

But, gentlemen, after you have said and accepted these obvious things your program of action is still to be formed. When will you act and how will you act?

The easiest thing is to strike. The brutal thing is the impulsive thing. No man has to think before he takes aggressive action; but before a man really conserves the honor by realizing the ideals of the Nation he has to think exactly what he will do and how he will do it.

Do you think the glory of America would be enhanced by a war of conquest in Mexico? Do you think that any act of violence by a powerful nation like this against a weak and [distracted] neighbor would reflect distinction upon the annals of the United States?

Do you think that it is our duty to carry self-defense to a point of dictation into the affairs of another people? The ideals of America are written plain upon every page of American history.

And I want you to know how fully I realize whose servant I am. I do not own the Government of the United States, even for the time being. I have no right in the use of it to express my passions.

I have no right to express my own ambitions for the development of America if those ambitions are not coincident with the ambitions of the Nation itself.

And I have constantly to remind myself that I am not the servant of those who wish to enhance the value of their Mexican investments, that I am the servant of the rank and file of the people of the United States.[103]

Freed from the threat of immediate war, the president sought a new way to accomplish his objectives in Mexico, objectives

---

[103] *Public Papers: The New Democracy*, 2: 218–219. Wilson included in this address a reiteration of his faith in moral force and opinion as the greatest and most permanent forces in the world.

which included but were not limited to the protection of the frontier. On July 3, Wilson asked Lansing to prepare a memorandum on Mexican policy. The next day Lansing sent the president a four-page handwritten memo that outlined the procedures for dealing with Mexico that the United States would employ until the very eve of its entry into World War I. Lansing suggested that a joint American-Mexican Commission be named to study the problems related to the border troubles and the methods to prevent them in the future. It was not a new idea, Lansing observed, but it might be worked out in a new way. "If the Carrizal incident was a clear case of Mexican aggression," he added, "I doubt if I would be favorable to this policy but it appears to me that Captain Boyd was possibly to blame. At least there is sufficient contradiction in the statements of those present to put us on inquiry as to the facts before taking drastic action."[104] He offered the following specific recommendations:

1st. The proposal for such a commission should be made by the *de facto* Government in answer to our note of June 25th as evidence of its friendly intentions. (I feel convinced that this can be accomplished through Arredondo and through the financial agent of Carranza, Dr. Rendón. In fact I know the latter is already making representations to his Chief in favor of a commission of some sort.)

2nd. The Commission should be composed of an equal number of Americans and Mexicans, and should sit in Washington as soon as possible.

3rd. The members should be diplomatic commissioners clothed with formal powers to negotiate a protocol or protocols and referendum and to make joint or several reports.

4th. The subjects to be considered by the Commission should embrace—

(*a*) The Carrizal incident.

(*b*) The raids which have taken place across the border.

(*c*) The general state of lawlessness and brigandage which has prevailed in Mexican territory contiguous to the international boundary.

(*d*) The treatment of Mexican citizens on the American side of the boundary.

(*e*) Efficient means of suppressing the lawless elements and restoring peace and safety by cooperation of the military and civil authorities of the two countries.

---

[104] Lansing to W.W., July 3, 1916, Wilson Papers, Ser. 2, and 812.00/17714½. The latter is marked "Original in longhand sent to President 9 A.M. July 4, 1916."

(*f*) The right to pursue marauders within a fixed or flexible zone without regard to territorial sovereignty, the pursuers to be properly restricted in dealing with the civil and military authorities of the other country.

(*g*) The use of the railroads in exercising the right of pursuit.

(*h*) A cooperative scheme of border protection which will insure safety to life and property.

(*i*) Any other pertinent subject which will aid in the accomplishment of the ends desired.

Subjects *a, b,* and *d* should be covered by a report or reports. The other subjects, included in a protocol or protocols.

5th. Until the Commission has met and completed its labors and the Governments have acted upon their reports and protocols, the *status quo* as to American troops in Mexico should continue, and in case of raids into American territory American military authorities should be permitted to cross the boundary in "hot pursuit" of the raiders.

This in crude form is the general scheme which I have in mind as offering a possible amicable solution of the present difficulty.

At the same time I would not abate for one hour the military preparations which we are making for this effort at peaceable settlement may in the end fail. If it does, we ought to be fully prepared—and I think that we will be by the time the Commission completes its work. We certainly would be better off than we are now if force is necessary. I believe too that our increasing show of strength would have a saluatory [*sic*] effect on the negotiations. It is what the Mexicans appreciate better than anything else.[105]

The day Lansing sent his proposal to the president a note arrived from the Mexican government that offered an opportunity to try out the idea for a joint commission. The note, signed by the Mexican foreign minister, Cándido Aguilar, stated that the immediate release of the Carrizal prisoners provided "additional" evidence of the Mexican government's desire to reach a peaceful settlement of the difficulties between Mexico and the United States. Since there were two causes of conflict—the insecurity of the border and the presence of American troops in Mexico—the two governments should concentrate their efforts on remedying both. "The Mexican Government is disposed to give quick as well as practical consideration in a spirit of concord to the remedies that may be applied to the existing condition." Aguilar also inquired whether the United States desired to accept the proposal of certain Latin American countries to mediate,

---

[105] *Ibid.*

a proposal the Mexican government had accepted in principle, or preferred direct negotiation. Aguilar stated that the Mexican government would do everything possible to avoid the repetition of incidents that might aggravate the situation and hoped the United States government would do the same.[106]

Lansing sent Aguilar's conciliatory note to the president and volunteered to discuss the joint commission with Arredondo.[107] The president approved, and on July 6 Lansing informed Arredondo officially that the United States would take under consideration any plan proposed by the Mexican government and invited suggestions and discussion of practical methods to settle the difficulties between the two nations.[108] The plan for a joint commission was thus set in motion. It remained to reach agreement on the scope of the commission's powers, and this problem would baffle and then defeat the commission's efforts.

At the risk of a war that dismayed him but that he was prepared to fight, President Wilson had regained the initiative in dealing with Mexico. Pershing stayed in Mexico to protect the border during an election year. The establishment of a joint commission promised to keep the Mexican situation safely neutralized until the election had passed. Unable to bluff or force the United States out of Mexico, the Mexican government found it necessary to change tactics. Its objective remained to rid Mexico of American troops and American interference in Mexican affairs.

---

[106] Arredondo to Lansing, forwarding note from C. Aguilar, July 4, 1916, 812.00/17715$\frac{1}{2}$.
[107] Lansing to W.W., July 5, 1916, Wilson Papers, Ser. 2.
[108] Lansing to Arredondo, July 6, 1916, 812.00/17716$\frac{1}{2}$. The president revised this note before it was delivered.

Progressivism at home and war in Europe dominated the presidential campaign in the summer and fall of 1916. Wilson's resolute, dangerous, and successful handling of the crisis over American troops in Mexican territory had effectively eliminated Mexico as a major campaign issue. The president, nonetheless, spoke and wrote about Mexico on a number of occasions and elaborated the policy he had followed consistently since 1913. Wilson told the voters that he supported the Mexican Revolution and the right of the Mexican people to change their government by whatever means they chose. He opposed the exploitation of Mexico by American or any other capitalists and would not serve the ambitions of such men. The conduct of the United States toward Mexico, he added, would influence not only the "knitting together" of the Americas but future world peace.

Belling the cat, he told the members of a Salesmanship Congress in Detroit on July 10:

What makes Mexico suspicious of us is that she does not believe as yet that we want to serve her. She believes that we want to possess her, and she has justification for the belief in the way in which some of our fellow citizens have tried to exploit her privileges and possessions. For my part, I will not serve the ambitions of these gentlemen, but I will try to serve all America, so far as intercourse with Mexico is concerned, by trying to serve Mexico herself. There are some things that are not debatable. Of course, we have to defend our border, that goes without saying. Of course, we must make good our own sovereignty, but we must respect the sovereignty of Mexico. I am one of those—I have sometimes suspected that there were not many of them—who believe, absolutely believe, the Virginia Bill of Rights, which was the model of the old bills of rights, which says that a people has a right to do anything they please with their own country and their own government. I am old-fashioned enough to believe that, and I am going to stand by that belief.[1]

Accepting renomination as the Democratic presidential candidate on September 2, Wilson said at Shadow Lawn, New Jersey:

Many serious wrongs against the property, many irreparable wrongs against the persons, of Americans have been committed within the territory of Mexico herself during this confused revolu-

---

[1] *Public Papers: The New Democracy,* 2: 231.

tion, wrongs which could not be effectually checked so long as there was no constituted power in Mexico which was in a position to check them. We could not act directly in that matter ourselves without denying Mexicans the right to any revolution at all which disturbed us and making the emancipation of her own people await our own interest and convenience.

For it is their emancipation that they are seeking—blindly, it may be, and as yet ineffectually, but with profound and passionate purpose and within their unquestionable right, apply what true American principle you will—any principle that an American would publicly avow. The people of Mexico have not been suffered to own their own country or direct their own institutions. Outsiders, men out of other nations and with interests too often alien to their own, have dictated what their privileges and opportunities should be and who should control their land, their lives, and their resources—some of them Americans, pressing for things they could never have got in their own country. The Mexican people are entitled to attempt their liberty from such influences; and so long as I have anything to do with the action of our great Government I shall do everything in my power to prevent anyone standing in their way. I know that this is hard for some persons to understand; but it is not hard for the plain people of the United States to understand. . . .

. . . The people of Mexico are striving for the rights that are fundamental to life and happiness—fifteen million oppressed men, overburdened women, and pitiful children in virtual bondage in their own home of fertile lands and inexhaustible treasure! Some of the leaders of the revolution may often have been mistaken and violent and selfish, but the revolution itself was inevitable and is right. . . .

. . . I am more interested in the fortunes of oppressed men and pitiful women than in any property rights whatever. Mistakes I have no doubt made in this perplexing business, but not in purpose or object.[2]

One month before the election, *Ladies' Home Journal* published an interview with Wilson in which he reiterated the same ideas:

If we should intervene in Mexico, we should undoubtedly revive the gravest suspicions throughout all the states of America. By intervention I mean the use of the power of the United States to establish internal order there without the invitation of Mexico and determine the character and method of her political institutions. We have professed to believe that every nation, every people, has the right to order its own institutions as it will, and we must live up to that profession in our action in absolute good faith.

[2] *Ibid.,* pp. 284–286.

Moreover, "order" has been purchased in Mexico at a terrible cost when it has been obtained by foreign assistance. The foreign assistance has generally come in the form of financial aid. The financial aid has almost invariably been conditioned upon "concessions" which have put the greater part of the resources of the country which have as yet been developed in the hands of foreign capitalists, and by the same token under the "protection" of foreign governments.

Those who have successfully maintained stable order in Mexico by such means have, like Díaz, found that they were the servants, not of Mexico, but of foreign *concessionaires*.

The economic development of Mexico has so far been accomplished by such "concessions" and by the exploitation of the fertile lands of the republic by a very small number of owners who have accumulated under one title hundreds of thousands of acres, swept within one ownership the greater part of the states, and reduced the population of the country to a sort of peonage. . . .

It goes without saying that the United States must do as she is doing—she must insist upon the safety of her borders; she must, so fast as order is worked out of chaos, use every instrumentality she can in friendship employ to protect the lives and the property of her citizens in Mexico.

But she can establish permanent peace on her borders only by a resolute and consistent adoption in action of the principles which underlie her own life. She must respect the liberties and self-government of Mexicans as she would respect her own. She has professed to be the champion of the rights of small and helpless states, and she must make the profession good in what she does. She has professed to be the friend of Mexico, and she must prove it by seeing to it that every step she takes is a step of friendship and helpfulness. . . .

Mexico must no doubt struggle through long processes of blood and terror before she finds herself and returns to the paths of peace and order; but other nations, older in political experience than she, have staggered through these dark ways for years together to find themselves at last, to come out into the light, to know the prize of liberty, to realize the compulsion of peace, and the orderly processes of law.[3]

These professions of faith, and they are moving and persuasive, emphasize only one aspect of Wilson's response to the Mexican Revolution. They explain both his sympathy for the revolution

---

[3] "The Mexico Problem Again: An Interview," *Ladies Home Journal,* October 1916, in *Public Papers: The New Democracy,* 2: 340–341, 342–343.

and his restraint in the use of force. Wilson's professions nonetheless only hint at the activism in his response. When he pledged, for example, to "serve" Mexico in "friendship and helpfulness," he promised to attempt to channel and control the Mexican Revolution by intervention and mediation in 1913, 1914, and 1915. The Joint Mexican-American Commission provides yet another example of the activist and unsuccessful aspect of Wilson's response to the Mexican Revolution.

THE SCOPE OF THE JOINT COMMISSION

The Mexican government picked up Lansing's cue and proposed on July 12 that a joint commission decide the evacuation of American troops from Mexico and prepare a referendum agreement on border protection.[4] The president and Lansing apparently intended from the outset to broaden the terms of the commission to include not only border problems but also the regulation of Mexico's internal political and economic affairs. The counselor of the State Department, Frank Polk, handled the early discussions of the commission's terms. Lansing suggested two days after the Mexican government had accepted the idea for a commission that, if necessary, Polk could add a general clause making the commission available for additional topics which might be submitted to it by mutual agreement. Lansing preferred making the terms specific and proposed the general clause as a last resort.[5]

Polk offered a general clause to Arredondo on July 19, suggesting that it might be added to the terms originally proposed by the Mexican government. The clause as revised by Polk and approved by President Wilson directed the commission to settle the border problems and evacuation of American troops and "consider such other matters as may be submitted to the Commission, the settlement of which tend to improve the relations of the two Governments; all of which shall be subject to the approval of both Governments."[6] Carranza turned down the proposal and, to bring pressure on the American government, released the original Mexican note. With the approval of the president, Polk protested the release of the note as discourteous

---

[4] See Polk to Rodgers, July 13, 1916, 812.00/18756a.
[5] Lansing to Polk, July 14, 1916, 812.00/18790½.
[6] Polk to W. W., July 19, 1916, 812.00/18790½A. A note attached is marked "Returned & approved W.W." in Wilson's handwriting.

and urged the Mexican government to broaden the scope of the joint commission's work:

There are, as the Carranza Government must be well aware, other and very important questions which have been raised by or have grown out of the disturbed conditions which have so long prevailed in Mexico. It is not the intention or desire of this Government to interfere in any way with the internal administration of Mexico. But American lives have been lost and American property injured and destroyed, and the Government feels that it is its duty to spare no effort to prevent a repetition of these occurrences; and it sincerely hopes to secure this as far as possible in friendly cooperation with the *de facto* Government after careful and impartial inquiry by the proposed Commission.[7]

The Mexican government dissented. Authorizing the joint commission to discuss internal affairs would be extremely difficult to explain inside Mexico. The Mexican government would agree informally to discuss the problems mentioned by the United States. Officially, the terms of the commission's inquiry must mention only withdrawal and the border difficulties.[8]

The president refused. He could be as stubborn as Carranza, and on July 28 Wilson directed Polk to accept the Mexican proposal for a joint commission on condition that following a satisfactory solution of the border problems and withdrawal of American troops the commission would consider "other matters the friendly arrangement of which would tend to improve the relation of the two countries."[9] The next day Rodgers reported that the Mexican government was "very anxious for a conference and will do much rather than have it abandoned."[10] On August 1, Polk directed Rodgers to inform the Mexican government that the United States had no intention of putting territorial or pecuniary claims before the commission. Carranza still refused to broaden the terms.[11] In an irregular and clever move, Carranza informed the American government on August 4 that he had appointed three commissioners—Ignacio Bonillas, Alberto Pani, and Secretary of the Treasury Luis Cabrera—to

---

[7] Polk to Rodgers, July 21, 1916, 812.00/18791½B. For the president's approval see W.W. to Polk, July 21, 1916, 812.00/18791½A. Polk kept Lansing informed, Polk to Lansing, July 21, 1916, 812.00/18791½C.
[8] Rodgers to Secretary of State, July 21, 1916, 812.00/18767.
[9] See Polk to Lansing, July 28, 1916, 812.00/24296.
[10] Rodgers to Secretary of State, July 29, 1916, *Foreign Relations, 1916,* p. 605.
[11] Rodgers to Secretary of State, August 3, 1916, 812.00/18851.

discuss "preferentially" the security of the frontier and the withdrawal of American troops.[12]

The Wilson administration was perplexed. Polk wrote Lansing: The opinion seems divided as to what course should be pursued. Some feel that Carranza should be told that the Note is not clear and ask definitely what his intentions are. Others suggest it might be well to send a Note stating that our Commissioners are being appointed on the assumption that the Commissioners have power to discuss all subjects. It has also been suggested that we accept the Note and see what happens. The objection to this was made that it would hurt politically to go ahead with every reason to believe that the Commission would be a failure.[13]

The president quickly decided to settle for an informal verbal promise from Arredondo, Carranza's representative in Washington, that the commission would be allowed to concern itself with the vague and sweeping "other matters" of concern to the United States. Arredondo made this promise on August 8 and repeated himself the next day.[14] With that, the president turned to selection of the American commissioners. He wanted Louis Brandeis, who could not serve because of his position on the Supreme Court,[15] and Richard Olney, who declined on the grounds of lack of familiarity with the issues. The president finally appointed his secretary of the interior, Franklin K. Lane, George Gray, a prominent attorney in Wilmington, Delaware, and Dr. John R. Mott, Wilson's original choice as ambassador to China and an activist in Christian missionary circles. A student of Latin American affairs, L. S. Rowe, was appointed secretary to the American commissioners.

Carranza had won a small but crucial diplomatic victory by refusing formally to broaden the terms of the commission's inquiry. Wilson and Lansing hoped for the best, but they realized that whether and to what extent the commissioners would discuss Mexico's internal problems lay with the Mexican government. Lansing wrote Richard Olney that:
One of the chief difficulties, probably the principal one, which

---

[12] Arredondo to Secretary of State, August 4, 1916, in Polk to Lansing, August 4, 1916, 812.00/24297.
[13] Polk to Lansing, August 4, 1916, 812.00/24297.
[14] See Polk to W.W., August 8, 1916, Wilson Papers, Ser. 2, and Polk to W.W., August 9, 1916, *ibid.*
[15] See Brandeis to Secretary of State, August 9, 1916, in Polk to W.W., August 9, 1916, Wilson Papers, Ser. 2, and W.W. to Polk, August 10, 1916, *ibid.*

the Mexican government has to face is the evil state of the present Government's finances. While, of course, that is not a matter for agreement between the two Governments it is a matter which may be informally discussed, provided the Mexican Commissioners are willing to do so. In fact, the financial problem enters into very many of the decrees and local exaction which form the bases of complaints by Americans having interests in Mexico. Just how far the conferees may go in the discussion of these subjects is uncertain as no definite arrangement has been made. . . .[16]

WILSON'S ATTEMPT TO BARGAIN WITHDRAWAL FOR CONTROL OF THE REVOLUTION

The commission met in New London, Connecticut. From the outset the Mexican and American commissioners pursued different objectives. At the first session of the commission on September 6, 1916, Cabrera stated that the Mexican commissioners had been instructed to take up withdrawal of the American troops and protection of the border and only then to consider the "other international and economic problems involved in [the] Mexican situation."[17] Secretary Lane described his purpose quite differently: "The principle of our negotiation has been and is— what is the wise thing to do now so as to help Mexico most without any sacrifice of American dignity, and so as to secure as speedily as possible such a re-establishment of conditions in Mexico as would permit the re-entry of Americans to their properties in that country. So we have talked facts, not theories . . . and worked with them as if we too were engaged in the government of Mexico."[18]

This divergence of viewpoint hardly promised productive discussions. Moreover, in mid-September Villa added to the embarrassments of the Mexican government by launching a series of destructive raids against a number of Mexican towns. The president quickly silenced all talk of military action by Pershing and allowed the stalemated discussions at New London to continue with the commissioners unable even to agree on an agenda.[19] Finally, on September 22, the American commissioners proposed the following approach:

---

[16] Lansing to Richard Olney, August 15, 1916, 812.00/24300.
[17] Lane to Secretary of State, September 6, 1916, 812.00/19093.
[18] Lane to Secretary of State, September 10, 1916, 812.00/19160½.
[19] See Arthur S. Link, *Wilson: Campaigns for Progressivism and Peace, 1916–1917* (Princeton, N.J.: Princeton University Press, 1965), pp. 122–123.

Would this be a satisfactory program for the Joint Commission:
That while the military details of a plan of border control formulated by us are under consideration at Washington, we pass to
the consideration of three questions:
1. Protection to life and property of foreigners in Mexico.
2. Establishment of a claims commission.
3. Religious tolerance.
It being understood between us that our effort shall be to reach
a tentative understanding upon these questions which the American
Commissioners regard as of certainly no less importance than that
of border control, and it being further understood that the border
control matter shall not be made dependent in any way upon
our agreement upon these above mentioned questions.[20]

The Mexican commissioners responded that despite the assurances of their American colleagues, as long as American troops
remained in Mexico they feared that an agreement on withdrawal would be made conditional on the conclusion of agreements on the other questions. They agreed to submit the proposal
to Carranza, but in the meantime insisted on settling the withdrawal of American troops. In a resounding understatement,
Lane reported on September 29: "After the first two or three
meetings we felt that there was a lack of sympathy between
the two commissions as to our program." In the same report
he revealed more of the nature of the proposals urged by the
American commissioners and how far they reached into Mexican
life and the Mexican Revolution. When discussing conditions
in Mexico, Lane reported, the Mexican commissioners grew eloquent about their needs but slighted their responsibilities.
We have persistently insisted that a sense of responsibility is a
basis for growth and that they must recognize their obligations
or we could not help them. And this talk has always led along
in this fashion: 1. Mexico must be pacified. 2. To pacify her
Mexico must have an army. 3. To maintain an army Mexico must
have good money. 4. To get good money Mexico must reopen
her mines and invite the return of the 50,000 Americans who were
there, and all other foreigners, as well as some of her own people.
5. To insure the return of Americans and other foreigners and
the opening up of industries we must have peace.[21]

Lane reported that the American commissioners had arranged
for Cabrera to meet with representatives of mining interests

---

[20] Lane to Secretary of State, September 22, 1916, 812.00/19265, copy
in Fletcher Papers, General Correspondence, Box 4.
[21] Lane to Secretary of State, September 29, 1916, 812.00/19416½.

affected by recent Mexican decrees. He hoped for good results. "Our purpose now," he added, "is to take up these internal questions which make Mexico so bad a neighbor, one by one and demand that manifest injustices shall be undone." The American commissioners sought a way to help Mexico achieve three objectives:

. . . Secure peace and a stable government; reopen their industrial and agricultural life upon a basis that will give employment to labor and secure revenue to the government, at the same time protecting foreign investments against unjust conditions of forfeiture and taxation, and reserving Mexico's right to control all the properties within her domain; and third, make a plan by which through primary education, industrial education, agricultural education, her people can be brought up to a higher level of civilization. This involves, as you will see, such matters as the re-establishment of a currency system, the construction of an educational system, a method by which the land may honestly be taken from those who do not use it and given to those who will, the return of an army composed of men who have pursued the policy of bandits to normal lives of labor, and an infinitude of matters and details involved in these larger problems.

It is not for us to do these things, but our problem is greater than the questions of withdrawal and border control. We must help these people to get upon a sure footing and to start right, or else Villa's raids and Zapata's raids will be of increasing frequency and one government after another will come up and go down in Mexico.[22]

On October 2, Cabrera told the American commissioners, when the commission reconvened, this time in Atlantic City, that Carranza was surprised to discover that no progress had been achieved on an agreement for withdrawal and border protection. Cabrera proposed that the commission work out a plan for the protection of the border. When this was approved by both governments, the American troops would withdraw, and then the commission could examine other questions.[23]

In reply the American commissioners submitted a revised program in which they agreed to discuss withdrawal first if the Mexican commissioners would agree to discuss the three topics submitted on September 22 as well as a fourth: "Prevention of causes likely to lead to misunderstanding, friction and strife between the American and Mexican peoples."[24] On October

[22] Ibid.
[23] Lane to Secretary of State, October 2, 1916, 812.00/19389.
[24] In Lane to W.W., October 6, 1916, Wilson Papers, Ser. 2.

6 the Mexican commissioners made a formal reply to the American proposals. In view of their instructions, said the Mexican commissioners, they could discuss only withdrawal of the American troops, safeguarding and patrolling of the border, and pursuit of outlaws at the border. If agreement should be reached on these questions, they would discuss any *international* questions submitted by the American commissioners.

This prompted Lane to write to the president and request an interview. The American commissioners believed the commission had reached a "fork in the road." Lane wrote the president:

From the first and continuously to date we have had a debate as to the powers of the Joint Commission. The Mexicans claim that the questions of withdrawal and border control must be settled and actual withdrawal effected before they can discuss what they regard as internal questions, such as the protection of life and property of foreigners in Mexico. We have contended that the whole problem is one problem, and that we could not decide to withdraw our troops or recommend a system of border control without at the same time giving consideration to and arriving at a tentative agreement as to the problems that particularly affect us. . . . They have refused to agree on any program which involves any obligation on their part. . . . They will not admit any obligation as superior to the success of the revolution, nor will they agree at this time to discuss such questions as the arbitrary forfeiture of mining claims until we are out of Mexico.[25]

The Mexican commissioners, Lane added, would not even permit the discussion of matters other than withdrawal and border protection to appear on the minutes of the commission.

Lane, Mott, and Gray believed that the Mexican commissioners were bluffing, and that the United States should call their bluff. Carranza's financial decrees had alienated the British and French governments, and conditions within Mexico were rapidly deteriorating. Yet if Carranza would only cooperate, Lane declared, the revolution could be saved.

We have pleaded with them daily that we might be given an opportunity to prove our friendship. The only answer they made is "Take your troops out and then we will talk." But they will not in writing stipulate the subjects which they will discuss. We have proposed that our troops should back out step by step as they prove their ability to command the territory. This at first they said they would not be willing to agree to as a plan of withdrawal, but today concede. They will not, however, agree that

---

[25] *Ibid.*

if we adopt such a plan they will take any measures which will open up their country to the 40,000 Americans who have their homes and working-places there.[26]

Lane described three possible courses of action. First, the United States might threaten to withdraw its recognition of the Mexican government unless Carranza agreed to the American demands. Second, the American commissioners might threaten to dissolve the conference or, third, they might proceed to devise a plan for withdrawal and border protection without receiving any guarantees of the protection of American lives and interests.[27] Lane confidently believed that the threat to withdraw recognition would bring the Mexican government to heel. Lansing had recommended, Lane told the president, that the American commissioners should go ahead and discuss the question of border safety and, if possible, draw up an agreement for withdrawal.[28] Lane put the choice to the president: "Should we act upon the theory of [Lansing's] telegram and deal with this question to a conclusion and actually withdraw our troops to the border before dealing with any of the questions which vitally affect Americans having interests in Mexico or relations with Mexico?"[29]

Lane met with the president at the president's summer home, Shadow Lawn, in New Jersey. Wilson apparently instructed Lane to continue the meetings, according priority to border safety and withdrawal, and to maintain pressure on the Mexican commissioners to discuss protection of American lives and property and the other internal questions. Accordingly, on October 11, the American commissioners proposed a three-point plan: (1) Each nation would assume responsibility for the protection of its own side of the border; (2) full military cooperation would be established between commanders on both sides, and each would be allowed to scout ten miles on either side of the border and to use the railroads of either nation to transport his troops from point to point; and (3) the American troops in Mexico would be withdrawn as rapidly as was consonant with the safety of the border. The Mexican commissioners were asked to indicate which of two methods of withdrawal they preferred: complete withdrawal by March 15, 1917, provided no raids had

---

[26] *Ibid.*
[27] *Ibid.*
[28] Lansing to Lane, October 3, 1916, quoted, *ibid.*
[29] *Ibid.*

occurred within one hundred miles of the existing American
lines in Chihuahua, or a staged withdrawal to reach Colonia
Dublán within ninety days and, if no attacks had occurred within
one hundred miles of existing lines, complete withdrawal by
the end of the next ninety days.[30] The Mexican commissioners
accepted the parts of the proposal that involved arrangements
for safety along the border and contended that acceptance must
be accompanied by immediate withdrawal.[31]

Though they accorded priority to discussions of withdrawal
and protection of the frontier, the American commissioners had
not abandoned their determination to commit the Mexican government to discuss Mexico's internal situation. On October 27
the American commissioners advanced a comprehensive plan.
They would agree to reach an immediate agreement on border
control and withdrawal if the Mexican government would give
"formal assurance" of its acceptance in principle of a group
of proposals touching Mexico's internal affairs. No public announcement of the agreement on internal affairs would be made
until after the plan of withdrawal had been ratified. The American commissioners proposed a staged withdrawal to be completed within ninety days, provided no raids occurred within
seventy-five miles of the present position at El Valle. Each nation
would guard its own side of the border and assume responsibility
for lawless acts perpetrated from its territory into the territory
of the other. This plan of withdrawal and border control would
come into effect if the Mexican government accepted in principle
the following proposals involving Mexico's internal affairs:
1. ENFORCEMENT OF NEUTRALITY LAWS.
The United States will use every means at its disposal to prevent
within its jurisdiction, conspiracies against the de facto government,
or against established order in Mexico.
2. PROTECTION OF LIFE AND PROPERTY OF FOREIGNERS.
The Government of Mexico solemnly agrees to afford full and
adequate protection to the lives and property of citizens of the
United States or other foreigners, and this protection shall be adequate to enable such citizens of the United States . . . [to operate]
industries in which they might be interested. The United States
reserves the right to re-enter Mexico and to afford such protection
by its military forces, in the event of the Mexican Government
failing to do so. In case Americans are killed in the United States

---

[30] Lane to Secretary of State, October 11, 1916, 812.00/19493.
[31] Lane to Secretary of State, October 12, 1916, 812.00/19502.

by marauders, the United States reserves the right to pursue such marauders until they are captured.

The United States Government agrees to use every means at its disposal to assure adequate protection to Mexican citizens resident on American territory.

3. RECOGNITION OF PROPERTY RIGHTS.

That all property rights heretofore acquired by citizens of the United States or other foreigners, in accordance with the established constitutional laws of the Mexican Republic, shall be regarded as valid. Should any question arise with reference to the validity of such property rights, the Mexican Government agrees that the determination of such rights shall be had through due process of law and adjudication by the regularly constituted tribunals of the country.

4. CLAIMS COMMISSION.

The Mexican Government agrees in principle to the establishment of a Mixed Claims Commission, which shall give proper consideration to all claims of citizens of the United States and other foreigners arising out of injury to persons or property subsequent to November 20, 1910. A subsequent protocol will determine the constitution of this Commission, the terms of submission, and the rules which shall govern the tribunal.

5. RELIGIOUS TOLERANCE.

The Mexican Government agrees to give effect to the constitutional provision relating to freedom of conscience in a broad spirit of religious tolerance.

6. ELIMINATION OF DISEASE AND RELIEF OF DISTRESS AND STARVATION.

The Mexican Government agrees to afford every facility to such agencies in the United States as may wish to combat disease and to relieve the distress and starvation now prevailing in many sections of the Mexican Republic.[32]

The American commissioners hardly expected the Mexican commissioners to accept. They refused, rejecting the reservation by the United States of the right to enter Mexican territory and expressing surprise that the withdrawal of troops had been made contingent on the acceptance of such far-reaching proposals involving Mexican internal affairs.[33]

The Wilson administration plainly sought to bargain the withdrawal of the Pershing expedition in exchange for sweeping promises from the Mexican government that touched the core

---

[32] Lane to Secretary of State, October 27, 1916, 812.00/19667.
[33] See 812.00/19700, October 27, 1916, apparently forwarded by mail to Secretary Lane.

of Mexican life and the Mexican Revolution. From a justified expression of national self-defense the presence of American troops in Mexico had been twisted into a vehicle for controlling Mexico's future. Although the commissioners managed to produce draft agreements on withdrawal and border control by November 13, the Mexican negotiators were told that the agreements would not be submitted unless they would agree to discuss the internal matters mentioned in the October proposals.[34]

A split developed among the Mexican commissioners. Pani and Bonillas made clear to Lane that they would accede to the American demands. Cabrera, who spoke for Carranza, remained adamant, and on November 12, Lane reported that Cabrera's stubbornness had created a crisis for the Commission.[35] On November 15, Lane reported: "Everything points to necessity of an ultimatum to Mexican Commissioners informing that plan of border control . . . is our last word on the subject."[36] The choice was doubly cruel for the Mexican government. Villa had now captured Parral and the town of Jiménez. With American financial and material assistance, the Mexican government's troops could easily destroy this threat to its power and to the revolution.

Lane met with the president and Lansing and Baker at the White House on November 18. The war in Europe overshadowed all other issues. Wilson's concern over the war was so great that on the eve of the election he had devised a plan to make Hughes president immediately if Hughes won. Wilson would appoint Hughes secretary of state, and Wilson and the vice-president, Thomas R. Marshall, would resign. Hughes would become president by constitutional succession, and the country would have been granted responsible government at a crucial moment in its history.[37] Wilson had won a narrow victory in the election, however, and could move with more freedom on Mexican matters.

---

[34] Lane to Secretary of State, November 13, 1916, 812.00/19856. See also Lane to Secretary of State, November 14, 1916, 812.00/19863. The drafts provided for withdrawal within forty days after approval of the agreements, allowed delays in the withdrawal in case of a recurrence of raids, and required military cooperation in protecting the border. See Wilson Papers, Ser. 2, November 11 and November 13.
[35] Lane to Secretary of State, November 12, 1916, 812.00/24314.
[36] Lane to Secretary of State, November 15, 1916, 812.00/19875.
[37] W.W. to Lansing, November 5, 1916, Wilson Papers, Ser. 2.

The American commissioners, the president, and his closest advisers persisted in the belief that the Mexican government could be bluffed. Lane returned to Atlantic City with the ultimatum he desired. On November 21, the commissioners met to discuss the proposed agreements on withdrawal and border control. Lane read into the minutes of the commission a reservation of the right of the United States to pursue marauders into Mexico. In accordance with the president's instructions the American commissioners formally requested an assurance from Carranza that, when the agreements on withdrawal and border control were approved, the Mexican commissioners would be allowed to discuss the other questions proposed by the American commissioners. Lane stated that when such an assurance had been received the American commissioners would submit the agreements to their government for approval.[38]

Cabrera objected both to the formal communication and to the reservation of rights. Lane told him that he was to blame for the insistence on formal assurances, and that as far as the American commissioners could tell, the Mexican government would discuss nothing until the American troops were withdrawn from Mexico. Discussion continued, and Cabrera finally declared, "I do not believe that you intend to withdraw the troops from Mexican soil until we have agreed to your proposals on the other questions which you desire to submit." He added that Carranza supported his views. Lane replied that if that was so then the negotiations should be broken off, "because, in our minds, questions such as the protection of life and property of foreigners were of far greater moment, not only to the United States but also to Mexico than the question of border control or withdrawal of American troops."[39] Lane then delivered Wilson's ultimatum:

The president's purpose and our purpose in coming into this conference was to draft with you a constructive program which would strengthen the Carranza Government, and would assist in the

---

[38] The formal communication, the reservation of the right to pursue, and the intention to submit the agreements only after receipt of assurances of further discussions are in Lane to W.W., December 1, 1916, Wilson Papers, Ser. 2. All official communications between the commissioners are in "American and Mexican Joint Commission Official Communications," prepared by L. S. Rowe, secretary to the American commissioners, n.d., 812.00/19861½.

[39] Lane to Secretary of State, November 21, 1916, 812.00/19983½.

restoration of order and prosperity in Mexico. This was our hope, and it is still our expectation.

I must inform you, in all solemnity, that the President's patience is at an end, and that he regards present conditions in Mexico as intolerable.

The plan of withdrawal of troops and border control which we are proposing to you this morning is but a step toward that larger constructive program which we confidently expect you to draw up with us in the same spirit of helpfulness and cooperation in which we approach these questions. Nothing short of this will satisfy either the Government or the people of the United States, and it is well for you to know this clearly and definitely at the present moment. We do not wish to do anything that will either hurt your pride or diminish your sovereignty. We have no designs on the integrity of your territory or your freedom of action in the determination of your national policy, but we are deeply and vitally interested in the fullfillment of your obligation to protect the lives and property of foreigners who have cast their lot with you, and in the satisfactory adjustment of every question which affects the cordial relations between the United States and your country. This can only be done through a policy characterized by frankness, cordiality, mutual trust and cooperation. If, however, you have reached the conclusion that you do not desire the cooperation of the United States, if you feel that you want to cut yourselves off completely, it is well for us to know this as soon as possible, as it will vitally affect our policy with reference to Mexico.[40]

At this point Cabrera declared that Mexico would have to "follow the road indicated by the United States." Lane again denied, with no sense of his own inconsistency, any desire to dictate to Mexico and concluded: "It is evident that many of the problems confronting you cannot be satisfactorily solved unless you have the friendship and the cooperation of the United States. It is up to you three gentlemen to determine whether Mexico is to have the benefit of such cooperation or, whether she desires to pursue a policy of isolation. This latter policy can only lead to but one result, namely the downfall of the Carranza Government with all the consequences that this will involve."[41] One of the Mexican commissioners, Alberto Pani, left the next day for Mexico City to communicate the agreement to Carranza. He was accompanied by David Lawrence.

Two days later Villa began his successful assault on the city

---

[40] *Ibid.*
[41] *Ibid.*

of Chihuahua. On November 24 the Mexican and American commissioners signed an agreement, ad referendum, for withdrawal of American troops and protection of the border. The terms called for withdrawal of American troops within forty days after approval of the agreement. Evacuation would begin when troops of the Mexican government had taken positions south of the American forces so as to guarantee protection of the border. Each of the governments assumed responsibility for protection of its side of the boundary.[42]

In December the president's primary concern was his note to the European belligerents asking them to define their war aims. Lansing sent the note on December 18. That day, the Mexican commissioners disclosed that Carranza rejected the agreement on withdrawal and border control and refused to allow discussion of internal matters until American troops withdrew from Mexico. Carranza found a major fault in the agreement itself: it permitted a conditional withdrawal that might be interrupted, and thus seemed to sanction foreign occupation. Carranza protested against the reservation of the right to enter Mexican territory and argued that an agreement could be reached that would obviate the need for such a reservation. "In brief," read the formal reply, "the Constitutionalist Government believes that any Agreement regarding the withdrawal of American troops from Mexican soil which may be reached, must be effected without implying consent, either express or tacit, with the present occupation, without sanctioning in the future the said occupation, and without authorizing or tolerating in the future a new expedition of American forces into Mexican territory."[43] The Mexican commissioners submitted a revised protocol that called for immediate, unconditional withdrawal.[44] The American commissioners refused to accept modifications in the original agreement. Then, softening their position somewhat, they assured the Mexican commissioners that if the agreement was approved and

---

[42] Lane to W.W., December 1, 1916, Wilson Papers, Ser. 2. Villa's successes again tempted the president and Generals Funston and Pershing to use force, but Villa was defeated south of Chihuahua on December 2 and the temptation passed. See Link, *Wilson: Campaigns for Progressivism and Peace,* pp. 332–333.

[43] Mexican Commissioners to American Commissioners, December 18, 1916, 812.00/19861½; copy in Fletcher Papers, General Correspondence, Box 4.

[44] Mexican Commissioners to American Commissioners, December 19, 1916, *ibid.*

if the assurance to discuss "other vital questions" was given, then the American government would not insist on settling those other questions before withdrawal was completed.[45] Lane immediately wrote the president that if the Mexicans responded favorably the conference might continue, if unfavorably the conference was at an end.[46] The American commissioners optimistically believed that Carranza would give in and authorize the immediate discussion of internal affairs.[47]

For several weeks the War Department had been recalling National Guard units from the border at the rate of about 6,000 men each week.[48] On December 23, Secretary Baker recommended to the president the complete recall of the Guard from the border. Baker made this proposal because he assumed that whatever the outcome of the Joint Commission's negotiations, Pershing's force would be withdrawn from Mexico. He wrote the president,

Whatever the outcome of the American-Mexican Commission's deliberations, the likelihood is that we will withdraw General Pershing's force from Mexico. That is to say, if the protocol is accepted this force will be withdrawn under its terms. If the protocol is not accepted, and the Commission's deliberations are terminated, it would seem that our attitude would have to be, having tried to help Mexico and failed to receive her cooperation, we were obliged to throw upon her the assumption of her full responsibilities as an independent government, retire to our own border, and hold her responsible for any encroachment upon our rights thereafter arising.[49]

Baker asserted that General Funston would be able to police the border adequately with regular troops and those of General Pershing. Only an occasional depredation in a remote place was to be feared, and no police force could protect against this. If intervention again became necessary in order to protect American citizens along the border, the forces under General Funston seemed adequate, and in any case the Guard could be called once more.

---

[45] Lane to Secretary of State, December 19, 1916, 812.00/20144½, and American Commissioners to Mexican Commissioners, December 19, 1916, 812.00/19861½.
[46] Lane to W.W., December 20, 1916, Wilson Papers, Ser. 2.
[47] L. S. Rowe to Fletcher, December 21, 1916, Fletcher Papers, General Correspondence, Box 4.
[48] Baker to W.W., December 9, 1916, Wilson Papers, Ser. 2.
[49] Baker to W.W., December 23, 1916, Wilson Papers, Ser. 2.

Baker's letter obscured his motives. There is no mention, for example, of the capacities of the Mexican government to protect the border or of a decline in unrest in Mexico, or of a desire to prepare for entry into the world war. Baker had relinquished, nonetheless, any hope of bargaining the withdrawal of Pershing's force in exchange for negotiated interference in Mexican affairs.

The reply of the Mexican commissioners, dated December 27, merely reiterated the old reasons why the American proposals were unacceptable. The Mexican commissioners were willing to continue the commission's work, but they left this decision up to the American government. As in the past, the Mexican commissioners indicated their willingness to discuss other questions as soon as American troops were withdrawn. Lane discussed the reply with the president on December 29. In a memorandum to the American commissioners on January 1, L. S. Rowe, their secretary, recommended withdrawal of Pershing's force and the dispatch of Ambassador Henry P. Fletcher. The presence of American troops, Rowe stated, had become an obstacle rather than a catalyst to better relations with Mexico.[50] On January 3 the American commissioners dispatched a letter to their Mexican colleagues and a report to President Wilson. The communication to the Mexican commissioners simply reviewed the course of negotiations and expressed the hope that the prolonged conferences might not, in the end, prove fruitless.[51] The commissioners reported to the president that no agreement satisfactory to Mexico and the United States could be reached on withdrawal or border control. They recommended that the president unilaterally withdraw American forces from Mexico. With this impediment removed, it might prove possible through direct negotiations with the Mexican government to deal wih the questions of vital concern to the United States government. The most important of these, in the commissioners' view, was the protection of the life and property of foreigners in Mexico. They declared:

The careful study of the mass of information submitted to us

---

[50] Rowe to American Commissioners, January 1, 1917, copy in Fletcher Papers, General Correspondence, Box 4. See also Rowe to Secretary of State, January 4, 1917, 812.00/24323. At this point even Canova was recommending withdrawal. See Canova to Secretary of State, January 3, 1917, 812.00/20525.

[51] American Commissioners to Mexican Commissioners, January 3, 1917, copy in Fletcher Papers, General Correspondence, Box 4.

through official and other channels, has created in our minds the
deepest misgivings with reference to the course of events in Mexico.
We have eagerly searched for indications that the revolutionary
government was fulfilling the avowed purposes of its platform,
but this has revealed to us most disquieting economic, financial,
sanitary and social conditions, which involve untold misery and
suffering for the masses of the people. Furthermore, the proceedings
of the Constitutional Convention now in session at Queretaro indicate a fixed and settled purpose to place in the organic law of
the republic provisions which tend to make the position of foreigners in Mexico intolerable, which open the door to confiscation
of legally acquired property and which carry with them the germs
of serious international friction.

It is this grave menace that creates in us the deepest anxiety
and a desire no less insistent to have these matters taken up with
the least possible delay.[52]

The president was unhappy with the report. When he met
with Lane, Gray, and Mott he implied they had not made any
constructive suggestions for future policy. Gray and Mott resented Wilson's reaction and concluded that he had lost the
generosity of spirit toward Mexico that he had displayed in his
article in *Ladies' Home Journal*. Gray and Mott wanted to
make public the recommendations to withdraw Pershing and
to send Ambassador Fletcher, but the president flatly refused
and instructed Lane to say nothing except that they had submitted a report.[53]

Wilson lived under the strain of his efforts to bring peace in
Europe, and he undoubtedly resented Carranza's intransigence.
Still, there was nothing to do but swallow the pill. On January
15 the Joint Commission met for its final session. The American
commissioners proposed adjournment and a recommendation
to both governments to reestablish full diplomatic relations so
that further negotiations might begin to secure the protection
of foreign lives and property, the establishment of an International Claims Commission, and the elimination of causes of con-

---

[52] American Commissioners to W.W., January 3, 1917, copy in Fletcher
Papers, General Correspondence, Box 4. For information about some
of the "other channels" of information and an account of some of the
efforts of American businessmen to influence the American Commissioners, see the Diary of Chandler P. Anderson, November 15, 19, December 26, 29, 1916, and January 3, 1917, The Papers of Chandler
P. Anderson, Library of Congress, Accession 5996, 2, Box 2 (hereinafter
cited as Anderson Papers).
[53] Lane to Lansing, January 4, 1917, 812.00/24733.

flict between Mexico and the United States. The Mexican commissioners refused to agree unless the American commissioners would recommend the withdrawal of all American troops. Lane, Gray, and Mott refused, in accordance with instructions from the president. The commission adjourned sine die. In their final report the American commissioners recommended the immediate reestablishment of full diplomatic relations in order to facilitate consideration of the protection of foreigners in Mexico and the other matters touching Mexico's internal affairs.[54] Three days after the final meeting of the Joint Commission, Baker directed Funston to inform Pershing that his command would be withdrawn from Mexico "at an early date."[55] Pershing began withdrawing on January 31, and the last American soldier crossed the border on February 5.[56]

EXCHANGE OF AMBASSADORS

For a time in December 1916 it appeared that Carranza would yield to the American demands and allow his representatives to discuss Mexico's internal affairs in the Joint Commission.[57] The rapprochement between Mexico and the United States became entangled in Mexican internal politics, however, and no agreement was possible.[58]

---

[54] Lane to W.W., January 16, 1917, 812.00/19861½.
[55] Baker to W.W., January 18, 1917, Wilson Papers, Ser. 2, forwarding copy of orders to General Funston.
[56] *Foreign Relations, 1917,* p. 908.
[57] David Lawrence reported on December 2 and on December 6 that Carranza would probably accept the American proposal with only minor revisions. See Thurston to Secretary of State, December 2, 1916, 812.00/20005, and Thurston to Secretary of State, December 6, 1916, 812.00/20029. A confidential agent, who signed his dispatches to Polk with the initial "M," also reported on December 6 that Carranza would sign the protocol "within a day or two," and that Carranza now realized that "it was essential not to antagonize the United States but to accept its good offices if his government was to stand any show of maintaining itself." Thurston to Secretary of State, December 6, 1916, 812.00/20025. I have been unable to identify "M." His reports indicated he had access to the highest Mexican officials and was well versed in Mexican affairs. His identity may be contained in the Polk Papers.
[58] "M" attributed Carranza's rejection of the protocol to pressure from the Mexican military leadership who desired to prolong the threat of American intervention in order to strengthen their control of the government and the constitutional convention in Querétaro. See Thurston to Secretary of State, December 13, 1916, 812.00/20075, and Thurston to Secretary of State, December 17, 1917, 812.00/20090.

The desire of important Mexican leaders to block a rapprochement with the United States was matched by the equally ardent desire of a number of influential Americans who desired to block recognition of Carranza's government until certain provisions of the new Mexican constitution aimed at foreign interests had been removed. This included the committee to protect American-owned properties in Mexico represented by the lobbyists Chandler P. Anderson, former counselor of the State Department, Frederic R. Kellogg, and Delbert J. Haff. Anderson, Kellogg, and Haff acted on behalf of some of the largest American interests in Mexico, including those of H. P. Whitney, John Hays Hammond, Bonbright and Company, E. L. Doheny, and the greatest mining, smelting, and rubber interests in Mexico.[59] On November 19 the committee had submitted a memorandum to the American members of the Joint Mexican-American Commission. The memorandum urged the United States to withhold recognition from the Mexican government if it adopted a constitution harmful to foreign rights and properties in Mexico.[60] On December 26, Anderson and Kellogg submitted a second memorandum to the American commissioners, stating that the constitution under consideration at Querétaro, particularly Articles 27, 28, and 33, would "incalculably and unjustifiably damage all foreign rights in Mexico." Anderson and Kellogg urged that the United States declare (1) that all steps taken under Articles 27, 28, and 33 were disapproved by the United States and would not be recognized as valid; (2) that the United States would not acquiesce in direct or indirect confiscation of foreign interests in Mexico; and (3) "that the United States Government will not accord its recognition to any Mexican government which may be elected or constituted upon the basis of such an anti-foreign and confiscatory program. . . ."[61] Anderson used his access to Lansing, Polk, and Canova to press the claims of his clients.[62] On January 9, 1917, Charles B. Parker, representing American interests in Mexico, was instructed by Lansing in al-

---

[59] See Diary of Chandler P. Anderson, November 15, 1916, Anderson Papers, Accession 5996, 2, Box 2.
[60] Discussed in Frederic R. Kellogg and Chandler P. Anderson to American Commissioners, "Memorandum Concerning the New Proposed Constitution of Mexico," dated December 26, 1916, 812.011/4.
[61] *Ibid.*
[62] See Anderson's Diary for December 29, 1916, January 3, 1917, and January 22, 1917, Anderson Papers, Accession 5996, 2, Box 2.

most the exact words of the committee's memorandum to protest to the Mexican government against Articles 27 and 33 and to demand that these articles be expunged or altered so as not to affect the treaty rights of Americans and all foreigners. The Mexicans went on with their constitution making, and on January 22, Parker was again instructed with the committee's words to protest against the provisions of the constitution affecting foreign interests:

You will immediately bring the foregoing [provisions of Articles 27 and 33] to the attention of General Carranza and say that the above mentioned provisions seem to indicate a proposed policy toward foreigners which is fraught with possible grave consequences affecting the commercial and the political relations of Mexico with other nations. You will point out that the Government of the United States cannot, of course, acquiesce in any direct or indirect confiscation of foreign owned properties in Mexico. You will further say that the Government of United States, with a view to avoiding the possibility of the disturbance of hitherto pleasant relations existing between the two Governments, and with a view to avoiding future serious difficulties with any government organized under the proposed constitution, earnestly desires General Carranza to give these matters his careful personal consideration.[63]

Predictably, Leon Canova, the chief of the State Department's Mexican division, lent his voice to those opposing the exchange of Ambassadors. On January 17 he warned Secretary Lansing to prepare for a clash with Mexico even if Ambassador Fletcher were sent immediately to Mexico City.[64] And on January 25, Canova submitted a memorandum describing the Mexican constitution as arbitrary and illegal and stressing the weakness of Carranza's government.[65]

The president had nonetheless decided to send Fletcher to Mexico City, and, toward the end of January, Fletcher began to prepare for his departure.[66] He left for Mexico City on February

---

[63] Lansing to Parker, January 22, 1917, 812.011/11a. Polk drafted this telegram. See Anderson's Diary, January 22, 1917, Anderson Papers, Accession 5996, 2, Box 2.

[64] Canova to Secretary of State, January 17, 1917, 812.00/20673.

[65] Canova to Secretary of State, January 25, 1917, 812.00/20674.

[66] On January 31, Parker was asked to find out the precise form for Fletcher's letters of credence. See U.S., National Archives, General Records of the Department of State, Record Group 59, Personal Records of Diplomatic Officers, Lansing to Parker, January 31, 1917, 123 F 63/120a, hereinafter cited by number and date. Lansing had informed the Mexican government in December 1915 of the intention to appoint

10, arriving on February 17. Before he could present his credentials, the publication of a telegram from the German foreign secretary, Arthur Zimmermann, to the German minister in Mexico shocked the American people and moved the United States closer to war with Germany.

Fletcher. The Mexican government had approved, and Fletcher's appointment was confirmed by the Senate on February 25, 1916. Fletcher was immediately instructed to return home and he took his oath of office and left Chile on March 9, the day of Villa's attack on Columbus. The exchange of ambassadors was delayed for a year as a consequence of Villa's raid and the dispatch of the Pershing expedition. See 123 F 63/111a, 113a, and 117.

The Entente powers and the United States had long feared Mexican involvement with Germany. In late October 1916, Sir Cecil Spring-Rice told Lansing that rumor indicated German submarines were active in the Gulf of Mexico. The allies, warned Spring-Rice, would take drastic action if it appeared that Mexico was furnishing assistance to Germany. Lansing instructed Parker to impress upon Carranza the necessity to prevent the use of Mexican territory as a base of operations for belligerent warships. "General Carranza must realize," Lansing warned, "that the least violation of Mexican neutrality in this connection can only have the most far reaching and disastrous results."[1] Lansing sent similar instructions to Secretary Lane in Atlantic City with the Joint Mexican-American Commission.[2] The Mexican government replied indignantly and equivocally. The operation of submarines in the Gulf could not constitute grounds for drastic action, the reply stated, for German submarines had entered American ports and sunk ships in American territorial waters without this causing any strain in British-American relations. Moreover, if the British government desired to communicate with the Mexican government it should do so directly.[3] The United States government apologized and observed that it had merely transmitted the information for what it was worth and was surprised at the Mexican government's response.

THE ZIMMERMANN TELEGRAM

There was reason for surprise. The Mexican government probably reacted so vehemently because it had nearly been caught in the act of making an offer of submarine bases to Germany.[4] In November, Carranza indicated a desire to cooperate with Germany and suggested, through Heinrich von Eckhardt, Ger-

---

[1] U.S., National Archives, General Records of the Department of State, Record Group 59, World War I and Its Termination, 1910–1929, Lansing to Parker, October 27, 1916, 763.72111/4185a, hereinafter cited by number and date only.
[2] Lansing to Lane, October 27, 1916, 763.72111/4185b.
[3] Parker to Secretary of State, November 4, 1916, 763.72111/4205.
[4] Friedrich Katz, *Deutschland, Díaz und die mexikanische Revolution, die deutsche Politik in Mexiko 1870–1920* (Berlin: Deutscher Verlag der Wissenschaften, 1964), cited in Link, *Wilson: Campaigns for Progressivism and Peace*, pp. 433–436.

man minister to Mexico, that Mexico would offer Germany submarine bases. The German government politely refused Carranza's overture. But when the decision was taken on January 9, 1917, to initiate unrestricted submarine warfare, the idea of Mexican-German cooperation was revived rather cynically in Berlin. On January 16 the German foreign secretary, Arthur Zimmermann, instructed von Eckhardt to propose an alliance between Germany and Mexico should the United States declare war on Germany as a result of the initiation of unrestricted submarine warfare on February 1.

The British government intercepted the telegram, which had been sent to Mexico through the German ambassador in Washington, and immediately began to decipher it with the aid of captured German code books.[5] The British foreign secretary, Arthur Balfour, gave Ambassador Page the decoded telegram in London on February 23, and on February 24 at 8:30 in the evening Page's telegram with the Zimmermann text arrived at the State Department. The text transmitted by Page read:

We intend to begin on the first of February unrestricted submarine warfare. We shall endeavor in spite of this to keep the United States of America neutral. In the event of this not succeeding, we make Mexico a proposal of alliance on the following basis: make war together, make peace together, generous financial support and an understanding on our part that Mexico is to reconquer the lost territory in Texas, New Mexico, and Arizona. The settlement in detail is left to you. You will inform the President of the above most secretly as soon as the outbreak of war with the United States of America is certain and add the suggestion that he should, on his own initiative, invite Japan to immediate adherence and at the same time mediate between Japan and ourselves. Please call the President's attention to the fact that the ruthless employment of our submarines now offers the prospect of compelling England in a few months to make peace. Signed ZIMMERMANN.[6]

President Wilson was indignant when Polk showed him the telegram, but he did not swerve from his plan to preserve Amer-

---

[5] For an account of the interception of the telegram and the circumstances of its decoding and disclosure to the American government, see Barbara Tuchman, *The Zimmermann Telegram* (New York: Dell, Laurel Edition, 1965).

[6] W. H. Page to Secretary of State, February 24, 1917, 862.20212/69. The original text is in *Official German Documents Relating to the War,* 2 vols. (New York: Oxford University Press, 1923), 2: 1337.

ica's neutrality by arming her merchant ships. On February 26 he asked Congress for authority to "supply our merchant ships with defensive arms, should that become necessary, and with the means of using them, and to employ any other instrumentalities or methods that may be necessary and adequate to protect our ships and our people in their legitimate and peaceful pursuits on the seas."[7] Nor did the president swerve from his subordination of Mexican-American relations to the war in Europe. The shape of the policy adopted by the president after the failure of the Joint Mexican-American Commission now began to appear. De facto recognition would be completed by the exchange of ambassadors, and the United States would protest any measures harmful to American interests in Mexico and attempt to commit the Mexican government to protect the rights of foreigners. Later, if the United States should become involved in the war in Europe, the American government would insist on Mexican neutrality. The president would go no farther.

Polk, acting for Secretary Lansing, who was still on vacation in White Sulphur Springs, informed Fletcher of the Zimmermann telegram on February 26. Fletcher was instructed:

You will at once see General Carranza or, if that cannot be arranged immediately, the Minister of Foreign Affairs. Read to him the substance of the German note and state that it is probable that the contents of this note will be made public in the United States immediately and suggest as your personal opinion that it might be well for the Mexican Government to make some comment. MERELY FOR YOUR GUIDANCE. The Department does not feel that it can properly withhold from the public the text of this German message. Its publication, however, may cause great consternation and it is possible, unfortunately, that, with the intense feeling aroused, there may be included a degree of uncertainty in regard to the attitude of Mexico unless the Mexican Government can make some statement which might be published simultaneously tending to show their disinterestedness.[8]

Fletcher saw the Mexican foreign minister, Cándido Aguilar, the same day. Aguilar denied any knowledge of the German proposal and stated that if such representations had been made, Eckhardt must have made them directly to Carranza. Carranza was then in Jalisco, and his absence from the capital had not only prevented Fletcher from presenting his credentials but had

---

[7] *Public Papers: The New Democracy,* 2: 431–432.
[8] Polk to American Embassy, Mexico, February 26, 1917, 11 A.M., 862.20212/70A.

deprived Eckhardt of an opportunity to make the German offer directly to Carranza. On February 5, Zimmermann had instructed Eckhardt to propose the alliance at once if there was no risk that the United States would learn of the negotiations.[9] The German minister had hesitated, and then on February 20 had broached the plan to Aguilar. Aguilar responded warmly and immediately took up the proposal with the Japanese minister.[10] Eckhardt renewed the discussions on February 26,[11] but on that day Fletcher made his query and revealed that the United States knew about the German offer.

By Wednesday morning, February 28, the president had decided to publish the Zimmermann telegram. At six that evening, Lansing released the story to the Associated Press. On the same day Lansing had also asked the Japanese ambassador in Washington what he knew of the German proposal. The ambassador replied that the proposal was "ridiculous" and that Japan could not be induced to consider it.[12] Ambassador Fletcher reported from Mexico City that he was leaving with Aguilar to meet Carranza at Guadalajara to discuss Mexico's attitude toward the German offer.[13]

The story broke in banner headlines across the United States on March 1 while Fletcher was on his way to meet Carranza. Two days later Zimmermann admitted that the telegram was genuine.[14] At noon the same day, March 3, Ambassador Fletcher presented his credentials to Carranza during a brief ceremony at the first chief's palace in Guadalajara. Carranza invited Fletcher to accompany him on the presidential train to Lake Chapala to attend a fiesta in Carranza's honor. During the journey Fletcher had a long talk with Carranza about the whole subject of Mexican-American relations. The president's party stayed at Chapala until March 8, when Carranza invited Fletcher to accompany him as far as Irapuato. Fletcher accepted and the two enjoyed another long conversation. Fletcher left Carranza's train at a small station en route and proceeded to

---

[9] *Official German Documents,* 2: 1338.
[10] Tuchman, *Zimmermann Telegram,* p. 160.
[11] *Ibid.,* p. 158.
[12] Lansing to American Embassy, Tokyo, March 1, 1917, 862.20212/76B.
[13] Fletcher to Secretary of State, February 28, 1917, 862.20212/74.
[14] See Lansing's Diary, March 4, 1917, Lansing Papers, for his account of the events leading up to the publication of the German note and his delight at Zimmermann's admission of the genuineness of the proposal.

Mexico City on another special train, arriving the evening of March 9.[15]

Carranza was very cautious during these extended discussions with the American ambassador. He would say only that Mexico had received no proposition of alliance from Germany which, of course, allowed him to tell the truth without admitting whether Eckhardt had discussed the proposal with him or Aguilar. Carranza turned the discussion to a proposal he had made on February 11 that the neutral powers offer their good offices to the belligerents and, if refused, force the war to a stop by embargoing all shipments to belligerents. At one point Fletcher asked him directly what he would do if Germany proposed an alliance against the United States. Carranza avoided giving a direct answer, saying only that Mexico desired to avoid becoming entangled in the war and returning to his peace plan. Fletcher doubted that Mexico would accept an alliance with Germany and believed that Carranza withheld an unequivocal reply in order to induce the United States to accept the plan for a conference of neutrals.[16]

Carranza and Aguilar pressed Fletcher to request the American government to lift the embargo on arms shipments to Mexico. Fletcher turned this to his own purposes by saying that unless Carranza would clarify what Mexico would do in case of war between Germany and the United States it would be very hard for President Wilson to allow the exportation of arms. During the return trip from Chapala, Fletcher drafted in Spanish a telegram to be sent to the State Department giving Carranza's views on the conference of neutrals and concluding with the categorical statement that Mexico would reject any proposal of alliance from Germany. Carranza refused to agree to this. He reiterated that no alliance had been proposed and asked for an answer to his peace proposal. Aguilar told Fletcher that if circumstances changed Carranza would define his position clearly. Fletcher understood this to mean that in case of war between the United States and Germany, Carranza would declare a strict neutrality.[17] Aguilar told Fletcher that in the mean-

---

[15] Fletcher to Secretary of State, March 13, 1917, 123 F 63/149.
[16] Fletcher to Secretary of State, March 10, 1917, 862.20212/89.
[17] Fletcher to Secretary of State, March 13, 1917, 862.20212/119, and Fletcher Papers, General Correspondence, Box 4. This is Fletcher's detailed report on his meetings with Carranza in regard to the Zimmermann note.

time he would be willing to transact any diplomatic business
that might arise. Aguilar declared, as Mexican officials had frequently declared, that the Mexican government would not give
a retroactive effect to its decrees, to the constitution, or to the
laws implementing the constitution.[18]

MEXICAN NEUTRALITY

It is tempting to view Carranza's peace plan as evidence of
the pro-German attitude of the Mexican government. In his
note of February 11 to the United States, Norway, Sweden,
Denmark, and Switzerland, Carranza proposed that the belligerent powers be invited

in common accord and on the basis of absolutely perfect equality
on either side, to bring this war to an end either by their own
effort or by availing themselves of the good offices or friendly
mediation of all the countries which would jointly extend that
invitation. If within a reasonable time peace could not be restored
by these means, the neutral countries would then take the necessary
measures to reduce the conflagration to its narrowest limit, by refusing any kind of implements to the belligerents and suspending
commercial relations with the warring nations until the said conflagration shall have been smothered.[19]

Any such action on the part of the United States would have
favored Germany and drastically weakened the Entente powers,
particularly Great Britain. On the other hand, the chief concern
of Carranza and the other Mexican leaders was not to strengthen
Germany but to protect Mexico against the United States. It
seems likely, therefore, that Carranza sought to entangle the
American government in a conference of neutrals in order to
keep the United States out of war and thus to remove all
pretexts for invading Mexico, whether to protect the property
of citizens of the Entente governments or to guarantee the avail-
ability of Mexican oil for war purposes.

Lansing gave the administration's reply on March 16, less than
a week before the president decided to ask Congress for a declaration of war.[20] Despite the efforts of the United States, the

---

[18] Lansing to W.W., March 7, 1917, forwarding a dispatch from Fletcher,
Wilson Papers, Ser. 2.
[19] Ramón P. de Negri to Secretary of State, February 12, 1917,
763.72119/468. The United States government forwarded this note on
behalf of the Mexican government to the neutral powers in Europe.
[20] See Link, "The Decision for War," *Wilson: Campaigns for Progressivism and Peace,* pp. 390–431.

reply declared, the war in Europe had intensified. The United States had been compelled to sever relations with Germany because of its unrestricted submarine warfare. The note continued:

To render the situation still more acute, the Government of the United States has unearthed a plot laid by the Government dominating the Central Powers to embroil not only the Government and people of Mexico, but also the Government and people of Japan in war with the United States. At the time this plot was conceived, the United States was at peace with the Government and people of the German Empire, and German officials and German subjects were not only enjoying but abusing the liberties and privileges freely accorded to them on American soil and under American protection.[21]

For these reasons the government of the United States could not participate in Carranza's proposal. Carranza replied the next day that joint action of the neutrals would be fruitless without the cooperation of the United States. The first chief offered the good offices of the Mexican government in any way they might be utilized to restore diplomatic relations between Germany and the United States or in any other way to prevent hostilities between the two nations. The Mexican reply stressed that the offer was made not to help Germany but to preserve peace in the Americas.[22]

On April 4, two days after the president's war message to Congress, General Obregón gave Fletcher a look at the viewpoint that had apparently prevailed in the counsels of the Mexican government. Fletcher reported to Lansing: "General Obregon in the course of a personal talk with me this afternoon said that he regarded the proposition of a Mexican alliance with Germany as absurd and that he believed that the Mexican Government, after six years of internal warfare, should devote itself to the pacification and reorganization of the country and would be very foolish to entangle itself with an European power

---

[21] Lansing to Negri, March 16, 1917, 763.72119/468. For the first three years of the war the United States allowed the German government to use American telegraphic facilities without censorship or close scrutiny. The Germans sent the proposal for war against the United States over American telegraph lines.

[22] Fletcher to Secretary of State, March 17, 1917, 763.72119/513. The United States warmly thanked Carranza for his offer on April 21, after Carranza had declared Mexico's neutrality. See Fletcher to Secretary of State, April 11, 1917, 763.72119/548, and Lansing to American Embassy, Mexico, April 21, 1917, 763.72119/513.

which would undoubtedly claim payment for services rendered."[23]

The Wilson administration continued to distrust Carranza's government. Three problems in particular troubled Mexican-American relations: Mexican oil, Mexican neutrality, and the new Mexican constitution with its provisions that threatened foreign interests. On April 10, Fletcher reported that the Mexican government contemplated prohibiting the export of petroleum.[24] Lansing immediately took up the question with the president. If the Mexican government attempted to prohibit shipment of oil from Tampico, Lansing observed, "I see no way but to occupy the territory with troops or else to allow the British naval forces to do so, even though it would be a technical violation of the Monroe Doctrine."[25] The president realized the importance of Mexican oil to the war effort, but he also recognized Mexico's rights. He replied to Lansing: "Unfortunately, the Mexican government has, no doubt, a legal right to prohibit exports; and I feel quite clear that we could not make such action on its part a justification for invasion and (virtual) war." His solution was, if the Mexican government attempted to halt exports, to allow the British to take control of the oil fields:

We have more than once allowed European governments to oblige Latin American governments to meet their financial obligations by a show of force, without deeming their action a violation of the Monroe Doctrine, because it involved no attempt at political control. The violations of British rights at Tampico might, on the same principle, without any disrespect to us, be prevented by a show of naval force on the part of the British government. In this instance, in view of the circumstances of the war, such action on their part would seem to be justified by necessity if not by the consideration that such a policy as they would be seeking to prevent on the part of the Mexican authorities, not being justified by the economic necessities of Mexico, would seem to be directed against Great Britain in hostile spirit.

Wilson instructed Lansing to inform the British government: "We would feel justified in leaving them free to take the neces-

---

[23] Fletcher to Secretary of State, April 4, 1917, 862.20212/177.
[24] U.S., National Archives, General Records of the Department of State, Record Group 59, Commercial Relations of Mexico: Export Trade, Embargo, Fletcher to Secretary of State, April 10, 1917, 600.129/7.
[25] Lansing to W.W., April 11, 1917, *ibid.,* and R. S. Baker Papers, State Department folder, Ser. 1, Box 11.

sary steps to safeguard their indispensable sources of oil supply against inimical action by the Mexicans."[26]

Fletcher took up the possibility of an embargo on Mexican oil with Aguilar on April 11. Aguilar replied in a highly conciliatory way and emphatically assured Fletcher that the Mexican government would not stop the export of oil. On the contrary, Aguilar declared that Carranza desired to "maintain and consolidate" friendly relations between the United States and Mexico.[27] Fletcher observed in his report of an interview with Luis Cabrera, Minister of Finance, that the Mexican government could be expected to take whatever advantage it could of the existing situation. He recommended that the best policy for the United States would be to help the Mexican government,

and to act as if we relied upon their friendly neutrality and good faith. . . . I think the advantages to be gained by pursuing this policy far outweigh such slight risks as may be involved. I have strong hopes that if we avail ourselves of every occasion to show a friendly disposition toward this Government, and help them whenever possible, that there will be a change of popular sentiment in Mexico, and that they will come to realize that their true and lasting interest is in friendly relations with the United States.[28]

Lansing took a considerably harsher view of the conduct of the Mexican government, particularly of its pro-German tendencies. He desired, for example, to bring Guatemala and Honduras into the war as allies of the United States in order to have a "constant check" on Mexico should the Mexican government's actions benefit Germany.[29] On April 18 he warned the president that the pro-German attitudes of the Mexican military, which he believed controlled the Mexican government, could involve the United States in war with Mexico over the Tampico oil fields.[30] Wilson reacted calmly. He wondered which party was

---

[26] W.W. to Lansing, April 11, 1917, 600.129/12½, and R. S. Baker Papers, State Department folder, Ser. 1, Box 11.
[27] Fletcher to Secretary of State, April 11, 1917, 763.72/3793, and Fletcher to Secretary of State, April 11, 1917, 763.72/3909.
[28] Fletcher to Secretary of State, April 11, 1917, 763.72/3909.
[29] See Leavell to Lansing, April 10, 1917, relaying a proposal of alliance from the Guatemalan government, and Lansing to W.W., April 12, 1917, recommending that the United States accept, both in 763.72/3773.
[30] U.S., National Archives, General Records of the Department of State, Record Group 59, Relations between the United States and Mexico, 1910–1929, Lansing to W.W., April 18, 1917, 711.12/43A, hereinafter cited by date and number; and R. S. Baker Papers, State Department folder, Ser. 1, Box 11.

anti-American, Carranza's or the military, and doubted the reliability of his information. Moreover, he was concerned to maintain the position of the United States as the defender of self-determination. He instructed Lansing: "The United States cannot afford to be too 'practical.' She is the leading champion of the right of self-government and of political independence everywhere. Only the most extraordinary circumstances of arbitrary injustice on the part of the Mexican government would make me feel that we had the right to take control at Tampico or at the Tehuantapec R.R. [the other trouble spot raised by Lansing]."[31]

On April 15, during an address before the Mexican congress, Carranza declared that Mexico would observe strict neutrality in the war. Two weeks before Carranza's declaration, Fletcher had asked to be instructed to inform Carranza that in the event of war between the United States and Germany the United States would rely on Mexico's neutrality.[32] Lansing forwarded Fletcher's request to the president on April 18.[33] The president approved the recommendations, although Carranza had already declared Mexico neutral. He took the occasion to vent his resentment toward Carranza: "All that Carranza has said and done shows his intense resentment towards this Administration. One could have written the reported conversation between Aguilar and any one of the representatives of other governments of whom Mr. Fletcher speaks oneself without difficulty after living with that pedantic ass the First Chief through all these anxious months."[34] Lansing instructed Fletcher to inform Carranza that the United States relied on Mexico's neutrality and expected the Mexican government to prevent Mexico from becoming a base for hostile acts against the United States. Lansing singled out German subjects in Mexico and warned Carranza to prevent their activities from compromising Mexico's neutrality in any way.[35] Fletcher discussed these matters with Carranza on April 25. He reported that Carranza realized the necessity of maintaining a strict neutrality and was willing to act against any acts

---

[31] W.W. to Lansing, April 19, 1917, 711.12/43½, and R. S. Baker Papers, State Department folder, Ser. 1, Box 11, on the president's personal typewriter.
[32] Fletcher to Secretary of State, March 30, 1917, 711.12/36.
[33] Lansing to W.W., April 18, 1917, ibid.
[34] W.W. to Lansing, April 19, 1917, 711.12/36½.
[35] Lansing to American Embassy, Mexico, April 21, 1917, 862.20212/270a.

by German subjects that might compromise Mexican neutrality.[36]

Last, doubts about how the Mexican government would implement the Querétaro constitution continued to trouble Mexican-American relations. Ambassador Fletcher prompted an intensive discussion of the problems connected with the constitution by asking whether he should attend Carranza's inauguration.[37] In a memorandum to Polk on April 19 the counselor of the State Department made the following points. The new Mexican constitution not only contained retroactive provisions, but certain sections seemed to be confiscatory. Carranza had given no binding assurances about these questions, and the attempt to implement the constitution retroactively would probably be made. The United States should avoid granting *de jure* recognition until certain that American interests would be protected. The counselor recommended that the American government try to have the Mexican constitution amended and tell Carranza that his government would not be recognized until this was done. The counselor advised against Fletcher attending the inaugural and said that if Fletcher were allowed to attend, he should inform Carranza that the United States maintained its opposition to the confiscation of or discrimination against the rights and interests of American citizens in Mexico.[38]

Lansing sent a recommendation to the president suggesting that Fletcher be allowed to attend the inaugural ceremonies. If necessary, he advised, a statement could be sent to the Mexican government along the lines of the counselor's memo. Lansing believed, however, that employing the words "de facto" in addressing the Mexican government after the inauguration would remove any indication that Fletcher's presence constituted formal recognition. Lansing believed that formal recognition should be avoided because of the war and because of the threat to American interests implicit in the new constitution. He advised the president, "Of course the advantage to be gained in preserving the *de facto* status is that the obligation to obey any mandate relating to neutrality issued by such a Government is far less than if it is *de jure*. Against an obligation of that sort we should endeavor to guard ourselves as far as possible. Furthermore it

---

[36] Fletcher to Secretary of State, April 25, 1917, 862.20212/273.
[37] Fletcher to Secretary of State, April 10, 1917, 123 F 63/151. Fletcher repeated his request for instructions on April 28, 1917, 123 F 63/153.
[38] Counselor to Polk, April 19, 1917, Wilson Papers, Ser. 2.

would be consistent with the reservation of rights improperly impaired by the new Constitution."[39]

Accordingly, Fletcher was permitted to attend the inauguration and was warned not to say or do anything that implied *de jure* recognition had been granted. The message authorizing his attendance carried secret instructions that defined American policy toward Mexico for the duration of World War I:

Strictly confidential. For your guidance: every thing should be done to hold the confidence and friendship of Carranza at this time. Although it may be impossible to accept those provisions of the new constitution which are in contravention of the international obligations of Mexico, it is desired for reasons of high policy not to force an issue on these questions. They will be met when they arise.

The Department relies upon your every effort to prevent matters of vital military importance coming to a head, in particular as regards the withdrawal of United States ships of war now in Mexican waters.[40]

The United States wanted peace with Mexico while it fought a war with Germany. The president had no intention of allowing the Mexican government to implement the new constitution as it wished, if that meant the confiscation or arbitrary reduction of American interests. Caught between his ideal of constitutional government and his passion for the Mexican people, the president desired to avoid intervention, to get on with the war against Germany, and to protect American interests in Mexico as well. By a judicious blend of threats and constant diplomatic pressure over the next four years the president succeeded far better in blocking the consummation of revolutionary reform than he had in controlling the course of revolutionary violence.

---

[39] Lansing to W.W., April 25, 1917, Wilson Papers, Ser. 2.

[40] Lansing to Fletcher, April 28, 1917, 123 F 63/151.

Conclusion

In responding to the Mexican Revolution, Taft sought to protect American lives and property, to maintain American neutrality, and to allow Congress to decide whether to use force. He escaped a profound crisis in Mexican-American relations largely because revolutionary civil war in Mexico developed only after he had left office. Taft based his foreign policy on protection of American interests, and in Mexico that required protection of the disproportionate share Americans had acquired in Mexico's economy. He successfully rationalized nonintervention by stressing that intervention would provoke the very destruction of American lives and property he desired to prevent. Had he remained in office with only this standard to guide his response, it seems likely that the much greater disorder and destruction that followed Madero's overthrow would have persuaded Taft either to intervene militarily against the Constitutionalists or to provide Huerta with the military and financial assistance the dictator needed to destroy the revolutionaries. Taft set order above reform and, though his policy appeared patient and farsighted in a time of relative tranquillity in Mexico, his motives reflected intolerance for revolutionary change that could well have involved the United States directly or indirectly in a war against the Mexican Revolution. The warnings about the costs of a war against another people that had been used successfully to rationalize noninvolvement might have been forgotten, as they were after 1954 in regard to Vietnam. Taft and the "party of order" he represented in the United States doubted the ability of Mexicans to achieve democratic government.[1] According to this view, Mexico was politically underdeveloped and suited only for coercive dictatorship. Taft naturally preferred a dictatorship of the right. As long as the level of revolutionary violence and destruction remained low, he was content to rely on neutrality, nonintervention, and diplomacy to accomplish his objectives.

Taft's greatest mistake was his failure to control Henry Lane Wilson, the American ambassador in Mexico City. By late January 1913, the president and his chief advisers in the State Department possessed indisputable evidence that Wilson disagreed

---

[1] The term "party of order" is from Arno J. Mayer, *Political Origins of the New Diplomacy, 1917–1918* (New Haven, Conn.: Yale University Press, 1959).

with the administration and was trying to use American policy
to drive Madero out of office. The logical step was to replace
the ambassador with someone less headstrong. But Taft and
Knox were playing their own game, designed to maintain American preponderance in Mexico. Toward this end Knox granted
Wilson permission to keep Mexican opinion in "a salutary equilibrium between a proper degree of wholesome fear and a dangerous and exaggerated apprehension."[2] These instructions arrived three days before Madero's arrest and five days before
his murder. Taft and Knox would not authorize the ambassador
to meddle in Mexican politics and to play kingmaker. But they
would not expressly forbid it either. Their conduct suggests they
hoped the ambassador could produce a peaceful Mexico and
a "friendly" government. If he had succeeded, it would have
been their victory. If he failed, the blame was his, for they had
not explicitly approved his course.[3]

If it was beyond the ability of the president to prevent revolution in Mexico, it was within his power to control the conduct
of his ambassador. By declining to exercise this power Taft
helped to defeat his own policy. He sought stability in Mexico
as a means to the end of protecting American lives and property.
Allowing Ambassador Wilson freedom of action actually speeded
the course of the Mexican Revolution toward civil war and
the confiscation of foreign investments.

Taft's policy possessed the well-defined objectives and rather
strict limits on the use of force peculiar to his understanding
of the national interest and his approach to foreign affairs. Still,
his conception of national interest could have dictated the most
far-reaching military involvement in Mexico, a contiguous country where American investments were large. In the case of Mexico, the restraints on Taft's action arose from the calm and
patient manner in which he implemented his principles rather
than from the principles themselves. The advantage of Taft's
response to revolution, like the approach to foreign affairs from
which it proceeded, was that it forbade involvement or at least
military involvement in countries whose welfare did not affect
America's economic and security interests, restrictively defined.
In its general application outside of the Americas, Taft's response
to revolution would have informed a policy that although not
sympathetic to revolution could have enabled the United States

---

[2] Supra, pp. 68.
[3] Supra, p. 90 n. 19.

to tolerate revolutionary change and adjust to it without becoming involved militarily or diplomatically.

From the beginning of his administration, Woodrow Wilson pursued an entirely different course. Ignoring the firm yet friendly insistence of the Constitutionalists that they would fight to the finish against Huerta, Wilson tried and failed to persuade the two sides to accept an armistice and a neutral provisional government until national elections could be held to establish a new constitutional government. When the victorious Constitutionalist movement split into warring factions, Wilson again attempted to pacify Mexico by appealing for a compromise among the revolutionaries. This effort proved equally unsuccessful, because once more the Mexican factions were engaged in a struggle to the death. Wilson then attempted to bargain the withdrawal of the Pershing expedition in exchange for the agreement of the Constitutionalist government to protect American lives and property and to establish a liberal, democratic government. This, too, proved unsuccessful. The Mexicans resolutely opposed all American interference in the revolution, and they were aided by the worsening of German-American relations in 1916 and early 1917 that culminated in war. After 1917 Wilson sought to moderate the economic reforms outlined by the Querétaro constitution and delayed recognition of Carranza and, later, Obregón, because neither would give "satisfactory" assurances that American interests in Mexico would be protected.

On the other hand, at no time did Wilson make war against either the objectives of the Mexican Revolution or the major revolutionary factions. He supported the Constitutionalists against Huerta, though they spurned his support, by launching a dilomatic campaign to topple the military dictator. When diplomatic opposition proved inadequate, Wilson arranged to supply the revolutionaries with arms. When this failed to produce sufficiently rapid change, and when Huerta seemed unshaken, Wilson seized on a minor incident at Tampico between Mexican soldiers and American sailors and, as part of his plan to overthrow Huerta, ordered the military occupation of the port of Veracruz. After the end of World War I, Wilson refused to give in to a movement to "punish" Mexico for damaging American interests, a movement which included many Senators. Wilson's secretary of state, Robert Lansing, and his ambassador to Mexico, Henry P. Fletcher. Fletcher resigned in protest in 1920 when his recommendations for drastic action against Mexico were rejected.

The problem, then, in dealing with Wilson's response to the
Mexican Revolution is to explain both Wilson's intervention
and his abstention, to explain what caused him to meddle constantly, with his unrealistic mediation proposals, and what caused
him to refuse to go to war against the Mexican Revolution
and instead to identify with and to support the aims of the
Mexican revolutionaries. The first part of the answer seems to
lie in a paradox. The same beliefs that hampered Wilson's Mexican policy were also its greatest sources of strength. Wilson
attempted to force the Mexican Revolution to conform to what
amounted to the pattern of American and British political development. With uncommon daring and brilliance the Mexican
revolutionaries refused to tolerate his interference. Again and
again they risked war with the United States and, in one way
or another, won the right to settle their own affairs. Wilson
did not oppose the aims of the Mexican Revolution, but he
differed with the revolutionaries over the best ways to achieve
those aims. Wilson tried to control developments in Mexico and
to force them into an American mold. But he avoided intervention against the Mexican Revolution because his belief in self-
determination and social justice, founded on his understanding
of the American Revolution and of contemporary American
political and economic life, proved stronger than his missionary's
desire to teach democracy to the world.

The tension between Wilson's sympathy for the Mexican Revolution and his desire to control Mexico's destiny determined
his response to the Mexican Revolution. There is no reason to
believe that this dilemma had been resolved when the United
States entered the war against Germany in April 1917. Rather,
the exigencies of great power politics led Wilson to turn away
from Mexico. He never again could devote the time and effort
to Mexican-American relations that marked his first years in
office. America's involvement with Germany thus constituted
a badly needed restraint on Wilson's intervention in Mexico.
The Mexican revolutionaries, despite the virtuosity they displayed in negotiation with the United States, gained a much-
needed respite when their stubborn "servant" led his country
into World War I.

The response of the Wilson administration, in particular, suggests several general conclusions with contemporary applicability.
Although Wilson desired to support the Mexican revolutionaries
his conspicuous failure to win their trust and cooperation suggests
how difficult it is for an outside government, however, pure its

motives, to control successfully the course of a foreign revolution, without resorting to overwhelming military force. The flow of revolutionary civil war opens itself to outside influence seldom and, if one were to judge from the Mexican experience, relatively early. Wilson's opposition to Huerta, culminating in allowing the revolutionaries to import arms and in occupying Veracruz, helped overthrow the tyrant. But these "services," as Wilson called them, to Mexico earned the enmity of the revolutionaries. Thereafter, the all-important political and organizational struggles, the crucial battles, and the radicalization of the Mexican Revolution were determined by internal factors and proceeded virtually immune from American influence. The lesson from the Mexican experience would seem to be that the choice for an outside government lies between intervention with overwhelming force at an early stage of a revolutionary civil war, along the lines of the Russian interventions in Hungary and Czechoslovakia or the American intervention in the Dominican Republic, and the frustrating pursuit of influence through diplomacy, with its necessarily smaller possibilities and lower priorities. Taft understood that these were his alternatives far better than did Wilson. Wilson's objectives in dealing with the revolutionaries—which amounted to controlling the Mexican Revolution—consistently overreached the means he was willing to employ. The revolutionaries perceived this and exploited brilliantly the inconsistency in American policy between means and ends. No such inconsistency existed in Wilson's opposition to Huerta. Wilson was determined to use whatever force necessary to overthrow Huerta and, in the end, resorted to a carefully controlled invasion of Mexican territory to accomplish his objective.

The second generalization concerns the importance of countervailing power in limiting the capricious exercise of superior power. Until 1916, the United States could act more or less independently in Mexico, though Wilson was always careful to court the European belligerents, particularly Great Britain. As war with Germany approached, Mexico's isolation diminished and she became a potential ally of Germany. The Mexican revolutionaries cleverly used the threat of a German alliance to enhance the importance to the American government of good relations with Mexico. Fortunately, the United States was not seeking a pretext to invade Mexico. One need only reflect on the difference in the reaction of the Wilson administration after the debacle at Carrizal and the reaction of the Johnson administration after the encounter between North Vietnamese and American warships in the Gulf of Tonkin. Had Wilson desired an excuse to make war on Mexico and the revolution, he could have found one easily in a battle deep in Mexican territory provoked by American troops or in Mexico's overtures to Germany.

By playing the German card in late autumn 1916, the Mexicans risked provoking war with the United States. From their standpoint, however, the choice lay between resisting the United States alone and resisting the United States with an ally. The offer of naval bases to Germany came shortly before Lane's ultimatum to the Mexican commissioners. The Mexicans sought the help of an external, countervailing power at a time when American policy was most capricious and most subject to the demands of domestic politics—in this case Wilson's need in an election year to demonstrate his intention to "stand up" to the Mexicans and to protect American investments in Mexico. Because of the war in Europe, Germany could not respond effectively to the Mexican initiative, and a German presence in Mexico never became a reality. The presence of countervailing power in Mexico could have curtailed the capriciousness of Wilson's Mexican policy, much as the Soviet and Chinese presence limits American freedom of action in Vietnam. This would not necessarily have excluded intervention. In fact, a threatening German presence in Mexico might have guaranteed massive American intervention. A German presence in Mexico would nonetheless have changed the criteria of action from considerations of domestic politics to questions of physical security. Wilson's response to the Mexican Revolution throughout 1916 supports the argument that in the absence of countervailing power or in situations of great disparity in power the stronger power tends to allow domestic political necessities to shape the tactics of intervention.

This raises a related point—the importance of the caliber of revolutionary diplomacy. Contrary to popular myth, successful revolutionaries seem to distinguish themselves as much by knowing when to accept as when to reject compromise. One thinks of Washington and Jay's treaty and Lenin and Brest-Litovsk and, on the unsuccessful side, Nasser and Sukarno and their provocative and disastrous diplomacies. The Mexican revolutionaries combined resistance and compromise in just the right amounts, as at Carrizal and the subsequent release of the American prisoners to forestall war and to make possible the formation of a Joint Commission. Again and again one marvels at the skill of Mexican diplomacy and at the depth of understanding of American politics it reflected. This skill clearly prevented war between the two countries and preserved Mexico's independence of body and spirit. On balance, the Mexican revolutionary experience would seem a far richer source than the Cuban for Latin Americans anxious to change their governments and to emancipate their countries from the United States psychologically as well as politically and economically. The Mexican revolutionaries won their battles against the United States without mortgaging their revolution to a third power, and in so doing they sowed the seeds of a future relationship based on equality and mutual respect.

Epilogue:
Toward a New American Response to Revolution

In order to exist, man must rebel. . . .
—Albert Camus, *The Rebel*

For the secret of man's being is not only to live but to have something to live for.
—Fyodor Dostoyevsky, *The Grand Inquisitor*

Most Americans expect foreign revolutionaries to be dedicated to the objectives sought and achieved by the Founding Fathers: independence, democracy, political freedom, constitutional government, and the sanctity of private property and individual enterprise. Americans also expect foreign revolutions to result in the relatively brief and painless attainment of internal harmony and material well-being. In short, Americans expect foreign revolutions to be liberal and successful, like their own. Most successful contemporary revolutions are not liberal, and many Americans explain this by finding such revolutions to be conspiratorial and externally originated and supported. According to this view, espoused by John Foster Dulles and Dean Rusk while secretaries of state, a "true" revolution cannot be at once communist and indigenous. This logic not only provides a rationale for intervention but also forecloses all inquiry into the relevance of the American experience to twentieth century revolutionaries. We avoid the painful introspection that accompanies self-knowledge and adjustment to changed circumstances.

It is not a peculiarly American fault to "universalize" one's own revolutionary experience. Frenchmen, Russians, Chinese, Cubans have all made the same mistake.[1] In this way, foreign

---

[1] The "universalization" of the French and Russian experiences is well documented. Fidel Castro's speeches and the involvement of Cuban revolutionaries in the internal affairs of other nations indicate the pretensions and illusions Cubans cherish for their experience. Régis Debray's *Revolution in the Revolution? Armed Struggle and Political Struggle in Latin America*, transl. by Bobbye Ortiz (New York: Grove Press, 1967), is an example of the universalization of the Cuban revolutionary experience. See especially pp. 106–107, 119–126. Frantz Fanon's *Wretched of the Earth* (London: MacGibbon & Kee, 1965) is an example of the universalization of the Algerian experience. For a discussion of Chinese "universalism" see my "Revolutionary Strategy and Chinese Foreign Policy," *SAIS Review* 11 (Autumn 1966), 5–12.

revolutions are tested against national doctrine instead of against indigenous determinants. The first step, then, in fashioning a new response to revolution is to resist the temptation to "universalize" one's own national revolutionary experience. Only the successful revolutionaries in a particular country can determine what assortment of principles and procedures they will utilize in creating and operating their revolutionary government. Elections, for example, played a crucial role in the American Revolution. They may or may not be relevant to the Vietnamese Revolution, but that decision will almost surely be made by the victorious revolutionaries, unless the United States undertakes to conquer all of Vietnam. Moreover, Wilson's inability to persuade any Mexican faction to agree to "honest" elections suggests that whatever role elections may play after a revolutionary seizure of power few if any revolutionaries will accept elections imposed from without as a means of determining the outcome of the revolutionary struggle. For three years Wilson tried unsuccessfully to persuade the Mexicans to settle the Mexican civil war by means of an armistice and national elections. The victorious Constitutionalists held elections, of course, but largely as a means of political mobilization and indoctrination to enable the people to endorse the accomplishments of the revolutionary government. The stakes of revolution are ill-suited to adjudication by election. It is as if the British had insisted at Paris that the American Revolution be settled by an election in which Tories and Patriots would have equal opportunities to campaign; as if the European powers had insisted that the Civil War be settled by an election in which followers of the United States of America and the Confederate States of America could have participated.

Second, present American policy in Asia and Latin America seems to be based in part on a misapplication to revolutionary situations of the doctrine of limited war. The concept and strategic doctrine of limited war arose after the Korean War in response to the growth of Soviet nuclear striking power, the introduction of thermonuclear bombs and missiles, and the emphasis by the major communist powers on national liberation war. Advocates of the concept argued that without effective means of conventional resistance the United States could not meet limited aggressions by communist powers undeterred by the bipolar nuclear balance. The concept of limited war was based on Clausewitz's dictum that unless war is controlled by overall political considerations it ceases to perform as an effective instrument of policy and becomes merely destructive. President

Kennedy and Secretary of Defense Robert McNamara "explicitly adopted the concept of limited war."[2] The result was a fundamental change in American strategy. The American army was increased in size, "special forces" were created to deal with guerrilla wars, a short-lived attempt was made to increase NATO conventional forces, and the capacity of the United States to airlift troops to deter or fight local wars was greatly increased.

For a number of reasons the concept and strategy of limited war are ill-suited as a basis for response to revolution. First, implicit in the strategy of limited war is the assumption that there are only two adversaries—communist and noncommunist—and that what one adversary loses the other always gains. While this may have been more or less true in Europe during the 1950s, the situation in Asia and Latin America has never been so easily explained. Even in the case of Vietnam, where the major adversary of the United States is tied by treaty to China and the Soviet Union, it is difficult to argue that a united, communist Vietnam would be all profit for China and the Soviet Union and all loss for the United States. Even if this were true, it would be even more difficult to argue that the proper American response to the Vietnamese revolution is to oppose the most successful revolutionary faction by the gradual introduction of American combat troops. The whole point of a strategy of limited war is to maintain a stalemate between countries. It seeks to confront a more or less equal adversary possessing limited objectives with the realization that to attain his objectives, however limited, would involve costs far out of proportion to the possible gains. The point of revolution is to overthrow the existing order within a country. The objectives of revolutionaries are thus unlimited, and the sort of conservative cost-risk calculus possible between the United States and the Soviet Union simply cannot be established between a superpower and a revolutionary movement. To say that the doctrine of limited war should not determine America's response to revolution is not to deny the vital importance in a nuclear age of subjecting war to the discipline of political considerations. Rather, it is to suggest that different political considerations should govern America's response to foreign revolution.

In order to fashion a new response to revolution, Americans

Social Sciences (New York: Macmillan, 1968), 9: 305.

---

[2] Robert E. Osgood, "Limited War," *International Encyclopedia of the*

must make a fresh attempt to reconcile the national interests of the United States with the revolutions that have occurred since the end of World War II and with those that are most likely to come. Many critics of America's involvement in Vietnam have suggested that the United States should emphasize national interests when responding to revolution abroad, believing that this would have prevented our involvement in Vietnam and will prevent similar involvements in the future. But will this necessarily keep the United States from going abroad, in the words of John Quincy Adams, "in search of monsters to destroy"? Or is the concept of national interest as capable of abuse and misinterpretation as, say, a concept of America's duty like that followed by Wilson? Different individuals thinking in terms of power and the national interest will often arrive at a wide variety of solutions to problems of national security. Germans, thinking in terms of power and the national interest, decided to initiate unlimited submarine warfare in February 1917. That decision, by bringing the United States into the war, assured the defeat of the Central Powers and precipitated a revolution that destroyed imperial Germany. Taft, thinking in terms of American interests, was prepared ultimately to intervene in the Mexican Revolution to protect American lives and investments, when to intervene promised to destroy American investments and to involve the two nations in a bloody, interminable war. The administrations of Eisenhower, Kennedy, and Johnson, thinking in terms of American power and national security, involved the United States deeper and deeper in a revolutionary civil war in Vietnam until American soldiers became the strongest support of an otherwise defeated Vietnamese faction.

The objection is, of course, that none of these acts was taken in accordance with the national interests of Germany or the United States. What is meant is that none of these actions was taken in accordance with the national interest "rightly understood."[3] This amounts to opposing different evaluations of the national interest without providing any sure means of deciding between them. In practice, of course, it is possible to reach agreement on the need to protect certain national interests. The process of determination nonetheless remains so vague that one man's peril is another man's security.

If approaching international affairs in terms of the national

---

[3] See Hans J. Morgenthau, "To Intervene or Not to Intervene," *Foreign Affairs,* April 1967, pp. 425–436.

interest provides no certain solution to such problems as when,
whether, and how much to intervene in foreign revolutions, the
approach does offer a rough standard of analysis and conduct
more reliable than any other, perhaps, though woefully inadequate by itself. To protect national interests is to assume certain
ideals, including the "preservation and continuity of the state."[4]
One must nonetheless ask, preservation "for what?" and continuity "to what end?" Only in this way can one achieve a
perspective sufficiently unprejudiced to understand and accept
justified change in national and international affairs. As Arnold
Wolfers observed,

Those who refuse to make the sacrifices of change or who having
brought about an unjust distribution of possessions and power,
are unwilling to correct such distribution may be guilty of provoking
enmity and aggression. Their opponents are not necessarily at fault,
then, merely because they want change urgently or because they
despair of any means short of violence. The *beati possidentes* may
be more peaceful and less inclined to initiate open hostility, but
their guilt may lie in their self-righteous and blind devotion to
the *status quo* or in the resentment they evoke in others.[5]

In responding to the Mexican Revolution, Woodrow Wilson
combined concern for his conception of America's national interests—the spread of democracy and "just treatment" of American
investments—with sympathy and respect for violent and radical
changes in Mexico's social order. Wilson found inspiration in
the American Revolution, particularly the emphasis on human
dignity and the right of a people to alter or abolish their government by whatever means most conducive to the public good.
A decade before he became president, Wilson took a conservative
view of the American Revolution, a view in keeping with his
conception of political development as an organic process whose
highest stage was democratic, constitutional government. In an
address in December 1902 he observed:

We look back to the great men who made our government as
to a generation, not of revolutionists, but of statesmen. They fought,
not to pull down, but to preserve—not for some fair and far-off
thing they wished for, but for a familiar thing they had and wished
to keep. Ask any candid student of the history of English liberty,
and he will tell you that these men . . . consecrated their lives

---

[4] Robert E. Osgood and Robert W. Tucker, *Force, Order, and Justice*
(Baltimore: Johns Hopkins Press, 1967), p. 323.
[5] Arnold Wolfers, *Discord and Collaboration: Essays on International
Politics* (Baltimore: Johns Hopkins Press, 1962), p. 63.

to the preservation intact of what had been wrought out in blood and sweat by the countless generations of sturdy free men who had gone before them.[6]

If this can be regarded as an Hamiltonian outlook, to which Wilson responded before coming to the presidency, his desire to accomplish reform at home and his need to cope with social revolution in Mexico inclined him toward a less confining, more innovative or Jeffersonian interpretation of the American revolutionary experience. He found inspiration, for example, in the Virginia Bill of Rights.[7] Dedicating Congress Hall in Philadelphia he declared:

I hear a great many people at Fourth of July celebrations laud the Declaration of Independence who in between July shiver at the plain language of our bills of rights. The Declaration of Independence was, indeed, the first audible breath of liberty, but the substance of liberty is written in such documents as the declaration of rights attached, for example, to the first constitution of Virginia which was a model for the similar documents read elsewhere into our great fundamental charters. That document speaks in very plain terms. The men cf that generation did not hesitate to say that every people has a right to choose its own forms of government—not once, but as often as it pleases—and to accommodate those forms of government to its existing interests and circumstances. Not only to establish but to alter is the fundamental principle of self-government. . . . Liberty inheres in the circumstances of the day. Human happiness consists in the life which human beings are leading at the time that they live. I can feed my memory as happily upon the circumstances of the revolutionary and constitutional period as you can, but I can not feed all my purposes with them in Washington now. Every day problems arise which wear some new phase or aspect, and I must fall back, if I would serve my conscience, upon those things which are fundamental rather than upon those things which are superficial. . . .[8]

---

[6] *Public Papers: College and State,* 1: 430.
[7] Article 3 of the Virginia declaration postulated: "That government is, or ought to be instituted for the common benefit, protection, and security, of the people, nation, or community; of all the various modes and forms of government that is best, which is capable of producing the greatest degree of happiness and safety, and is most effectually secured against the danger of mal-administration; and that when any government shall be found inadequate or contrary to these purposes, a majority of the community hath an indubitable, unalienable, and indefeasible right *to reform, alter, or abolish it, in such manner as shall be judged most conducive to the public weal.*" (Italics added.)
[8] *Public Papers: The New Democracy,* 1: 59–60. Cf. Hans J. Morgenthau, *The Purpose of American Politics* (New York: Random House, Vintage

273 Epilogue

In this way, Wilson insisted on the relevance of the American revolutionary experience to the troubled American domestic scene and to Mexico's social revolution. Though Wilson allowed his tutelary bent to dictate unnecessary and unsuccessful intervention in Mexico's internal affairs, he returned again and again to an understanding of revolution grounded in the American experience that prevented his meddling from passing into hegemony and military domination. Now, more than a half-century later, we need not repeat Wilson's errors. Nor should we forget his insistence on the relevance of the American revolutionary experience to twentieth-century revolutions. It now seems certain that the institutional modes of the American Revolution retain little relevance for most parts of the world. It is time to concentrate instead on fundamentals, as Wilson did, and to recognize that the fundamentals of the American revolutionary heritage remain relevant to contemporary circumstances. It is time to recognize as potential allies all people striving for dignity and a better life, all of the Vietnamese people, all of the people of Cuba, Guatemala, and the Dominican Republic, as well as the people of Czechoslovakia, Yugoslavia, and the writers and intellectuals of the Soviet Union. Freedom, human dignity, and the right of a people to alter their government—fundamental ideals of the American Revolution—have never been so universally accepted.

There is no intention here to slight national security or to imply that great nations may always choose their allies without regard to the realities of power and interest. Rather, my purpose is to reinforce the belief that America's revolutionary ideals can and should inform the pursuit of its national interests in the twentieth century. The danger raised by extreme advocates of the national interest is nothing less than the loss of the nation's soul. An imperial America would be a soulless America. Fortunately the task is too great and American power too small for the nation long to attempt to maintain order among and within

Books, 1960), p. 6: "Thus, the ideas molded by the historic experience of the eighteenth and nineteenth centuries encounter the world-wide tasks of the present and find it hard to give meaning to the thoughts and actions of the nation. The crisis of the national purpose has its roots in this inadequacy of the traditional body of ideas, yet that inadequacy need not by itself have created that crisis. For a nation must continuously reexamine and reformulate the ideas of the past in the light of the experience of the present and the anticipated demands of the future, always risking failure."

the countries of the world. On the other hand, the danger posed by the current unrestrained criticism of American policy is that Americans will become so alienated from themselves and their ideals that they will fall prey to internal reaction and external adventure.

Another course exists, founded neither on ignoring nor on overthrowing the nation's ideals. This course depends on the great strength and security of the United States and on the movement of revolution in Asia, Africa, Latin America, and Europe. The United States government is in a position to say to revolutionaries and dictators around the world: "To the extent that you dignify the lives of your people and free their minds and bodies you will have our respect." It is in a position to support revolution in certain vital areas, remembering only that those revolutionaries most likely to succeed will accept aid but will reject and oppose militarily if necessary any outside interference in the internal affairs of their nation.

Made safe against external attack by its preponderant nuclear and conventional forces, the United States can afford to welcome each outburst of revolution as a buttress of its own liberty, not as a threat to its existence. With a foreign policy firmly rooted in a restrained understanding of national interests and informed and inspired by the fundamental ideals of the American Revolution, the United States need never fear obsolescence or isolation.

Nonintervention would seem to be the most desirable course for all nations to pursue and the standard against which one should measure their actions. For thousands of years, nonetheless, powers have engaged in internal intervention—interference between disputant factions in another state—and revolutionaries within countries have associated themselves with outside powers.[9] The combination of these two conditions, as in Vietnam, presents the most troublesome case for American policy. What to do, for example, when China and the Soviet Union have extended aid to a faction that has an excellent chance of winning power and that seems likely to align the country with the Soviet Union or China after coming to power? It would seem that only one situation would require immediate military action by United States forces: if the shift in allegiance resulted in a threat to the physical security of the United States or the integrity of its institutions.

[9] See in particular the accounts of the Corcyraean Revolution in Thucydides, *The Peloponnesian War*, 3.70–3.85 and 8.46–8.48.

Foreign revolutions can threaten the United States only if they have the potential to cause a dangerous accretion of power to the Soviet Union or to heighten the risk of nuclear war by establishing an aggressively revisionist government in a powerful state, say Germany or Japan. America's relations with the Soviet Union, Japan, and Western Europe far outweigh in importance any developments that may soon take place in Africa, Asia, and much of Latin America. Many countries in these areas stand at the beginning of a long and difficult path to political and economic stability. They face terrible problems of poverty, ignorance, and internal strife, often exacerbated by tribal and ethnic hatreds. What happens in these countries cannot compare in importance for American security with the manner in which Japan assumes a role in Asia and the world commensurate with her great wealth and power or with the way in which Western Europe progresses toward political and economic unity.

That certain areas of the world are more important to United States security than others can be seen by examining existing security arrangements (compare the Southeast Asian with the North Atlantic treaty), trade statistics, or cultural and historical affinities. Only in a few parts of the world do the skills, resources, markets, and technology exist which, if controlled by a government bent on conquest or world domination, would endanger American security. They exist in Japan, Russia, Western Europe, and North America. Australia may, in the next generation, become a great industrial power. China seems intent on acquiring a large nuclear arsenal. China and Australia do not now rank in importance or strength with the areas and nations already mentioned.

People outside the few vital areas do not feel deprived by their status. They know they are less important to Russian and American security than Europe or Japan, and they rather enjoy their consequent freedom of action. The relative unimportance of these areas for American security and the unpredictable and difficult years ahead as the countries of Asia and Africa work out their destiny justify a relaxed approach on the part of the United States in responding to revolutionary violence. Americans bear the responsibilities that accompany power, but they should meet these responsibilities in ways commensurate with their needs, abilities, and resources.

If there is no threat to the security of the United States involved in the outcome of a revolution it would seem that nonintervention should be the rule. The United States might first attempt to establish with the Soviets and the Chinese a reciprocal agreement, implicit or explicit, not to intervene. Should this prove impossible and some sort of intervention still seem necessary, the United States could then follow the Soviet pattern of extending money, arms, and diplomatic support to that faction whose program and chances for success best harmonized with its long-range objectives.

Any American assistance to revolutionary factions should be made with the understanding that no American troops will wait in the wings to "save" the cause, barring foreign military intervention. The Mexican, Russian, Vietnamese, Algerian, and Cuban experiences suggest that those revolutionaries with a chance at success would not tolerate any other sort of arrangement. In the absence of other foreign intervention they would almost certainly insist on it. If the decision is to aid an existing regime against revolutionary overthrow, a similar restraint should condition American policy. Money and arms can be supplied by an outside power. No technical or material assistance can supply a cause worth dying for or create the organization and élan essential to win a revolutionary war. A restrained construction of American interests should guide intervention against foreign revolution, and virtually every revolution likely to occur falls outside this standard.

An Egyptian myth describes the phoenix as a beautiful, lone bird that lives for centuries and then consumes itself in fire, rising renewed from the ashes of its nest. The myth touches the nature of man and society. However long men would live, however eternal they would build their systems, change and death come to all. Yet men and societies have always risen from the ruins to renew life. Whether the prophecies of unending revolution in Asia, Africa, and Latin America now made by everyone from despondent conservatives to euphoric guerrilla leaders prove true or only half-true, the future will certainly reinforce the myth of the phoenix as men everywhere express their humanity in unending immolation and renewal. Despite the threat of nuclear destruction and technological sterilization, history justifies faith in man and his capacity to rebel. Americans have every reason to share that faith.

Selected Bibliography

MANUSCRIPTS
Library of Congress
Chandler P. Anderson Papers
Ray Stannard Baker Papers
Tasker H. Bliss Papers
Wilbur J. Carr Papers
Henry Prather Fletcher Papers
Philander C. Knox Papers
Robert Lansing Papers
William G. McAdoo Papers
John Bassett Moore Papers
Elihu Root Papers
Hugh Lennox Scott Papers
William H. Taft Papers
Woodrow Wilson Papers

PUBLIC DOCUMENTS
The National Archives of the United States
General Records of the Department of State. Record Group 59:
Decimal File: "Commercial Relations of Mexico: Export Trade, Embargo"; "Internal Affairs of Mexico, 1910–1929"; "International Affairs of Germany, Military Activities of Germany in Mexico"; "Personal Records of Diplomatic Officers"; "Political Relations between Mexico and Other States, 1910–1929"; "Relations between the United States and Mexico, 1910–1929"; "World War I and its Termination, 1914–1929."

"Correspondence of Secretary of State Bryan with President Wilson, 1913–1915."

"Personal and Confidential Letters from Secretary of State Lansing to President Wilson, 1915–1918."

General Records of the Department of the Navy. Record Group 80:

"Reports from Commanding Officer, U.S.S. *Annapolis* to Chief of Naval Operations on Situation along the East Coast of Mexico, 4225."

"Reports on Tampico, Mexico: 27820 to 27824."

"General Information on Mexican Coastal Waters, 5006."

"Correspondence of the Secretary of the Navy and Chief of Naval Operations, C-12-95 to C-12-247."

Naval Records Collection of the Office of Naval Records and Library. Record Group 45:

"Subject File, 1911–1927."

"WE-5, East Coast of Mexico, Boxes 655, 656, 659–661."

Records of the Adjutant General's Office. Record Group 94:

"Mexican Revolution, 208188."

"Mexican Intervention, 214991."

Records of United States Participation in International Conferences, Commissions, and Expositions. Record Group 43:

"Records of the United States Commissioners of the American and Mexican Joint Commission, 1916. Preliminary Inventory 76."

Records of the War Department General Staff. Record Group 165: "Records of the War College Division."

Publications of the United States Government

Department of State. *Papers Relating to the Foreign Relations of the United States, 1910.* Washington, D.C.: Government Printing Office, 1915.

————. *Papers Relating to the Foreign Relations of the United States, 1911.* Washington, D.C.: Government Printing Office, 1918.

————. *Papers Relating to the Foreign Relations of the United States, 1912.* Washington, D.C.: Government Printing Office, 1919.

————. *Papers Relating to the Foreign Relations of the United States, 1913.* Washington, D.C.: Government Printing Office, 1920.

————. *Papers Relating to the Foreign Relations of the United States, 1914.* Washington, D.C.: Government Printing Office, 1922.

————. *Papers Relating to the Foreign Relations of the United States, 1915.* Washington, D.C.: Government Printing Office, 1924.

————. *Papers Relating to the Foreign Relations of the United States, 1916.* Washington, D.C.: Government Printing Office, 1925.

————. *Papers Relating to the Foreign Relations of the United States, 1917.* Washington, D.C.: Government Printing Office, 1926.

————. *Papers Relating to the Foreign Relations of the United States, The Lansing Papers, 1914–1920.* 2 vols. Washington, D.C.: Government Printing Office, 1939–1940.

————. *The Mexican Oil Controversy as Told in Diplomatic Correspondence between the United States and Mexico.* Washington, D.C.: Government Printing Office, 1920.

Publications of Foreign Governments

Germany. National Constituent Assembly. *Official German Documents Relating to the World War.* Translated under the supervision of the Carnegie Endowment for International Peace. 2 vols. New York: Oxford University Press, 1923.

Mexico. Foreign Office. *Labor Internacional de la Revolución Constitucionalista de México.* México: Press of Secretaría de Gobernación, n.d.

BOOKS AND ARTICLES

Adler, Selig. "Bryan and Wilsonian Caribbean Penetration." *Hispanic American Historical Review* 20 (May 1940): 198–226.

Alden, John Richard. *The American Revolution, 1775–1783.* New York: Harper & Row, Torchbook edition, 1962.

Arendt, Hannah. *On Revolution.* New York: Viking Press, Compass edition, 1963.

Bailey, Thomas A. *A Diplomatic History of the American People.* 7th ed. New York: Appleton-Century-Crofts, 1964.

Bailyn, Bernard. *The Ideological Origins of the American Revolution.* Cambridge, Mass.: Harvard University Press, Belknap Press, 1967.

Baker, Ray Stannard. *Woodrow Wilson: Life and Letters.* 8 vols. Garden City, N.Y.: Doubleday, 1927–1939.

Baker, Ray Stannard, and Dodds, William E., eds. *The Public Papers of Woodrow Wilson.* 6 vols. New York: Harper, 1925–1927.

Becker, Carl. *The Heavenly City of the Eighteenth Century Philosophers.* New Haven, Conn.: Yale University Press, 1932.

Bemis, Samuel F. *A Diplomatic History of the United States.* 5th ed. New York: Holt, Rinehart & Winston, 1965.

——. *The Latin American Policy of the United States, an Historical Interpretation.* New York: Harcourt, Brace, 1943.

Billias, George Athan, ed. *The American Revolution: How Revolutionary Was It?* New York: Holt, Rinehart & Winston, 1965.

Blum, John M. *Woodrow Wilson and the Politics of Morality.* Boston: Little, Brown, 1956.

Brandenburg, Frank. *The Making of Modern Mexico.* Englewood Cliffs, N.J.: Prentice-Hall, 1964.

Brinton, Crane. *The Anatomy of Revolution.* Revised and expanded ed. New York: Random House, 1965.

Buehrig, Edward H. *Woodrow Wilson and the Balance of Power.* Bloomington: Indiana University Press, 1955.

Callahan, James M. *American Foreign Policy in Mexican Relations.* New York: Macmillan, 1932.

Camus, Albert. *The Rebel: An Essay on Man in Revolt.* Revised and complete translation by Anthony Bower. New York: Random House, Vintage Books, 1956.

Chambers, William Nisbet. *Political Parties in a New Nation: The American Experience, 1776–1809.* New York: Oxford University Press, 1963.

Clendenen, Clarence C. *The United States and Pancho Villa: A Study in Unconventional Diplomacy.* Ithaca, N.Y.: Cornell University Press, 1961.

Cline, Howard. *The United States and Mexico.* Revised and enlarged ed. Cambridge, Mass.: Harvard University Press, 1963.

Crévecoeur, Hector St. John de. *Letters from an American Farmer.* London: J. M. Dent, 1951.

Cumberland, Charles Curtis. *Mexican Revolution: Genesis under Madero.* Austin: University of Texas Press, 1952.

——. *Mexico: The Struggle for Modernity.* New York: Oxford University Press, 1968.

Curry, Roy M. *Woodrow Wilson and Far Eastern Policy, 1913–1921.* New York: Bookman Associates, 1957.

Curti, Merle. *Austria and the United States 1848–1852*. Smith College Studies in History. Northampton, Mass., 1926.

Curtis, Eugene N. "American Opinion of French Nineteenth Century Revolutions," *American Historical Review* 29 (January 1924) : 249–270.

Debray, Régis. *Revolution in the Revolution? Armed Struggle and Political Struggle in Latin America*. Translated from the author's French and Spanish by Bobbye Ortiz. New York: Grove Press, Evergreen edition, 1967.

Dinerstein, Herbert S. *Intervention Against Communism*. Baltimore: Johns Hopkins Press, 1967.

Dostoyevski, Fyodor. *The Brothers Karamazov*. Translated by Constance Garnett. New York: Modern Library, 1950.

Dulles, John W. F. *Yesterday in Mexico: A Chronicle of the Revolution, 1919–1936*. Austin: University of Texas Press, 1961.

Fabela, Isidro. *Historia Diplomática de la Revolución Mexicana*. 2 vols. México: Fondo de Cultura Económica, 1959.

Fanon, Frantz. *The Wretched of the Earth*. London: MacGibbon & Kee, 1965.

Fay, Bernard. *The Revolutionary Spirit in France and America, A Study of Moral and Intellectual Relations between France and the United States at the End of the Eighteenth Century*. New York: Harcourt, Brace, 1927.

Gazely, John Gerow. *American Opinion of German Unification, 1848–1871*. New York: Columbia University Press, 1926.

Graebner, Norman A., ed. *An Uncertain Tradition: American Secretaries of State in the Twentieth Century*. New York: McGraw-Hill, 1961.

Gruening, Ernest Henry. *Mexico and Its Heritage*. New York: Appleton-Century-Crofts, 1928.

Hackett, Charles Wilson. *The Mexican Revolution and the United States, 1910–1926*. World Peace Foundation Pamphlet 9 (1926) : 5.

Harrington, Michael. *The Accidental Century*. New York: Macmillan, 1965.

Hartz, Louis. *The Liberal Tradition in America: An Interpretation of American Political Thought Since the Revolution*. New York: Harcourt, Brace, 1955.

——. "The Basis of the American Response." Unpublished statement at the Hearings before the Committee on Foreign Relations of the United States Senate, February 26, 1968, on "The American Attitude toward Revolution."

Hazen, Charles Downer. *Contemporary American Opinion of the French Revolution*. Originally published in 1897. Gloucester: Peter Smith, 1964.

Hobsbawm, E. J. *The Age of Revolution: Europe 1789–1848*. London: Weidenfeld and Nicolson, 1962.

Jameson, J. Franklin. *The American Revolution Considered as a Social Movement*. Princeton, N.J.: Princeton University Press, Princeton Paperback, 1967.

Johnson, Chalmers. *Revolution and the Social System.* Hoover Institution Studies. Stanford, Calif.: Hoover Institution, 1964.

Just, Ward S. *To What End: Report from Vietnam.* Boston: Houghton Mifflin, 1968.

Kahle, Louis G. "Robert Lansing and the Recognition of Venustiano Carranza," *Hispanic American Historical Review* 38 (August 1958): 353–372.

Kennan, George F. *American Diplomacy: 1900–1950.* Chicago: New American Library, 1951.

Kenyon, Cecilia M. "Republicanism and Radicalism in the American Revolution: An Old-Fashioned Interpretation," *William and Mary Quarterly* 19 (April 1962): 153–182.

Ketcham, Ralph L. "France and American Politics, 1763–1793," *Political Science Quarterly* 78 (June 1963): 198–223.

Latham, Earl, ed. *The Philosophy and Policies of Woodrow Wilson.* Chicago: University of Chicago Press, 1958.

Link, Arthur S. *Wilson: The New Freedom.* Princeton, N.J.: Princeton University Press, 1956.

——. *Woodrow Wilson: A Look at His Major Foreign Policies.* Baltimore: Johns Hopkins Press, 1957.

——. *Wilson: The Struggle for Neutrality, 1914–1915.* Princeton, N.J.: Princeton University Press, 1960.

——. *Wilson: Confusions and Crises, 1915–1916.* Princeton, N.J.: Princeton University Press, 1964.

——. *Wilson: Campaigns for Progressivism and Peace, 1916–1917.* Princeton, N.J.: Princeton University Press, 1965.

Link, Eugene Perry. *Democratic-Republican Societies, 1790–1800.* New York: Octagon Books, 1965.

Liska, George, *Imperial America: The International Politics of Primacy.* Baltimore: Johns Hopkins Press, 1967.

Lowry, Philip H. "The Mexican Policy of Woodrow Wilson." Unpublished Ph.D. dissertation, Yale University, 1949.

McMaster, John Bach. *A History of the People of the United States from the Revolution to the Civil War.* 8 vols. New York: D. Appleton-Century, 1936.

Malraux, André. *Man's Fate (La Condition Humaine).* Translated by Haakon M. Chevalier. New York: Modern Library, 1961.

Marx, Karl. *The Class Struggles in France.* New York: International Publishers, n.d.

——. *The Eighteenth Brumaire of Louis Bonaparte.* New York: International Publishers, 1963.

Masters, Roger D. "The Lockean Tradition in American Foreign Policy," *Journal of International Affairs* 21 (1967): 253–277.

Maurice, C. Edmund. *The Revolutionary Movement of 1848–9 in Italy, Austria-Hungary, and Germany with Some Explanation of the Previous Thirty Years.* New York: G. P. Putnam's Sons, 1887.

Mayer, Arno J. *Political Origins of the New Diplomacy, 1917–1918.* New Haven, Conn.: Yale University Press, 1959.

Miller, John C. *Crisis in Freedom: The Alien and Sedition Acts.* Boston: Little, Brown, 1951.

——. *Origins of the American Revolution.* Revised ed. Stanford, Calif.: Stanford University Press, 1959.

Morgan, Edmund S., ed. *The American Revolution: Two Centuries of Interpretation.* Englewood Cliffs, N.J.: Prentice-Hall, 1965.

Morgenthau, Hans J. *In Defense of the National Interest: A Critical Examination of American Foreign Policy.* New York: Alfred A. Knopf, 1951.

——. *The Purpose of American Politics.* New York: Random House, Vintage Books, 1960.

——. "To Intervene or Not to Intervene," *Foreign Affairs* 45 (April 1967): 425–436.

Morris, Richard B. "Class Struggle and the American Revolution," *William and Mary Quarterly* 19 (January 1962): 3–29.

——. *The American Revolution Reconsidered.* New York: Harper & Row, 1967.

Munro, Dana G. *Intervention and Dollar Diplomacy in the Caribbean, 1910–1921.* Princeton, N.J.: Princeton University Press, 1964.

Nelson, William H. "The Revolutionary Character of the American Revolution," *American Historical Review* 70 (July 1965): 998–1014.

Notter, Harley. *The Origins of the Foreign Policy of Woodrow Wilson.* Baltimore: Johns Hopkins Press, 1937.

Oliver, John W. "Louis Kossuth's Appeal to the Middle West—1852," *Mississippi Valley Historical Review* 14 (March 1928): 481–495.

Osgood, Robert E. *Ideals and Self-Interest in America's Foreign Relations: The Great Transformation of the Twentieth Century.* Phoenix edition. Chicago: University of Chicago Press, 1953.

Osgood, Robert E., and Tucker, Robert W. *Force, Order, and Justice.* Baltimore: Johns Hopkins Press, 1967.

O'Shaughnessy, Edith. *A Diplomat's Wife in Mexico.* New York: Harper, 1916.

Palmer, R. R. *The Age of the Democratic Revolution: A Political History of Europe and America, 1760–1800.* 2 vols. Princeton, N.J.: Princeton University Press, 1959 and 1964.

Parkes, Henry Bamford. *A History of Mexico.* 3rd ed., revised and enlarged. Boston: Houghton Mifflin, 1960.

Pringle, Henry F. *The Life and Times of William Howard Taft.* 2 vols. New York: Farrar & Rinehart, 1939.

Quirk, Robert E. *An Affair of Honor: Woodrow Wilson and the Occupation of Veracruz.* Lexington: University of Kentucky Press, 1962.

——. *The Mexican Revolution, 1914–1915: The Convention of Aguascalientes.* Bloomington: Indiana University Press, 1960.

Reinhardt, Kurt F. *The Existentialist Revolt: The Main Themes and Phases of Existentialism.* 2d ed. New York: Frederick Ungar, 1960.

Rippy, J. Fred. *The United States and Mexico.* Revised ed. New York: F. S. Crofts, 1931.

Ross, Stanley R. *Francisco I. Madero: Apostle of Mexican Democracy.* New York: Columbia University Press, 1955.

Sáenz, Aarón. *La Política Internacional de la Revolución: Estudios y Documentos.* México: Fondo de la Cultura Económica, 1960.

Seymour, Charles, ed. *The Intimate Papers of Colonel House.* 2 vols. Boston: Houghton Mifflin, 1926.

Shaplen, Robert. *The Lost Revolution: The Story of Twenty Years of Neglected Opportunities in Vietnam and of America's Failure to Foster Democracy There.* New York: Harper & Row, 1965.

Steel, Ronald. *Pax Americana.* New York: Viking Press, 1967.

Stillman, Edmund, and Pfaff, William. *Power and Impotence: The Failure of America's Foreign Policy.* New York: Random House, 1966.

Tannenbaum, Frank. *Mexico: The Struggle for Peace and Bread.* New York: Alfred A. Knopf, 1950.

———. *Peace by Revolution: An Interpretation of Mexico.* New York: Columbia University Press, 1933.

Tatum, Edward Howland, Jr. *The United States and Europe, 1815–1823: A Study in the Background of the Monroe Doctrine.* Berkeley: University of California Press, 1936.

Tocqueville, Alexis de. *Democracy in America.* 2 vols. New York: Alfred A. Knopf, Vintage Books, 1958.

Tolles, Frederick B. "The American Revolution Considered as a Social Movement: A Re-Evaluation," *American Historical Review* 60 (October 1954): 1–12.

Trevelyan, George Otto. *The American Revolution.* Condensed and edited by Richard B. Morris. New York: McKay, 1964.

Tuchman, Barbara. *The Zimmermann Telegram.* New York: Dell, 1965.

Turner, Frederick Jackson. "The Policy of France Toward the Mississippi Valley in the Period of Washington and Adams," *American Historical Review* 10 (January 1905): 249–279.

Walworth, Arthur. *Woodrow Wilson.* 2d ed., revised. Baltimore: Penguin Books, 1965.

Whitaker, Arthur P. *The United States and the Independence of Latin America, 1800–1830.* New York: W. W. Norton, 1964.

Whitridge, Arnold. *Men in Crisis: The Revolutions of 1848.* New York: Scribner's, 1949.

Williamson, Harold F., Andreano, Ralph L., Daum, Arnold R., and Klose, Gilbert C. *The American Petroleum Industry.* 2 vols. Evanston, Ill. Northwestern University Press, 1959 and 1963.

Wilson, F. M. Huntington. *Memoirs of an Ex-Diplomat.* Boston: Bruce Humphries, 1945.

Wilson, Henry Lane. *Diplomatic Episodes in Mexico, Belgium, and Chile.* Garden City, N.Y.: Doubleday, 1927.

Wolfers, Arnold. *Discord and Collaboration: Essays on International Politics.* Baltimore: Johns Hopkins Press, 1962.

Womack, John. *Zapata and the Mexican Revolution.* New York: Alfred A. Knopf, 1968.

Yglesias, José. "Che Guevara: 'The Best Way to Die,' " *The Nation,* November 6, 1967, pp. 463–465.

Index